2302

THE LATE MEDIEVAL INTERLUDE

THE DRAMA OF YOUTH
AND ARISTOCRATIC MASCULINITY

The commercial theatre of the late sixteenth century is often credited with introducing its audiences to new, 'modern' modes of thought about the self, society and the nation, making them conscious that the self is performed, as an actor performs a role. Yet the earlier interlude drama, originally performed in households and other institutions of the late fifteenth and sixteenth centuries, indicates that the late medieval period was fully aware of the theatricality of identity.

This book argues that ideas of performance inform the concepts of aristocratic masculinity developed in the plays *Nature, Fulgens and Lucres, The Worlde and the Chylde, The Interlude of Youth* and *Calisto and Melebea*. It examines how the depiction of young male aristocrats in these texts is shaped by ideas of male youth constituted in the middle ages and associated with a range of moral, social and political meanings, and shows them as failing or succeeding to perform an adult noble masculinity in the aristocratic body and in aristocratic household. The book also suggests ways in which the plays offer discreet praise and censure of the manner in which their noble patrons performed as aristocrats. Throughout, it brings out the subtle qualities of the interludes, which, the author shows, have been unjustly neglected.

Dr FIONA S. DUNLOP is Research Associate of the Centre for Medieval Studies, University of York

YORK MEDIEVAL PRESS

York Medieval Press is published by the University of York's Centre for Medieval Studies in association with Boydell & Brewer Ltd. Our objective is the promotion of innovative scholarship and fresh criticism on medieval culture. We have a special commitment to interdisciplinary study, in line with the Centre's belief that the future of Medieval Studies lies in those areas in which its major constituent disciplines at once inform and challenge each other.

All inquiries of an editorial kind, including suggestions for monographs and essay collections, should be addressed to: The Director, University of York, Centre for Medieval Studies, The King's Manor, York YO1 7EP (E-mail: lah1@york.ac.uk).

Publications of York Medieval Press are listed at the back of this volume.

THE LATE MEDIEVAL INTERLUDE

THE DRAMA OF YOUTH
AND ARISTOCRATIC MASCULINITY

Fiona S. Dunlop

THE UNIVERSITY *of York*

YORK MEDIEVAL PRESS

First published 2007

A York Medieval Press publication
in association with The Boydell Press
an imprint of Boydell & Brewer Ltd
PO Box 9   Woodbridge   Suffolk IP12 3DF   UK
and of Boydell & Brewer Inc.
668 Mt Hope Avenue   Rochester   NY 14620   USA
website: www.boydellandbrewer.com
and with the
Centre for Medieval Studies, University of York

ISBN 1 903153 21 2
ISBN 978 1 903153 21 5

A CIP catalogue record for this book is available
from the British Library

This publication is printed on acid-free paper

Printed in Great Britain by
Antony Rowe Ltd, Chippenham, Wiltshire

CONTENTS

To Mary Sloan

and

In memory of Evelyn Dunlop

2 Timothy 1:5

ACKNOWLEDGEMENTS

My grateful thanks go to Jeremy Goldberg and Nick Havely at the Centre for Medieval Studies of the University of York, my supervisors for the thesis on which this book is based. To them I am indebted for many years of patient good humour, unfailing helpfulness and support. Jocelyn Wogan-Browne's tireless efforts in editing the typescript were invaluable for the preparation of the present volume. Greg Walker's advice on revising the original thesis and Mark Ormrod's help in writing the proposal for publication were also very much appreciated.

I owe a great deal to the research students and staff at the Centre for Medieval Studies, who have always been generous with their time and their ideas. In particular, I should like to thank Isabel Davis, Matthew Holford, Felicity Riddy, Sharon Wells and Sarah Williams.

My parents have provided both moral and financial support over many years of study. Indeed, I would probably have never ventured on postgraduate research without their encouragement.

I am also grateful to the Arts and Humanities Research Board for two years' funding, which helped me to complete the original thesis.

ABBREVIATIONS

BIHR   *Bulletin of the Institute of Historical Research*
EETS   Early English Text Society
  ES   Extra Series
  OS   Original Series
  SS   Supplementary Series
ELR   *English Literary Renaissance*
JEGP   *Journal of English and Germanic Philology*
MED   *Middle English Dictionary*. Ed. H. Kurath and R. E. Lewis. 118
       fascicles Ann Arbor, 1953–2001.
METh   *Medieval English Theatre*
MLQ   *Modern Language Quarterly*
OED   *Oxford English Dictionary*. Ed. J. A. Simpson and E. S. C. Weiner. 2nd
       edn 20 vols. Oxford, 1989.
PMLA   *Publications of the Modern Language Society of America*

INTRODUCTION

The end of the fifteenth century has long been perceived by scholars of literature and history as a crucial turning point – as the frontier between the 'medieval' and 'modern'.[1] This period of transition has been associated with political and administrative innovation, religious Reformation and literary Renaissance: in other words, with new modes of thinking about the self, society and the nation. Many scholars of the early modern period have explored the connections between the development of concepts of individuality and the development of the commercial theatre in the late sixteenth century. According to them, a new kind of drama instigated a new awareness that aspects of the self might be put on or performed, as an actor adopts a role for an audience. In the influential *Renaissance Self-Fashioning*, recently reissued in a new edition, Stephen Greenblatt first drew attention to metaphors drawn from theatre and spectacle in the work of Thomas More and others which indicate a self-conscious awareness of acting out an identity for the benefit of an audience.[2] Frank Whigham has also discussed the elaborate performances of Elizabethan courtiers who carefully turned out gestures and costumes in order to project finely tuned images of themselves.[3] Building on this work, David Posner has explored the 'link between theatricality and ideas of nobility and courtly behaviour in the late Renaissance' amongst nobles driven by an 'imperative of display'.[4] In turn, Peter Womack saw the commercial theatre of the late sixteenth century as instrumental in the renegotiation of concepts of the nation and the individual's relationship to it, as the theatre takes on a key role in the 'imagining' of a much greater body politic.[5] These kinds of studies have seen the medieval period, in contrast, as one where a sense of individuality was subordinated to communal identity, and where in any case concepts

---

1 L. Patterson, 'On the Margin: Postmodernism, Ironic History, and Medieval Studies', *Speculum* 65 (1990), 87–108; D. Aers, 'A Whisper in the Ear of Early Modernists', in *Culture and History, 1350–1600*, ed. D. Aers (Detroit, 1992), pp. 177–202; J. L. Watts, 'Introduction: History, the Fifteenth Century and the Renaissance', in *The End of the Middle Ages? England in the Fifteenth and Sixteenth Centuries*, ed. J. L. Watts (Thrupp, 1998), pp. 1–22; J. L. Watts, 'Politics, War and Public Life', in *Gothic: Art for England, 1400–1547*, ed. R. Marks and P. Williamson (London, 2003), pp. 26–36.
2 S. Greenblatt, *Renaissance Self-Fashioning: From More to Shakespeare* (Chicago, 1980, 2nd edn 2005).
3 F. Whigham, *Ambition and Privilege: The Social Tropes of Elizabethan Courtesy Theory* (Berkeley, 1984).
4 D. M. Posner, *The Performance of Nobility in Early Modern European Literature* (Cambridge, 1999), p. 1.
5 P. Womack, 'Imagining Communities: Theatres and the English Nation in the Sixteenth Century', in *Culture and History*, ed. Aers, pp. 91–145.

of identity were static and unchanging, because understood to be fixed at birth. They present the performance of self-hood as something quintessentially modern, a habit of thought alien to the medieval period which went before.

But how new were such concepts of identity? This book investigates issues of youth, masculinity and nobility in five play-texts written around the end of the fifteenth and the beginning of the sixteenth centuries: *Fulgens and Lucres* and *Nature*, by Henry Medwall (both written in the 1490s), *The Worlde and the Chylde* (c. 1509), *The Interlude of Youth* (c. 1514) and *Calisto and Melebea* (c. 1525). Each of these plays invites us to consider a young nobleman or men in the process of growing up and to categorize each as a failure or (more rarely) as a success in their attempts to make the transition to adult identities. As sociologists remind us, the depiction and analysis of problematic young people is often a symptom of adults' own deep-seated fears about identity and the threat of change.[6] These Tudor plays also offer us many opportunities to examine the medieval origins of their thinking about identity and individuality, society and nation, since their representations of the young are affiliated with later medieval literary genres of various kinds. In other words, the plays are closely engaged with questions of what it means to be an adult and aristocratic man, and they suggest that notions of noble masculinity in particular were subject to complex processes of reformulation and debate in the late medieval period.

The interlude as a literary genre

The five plays which I shall consider are commonly categorized as interludes. This term is used throughout the late medieval period and into the sixteenth century to denote entertainments in the accounts of households, colleges, towns and the royal court. Since many simply record payments to actors and troupes for performances, but give no details of the nature of the piece offered, it is difficult to be precise about the medieval meanings of the word.[7] It has, however, been borrowed by modern scholars for a group of play-texts from the late fifteenth and sixteenth centuries since, in the words of Davis, the term is 'the most convenient label for all those shortish late-medieval and early-Tudor plays, mainly preserved for us in printed editions, which we have grown used to regarding as comparable and to differentiating in our minds from other groupings of plays'.[8] It is not clear how representative these texts

---

[6] C. Jenks, *Childhood* (London, 1996); A. James, C. Jenks and J. Prout, *Theorizing Childhood* (Cambridge, 1998).

[7] E. K. Chambers, *The Mediaeval Stage*, 2 vols. (London, 1903), II, 181–2; N. Davis, 'The Meaning of the Word "Interlude": A Discussion', *METh* 6 (1984), 5–15; M. Jones, 'Early Moral Plays and the Earliest Secular Drama', in *The Revels History of Drama in English, Vol. 1: Medieval Drama*, ed. L. Potter (London and New York, 1983), pp. 213–91 (pp. 235–6).

[8] Davis, 'Meaning of the Word "Interlude" ', pp. 5–6.

are of the much larger body of interlude texts which have been lost, never mind any other kinds of performance which the term may originally have designated.[9]

However, for the first modern scholars of drama the category of the interlude occupied an awkward and liminal space, because it was seen as straddling the key literary historical boundary between the medieval period and the Renaissance. Nineteenth and twentieth-century literary historians constructed narratives of the development of dramatic forms, where the interlude stood as a stage of progression towards the Shakespearean drama. Since the plays of Shakespeare represented the pinnacle of dramatic achievement for these scholars, inevitably the interlude emerged as a lesser form. For instance, John Addington Symonds made an analogy with the theory of evolution in describing the interlude as 'one of those imperfect organisms which have long since perished in the struggle for existence, but which interest the physiologist both as indicating an effort after development upon a line which has proved to be the weaker, and also as containing within itself evidences of the structure which finally succeeded'.[10] In this account, the interlude is a kind of missing link or genetic freak of literary history, of interest only because it explained the origins of a more highly valued form of literature.

Such thinking about the interlude has had a particular influence on the reception of those texts associated with the end of the fifteenth and beginning of the sixteenth centuries, which have frequently been judged on the extent to which they exhibited 'Renaissance' qualities, as opposed to 'primitive', 'medieval' ones. For instance, *Nature*, *The Worlde and the Chylde*, and *The Interlude of Youth* share many features of the later medieval morality.[11] They focus on protagonists comparable to Everyman: universal figures whose experiences were meant to stand for those of all mankind, and whose experiences offer explicit moral and religious teaching on the nature of sin and the mechanics of repentance.

Critics who saw these interludes as representing the end of the morality form, often described them as the last gasp of an outmoded and obsolete form.[12] Those who viewed them more positively often did so on the basis of the new, 'humanist' qualities which they discerned in the texts. *Nature*, for example, explains man's sinfulness as a result of the fact that the young man is

---

9   G. Walker, 'Playing by the Book: Early Tudor Drama and the Printed text', in G. Walker, *The Politics of Performance in Early Renaissance Drama* (Cambridge, 1998), pp. 6–50.

10 J. A. Symonds, *Shakspere's* [sic] *Predecessors in the English Drama* (London, 1900), p. 118.

11 R. A. Potter, *The English Morality Play: Origins, History and Influence of a Dramatic Tradition* (London and Boston, 1975).

12 Jones, 'Early Moral Plays', pp. 223–4; J. E. Petersen, 'The Paradox of Disintegrating Form in *Mundus et Infans*', *ELR* 7 (1977), 3–16; A. W. Reed, *Early Tudor Drama: Medwall, The Rastells, Heywood and the More Circle* (London, 1926), p. 100; A. B. Righter, *Shakespeare and the Idea of the Play* (London, 1964), pp. 29–31; B. Spivack, *Shakespeare and the Allegory of Evil: The History of a Metaphor in Relation to his Major Villains* (New York, 1958), p. 215.

not yet governed by reason. Several scholars have read this feature of the play as a sign of the development of modern notions of individualism, where sin is an aspect of an individual's rational choice, rather than being the universal condition of mankind.[13] Indeed, Ian Lancashire has favourably contrasted Medwall's 'humanism' with *The Interlude of Youth*'s 'medieval view of human nature'.[14] The plays have also been regarded as humanist in their interest in particular kinds of learning. Scholars have drawn attention to the opening speech of *Nature* – which discusses the role of nature in creation – as a piece of humanist thinking which reveals a new and scientific approach to the natural world.[15] In more general terms, many critics have noted with approval the realistic representation of secular life in these interludes, which seem to indicate a movement away from the allegory of medieval morality drama, and towards the depiction of secular life in the Renaissance drama.[16]

On the other hand, *Fulgens and Lucres* and *Calisto and Melebea* have often been classed as 'Renaissance' plays, because they draw on continental sources, and deal with ostensibly secular themes, such as love and marriage. Moreover, Medwall's *Fulgens and Lucres* seems to exhibit an innovative dramatic technique, opening with a particularly striking frame.[17] The action is introduced by two figures who emerge from the audience (clearly in a great hall of a noble household or other institution) and who discuss the action of the play to follow. These characters are named only A and B in the speech headings, following the conventions of contemporary transcriptions of court cases. They abandon their roles as members of the audience and enter the world of the play, taking service with the two rival noble suitors, Gaius and Cornelius respectively. They are used to generate a comic sub-plot (the first known example in an English play), where A and B compete (though in much less refined ways than their noble masters) for the favours of Jone, servant of Lucres, herself the love object of Gaius and Cornelius.

Neither of the plays seems to exhibit many features of the medieval drama. *Calisto and Melebea* has been described as a product of the new 'humanist

[13] A. P. Rossiter, *English Drama From Early Times to the Elizabethans: Its Background Origins and Developments* (London, 1950), p. 104; Spivack, *Shakespeare and the Allegory of Evil*, p. 214; Potter, *English Morality Play*, p. 60.

[14] *Two Tudor Interludes: Youth and Hick Scorner*, ed. I. Lancashire (Manchester, 1980), p. 38.

[15] F. S. Boas, *Introduction to Tudor Drama* (London, 1933), p. 3; J. B. Altman, *The Tudor Play of Mind: Rhetorical Enquiry and the Development of Elizabethan Drama* (Berkeley, 1978), p. 13.

[16] Boas, *Introduction to Tudor Drama*, p. 3; Rossiter, *English Drama from Early Times*, p. 103; Altman, *Tudor Play of Mind*, p. 13; Jones, 'Early Moral Plays', pp. 223–4.

[17] R. C. Johnson, 'Audience Involvement in the Tudor Interlude', *Theatre Notebook* 24 (1970), 101–111; R. C. Jones, 'The Stage World and the "Real" World in Medwall's *Fulgens and Lucres*', *MLQ* 32 (1971), 131–42; J. S. Colley, '*Fulgens and Lucres*: Politics and Aesthetics', *Zeitschrift für Anglistik und Amerikanistik* 23 (1975), 322–30; W. Tydeman, *English Medieval Theatre, 1400–1500* (London, 1986), pp. 137–48; M. Twycross, 'The Theatricality of Medieval English Plays', in *The Cambridge Companion to Medieval English Theatre*, ed. R. Beadle (Cambridge, 1994), pp. 37–84 (pp. 74–5); P. Happé, *English Drama Before Shakespeare* (London and New York, 1999), pp. 57–8.

learning', in its reliance on the Spanish prose work *La Celestina*, and has been associated with the humanist Vives's sojourn at the English royal court in the early sixteenth century.[18] The repentance of its heroine Melebea, so nearly seduced by Calisto, has been read as an example of Renaissance self-fashioning, rather than a didactic model of a universal experience, since it is addressed directly to God, and not through a priest.[19] Yet the play ascribes Melebea's change of heart to early habits of regular prayer imposed by her father: it can be seen as promoting devotional practices altogether familiar to later medieval noblewomen. *Fulgens and Lucres* came to be viewed as the first purely secular play in English, one with a commitment to depicting individuals or social types rather than universal figures or personified sins.[20] Not only is there a lack of overt religious didacticism in *Fulgens and Lucres*, but it has been seen to embody a new interrogative philosophical stance, characteristic of the Renaissance.[21] It also seemed to prefigure the romantic comedies of Shakespeare in its matter (the story of the competition of two suitors for the hand of a young noblewoman) and its use of a sub-plot.[22] However, the depiction of at least one character, the suitor Cornelius, is heavily influenced by that of the personified universal sins and types of 'medieval' dramatic tradition.[23] Moreover, the conclusion of the play declares its didactic intent in resolutely moral terms – to encourage the pursuit of virtue and the suppression of vice amongst gentlemen. Its plot of two rival suits for the hand of a noblewoman is also a familiar one from medieval romance.[24]

The effect of this kind of discussion was to categorize *Fulgens and Lucres* and *Calisto and Melebea* as essentially modern plays, and the other early interludes as essentially medieval. The most recent editors of Medwall's plays have felt it necessary to stress that there is in fact no evidence to show whether *Nature* was written prior to *Fulgens and Lucres*, since so many discussions

---

18 D. Bevington, *From Mankind to Marlowe: Growth of Structure in the Popular Drama of Tudor England* (Cambridge MA, 1962), p. 45; G. Ungerer, *Anglo-Spanish Relations in Tudor Literature* (Madrid, 1956), pp. 9–25.

19 J. Watkins, 'The Allegorical Theatre: Moralities, Interludes, and Protestant Drama', in *The Cambridge History of Medieval English Literature*, ed. D. Wallace (Cambridge, 1999), pp. 767–92 (pp. 781–2).

20 Boas, *Introduction to Tudor Drama*, pp. 4–5; Reed, *Early Tudor Drama*, pp. 95–100; Righter, *Shakespeare and the Idea of the Play*, p. 36.

21 F. P. Wilson, *The English Drama, 1485–1585* (Oxford, 1969), p. 7; Altman, *Tudor Play of Mind*, pp. 13–30.

22 *Five Pre-Shakespearean Comedies*, ed. F. S. Boas (London, 1934), pp. vii–ix; Boas, *Introduction to Tudor Drama*, p. 36; Reed, *Early Tudor Drama*, p. 100.

23 T. W. Craik, *The Tudor Interlude: Stage, Costume and Acting* (Leicester, 1958), pp. 58–9; D. Bevington, *Tudor Drama and Politics: A Critical Approach to Topical Meaning* (Cambridge MA, 1968), pp. 51–2; Jones, 'Early Moral Plays', p. 245; H. B. Norland, *Drama in Early Tudor Britain, 1485–1558* (Lincoln NB, 1995), p. 237.

24 C. R. Baskervill, 'Conventional Features of Medwall's *Fulgens and Lucres*', *Modern Philology* 24 (1905), 419–42.

implied that this must be the case.[25] This school of thought assumed that once Medwall had made the great leap forward into the Renaissance there could be no going back to 'medieval' notions such as are evinced in *Nature*. In stressing that *Fulgens and Lucres* is so different in kind from *Nature* and other early interludes, such scholarly work tended to obscure what the interludes might have in common with each other, and what might make them a distinctive genre in their own right.

This book contends that, far from being clunky, didactic pieces, plays like *Nature*, *The Worlde and the Chylde* and *The Interlude of Youth* are just as actively engaged in sophisticated discussions of identity as *Fulgens and Lucres* and *Calisto and Melebea*. Indeed, the fact that any of these plays is able to access a sophisticated level of discussion and debate is because they rely on a large body of medieval thought – developed in scientific discourse, political writing and courtesy books as well as morally didactic works. These traditions had already made familiar the notion that one's identity was something which had continually to be performed, especially if one was an aristocratic man. The plays assume an audience with a working knowledge of these later medieval concepts. The figure of the young and noble man was already charged with meaning, so the depiction of such characters offered a convenient way of alluding to a framework on which ideas about the body, the moral and spiritual being, social status and the exercise of political power could be held together, though admittedly often in a state of considerable tension.

The opening chapters of this book examine some of the ways in which concepts of 'youth' had already been constituted as an object of study and knowing in the later medieval period. Chapter One discusses how the period of (male) youth came to be defined by medieval medical and scientific traditions, and how the plays make use of the life-cycle models they offer. Chapter Two investigates the ways in which later medieval moral and devotional works, courtesy literature, and political texts constructed images of young men, often founded on an understanding of male development derived from natural philosophy and medicine. It shows how these images influenced the depiction of the young male characters in the interludes.

Chapters Three and Four read the interludes' presentation of young noblemen in the context of the ideologies of the later medieval noble household. The household – as a physical space, administrative unit, and as a social and political institution – already carried its own ideological baggage on which the interludes draw and to which they contribute. Chapter Three considers what the interludes have to say about successful and unsuccessful methods of performing noble masculinity. In particular, it shows how they teach young men to enact their nobility through the management of a noble household. Chapter Four develops the ways in which the depictions of young

25 H. Medwall, *The Plays of Henry Medwall*, ed. M. E. Moeslein (New York and London, 1981), p. 6; H. Medwall, *The Plays of Henry Medwall*, ed. A. H. Nelson (Cambridge, 1980), pp. 20–1.

men in the interludes may be interpreted in political terms. First, it discusses why the interludes attempt to provoke high levels of anxiety about noble masculinity. Secondly, it considers the young male characters in relation to concepts of rule and authority, as symbols for political competence or (more frequently) ineptitude. The chapter goes on to show how individual interludes can be said to exploit the multiple meanings of young men in order to comment on personalities and politics of the period. Since the foregoing chapters will tend to stress what the depictions of young men have in common, I examine some of the idiosyncratic features of the depiction of young men in *Nature*, *Fulgens and Lucres*, and *The Interlude of Youth*, and indicate ways that the figures of young men might relate to the political strategies of the nobles with whom they have been associated.

CHAPTER ONE

Defining Youth

Early interludes did not invent a concept of youth. Their depiction of the young is informed by several intersecting traditions of thought about age and ageing, ideas so familiar to the audience that they do not need to be spelled out. The unspoken principles on which the representations rest have important implications for our understanding of the young men of the plays. Late medieval theories of the development of male bodies constituted youth first of all as a biological category.

Late medieval knowledge about age and ageing was articulated most succinctly in schemes of the Ages of Man, a means of presenting the body's growth and development in a paradigmatic, universalizing form. Ages of Man schemes construct a model of the typical life-span which divides it up into stages. Each stage of life, or 'Age', is defined in terms of years and labelled with a specific name.[1] Three early interludes evidently adopt this structural principle in their presentation of a universal central figure: two – Nature and The Worlde and the Chylde – depict the complete life-cycle of their male protagonists, Man and Infans, so that as the plays progress we see them grow from childhood to old age, passing through identifiable Ages.[2] The Interlude of Youth depicts one stage from that life-cycle.

Such schemes were not only academic, but were generally popular in art and writing in medieval England. The Ages of Man were depicted in stained glass, such as the scheme of c. 1180 extant in Canterbury Cathedral;[3] in manuscript illuminations, such as the Wheel of Life in the De Lisle Psalter (c. 1310);[4] in wall paintings such as that at Longthorpe Tower (c. 1330);[5] in moral and devotional poetry, such as the late fourteenth century The Parlement of the Thre

---

1 F. Böll, 'Die Lebensalter', *Neue Jahrbücher für das klassische Altertum* 31 (1913), 89–145; A. Hofmeister, '*Puer, Iuvenis, Senex*: Zum Verständnis der mittelalterlichen Altersbezeichnungen', in *Papstum und Kaisertum*, ed. A. Brackman (Munich, 1926), pp. 288–316; J. A. Burrow, *The Ages of Man: A Study in Medieval Writing and Thought* (Oxford, 1986); M. Dove, *The Perfect Age of Man's Life* (Cambridge, 1986); E. Sears, *The Ages of Man: Medieval Interpretations of the Life Cycle* (Princeton, 1986).

2 Medwall, *Plays of Henry Medwall*, ed. Nelson, p. 24; *The Worlde and the Chylde*, ed. C. Davidson and P. Happé (Kalamazoo, 1999), pp. 10–15; *Two Tudor Interludes*, ed. Lancashire, p. 49.

3 Burrow, *Ages of Man*, pp. 90–2; Sears, *Ages of Man*, pp. 72–4.

4 Burrow, *Ages of Man*, pp. 45–7; Sears, *Ages of Man*, pp. 146–8.

5 Burrow, *Ages of Man*, pp. 43–6; Sears, *Ages of Man*, pp. 137–8.

Ages and the fifteenth-century works *The Mirror of the Periods of Man's Life* and 'Of the seuen ages';[6] and in painted wall hangings, such as those belonging to Thomas More's father in the late fifteenth and early sixteenth centuries.[7] Both together and separately, these works engaged in a process of defining and naming a conception of youth as a period of life.

It should be said that the Ages of Man offered *one* way of understanding and dividing the male life-cycle. In the Middle Ages, as in the modern world, alternative periods of male youth were produced by other intellectual traditions and through a variety of social practices. The different periods of youth, constructed in relation to various first principles, do not necessarily dovetail neatly into one stable category. For example, legal discourses of medieval England produce a model of the life-cycle where there is a sharp distinction between a period of non-adulthood, known in the common law as 'infancy' or 'non-age', and a period of adulthood known as 'full age'.[8] In this case, a period of youth is constructed in relation to an adult status: it is a period when people are not subject to particular obligations and are not permitted to avail themselves of particular privileges. However, different legal codes established a wide variety of ages at which children might in different contexts be regarded as adults, and even within the same code different ages of maturity were established on the basis of gender and/or status.[9] Under canon law, for example, minimum ages for marriage came to be fixed at fourteen for boys and twelve for girls.[10] The treatise known as 'Bracton' on English common law, which dates from around the second quarter of the thirteenth century, presents a sliding scale of ages of majority, so that the heirs of knights and tenants under military fee came of age at twenty-one, while the heirs of sokemen did so at fifteen.[11]

Despite the variety of ages they invoke, canon law and common law are based on a similar internal logic, as the establishment of particular ages of adulthood is justified by reference to a principle of capacity. The ages specified

---

6   For *The Parlement of the Thre Ages*, see *Wynnere and Wastoure and The Parlement of the Thre Ages*, ed. W. Ginsberg (Kalamazoo, 1992). For *The Mirror of the Periods of Man's Life*, see *Hymns to the Virgin and Christ; The Parliament of Devils; and Other Religious Pieces*, ed. F. J. Furnivall, EETS OS 24 (1868), pp. 58–78. For 'Of the seuen ages', see A. H. Nelson, ' "Of the seuen ages": An Unknown Analogue of *The Castle of Perseverance*', *Comparative Drama* 8 (1974), 125–38. See also Burrow, *Ages of Man*, pp. 46–7; Sears, *Ages of Man*, pp. 139–40; *Worlde and the Chylde*, ed. Davidson and Happé, pp. 6–10.

7   T. More, *The Complete Works of Sir Thomas More*, ed. A. S. G. Edwards, 15 vols. (New Haven, 1963–1997), I, 3–7.

8   F. Pollock and F. W. Maitland, *The History of English Law Before the Time of Edward I*, 2 vols., 2nd edn (Cambridge, 1898), II, 438.

9   N. Orme, *Medieval Children* (New Haven and London, 2001), pp. 325–8.

10 Pollock and Maitland, *History of English Law*, II, 389–91; K. M. Phillips, *Medieval Maidens: Young Women and Gender in England, 1270–1540* (Manchester, 2003), p. 32.

11 *Bracton on the Laws and Customs of England*, ed. G. E. Woodbine, trans. S. E. Thorne, 4 vols. (Cambridge MA, 1968), II, 250–1; Pollock and Maitland, *History of English* Law, II, 438–9; Phillips, *Medieval Maidens*, pp. 26–8.

are those at which the individual should display the physical, intellectual or moral abilities necessary for them to function as adults in adult roles with all their attendant rights and responsibilities. Under canon law, individuals had to be sexually mature in order to contract a marriage, so that a marriage was not valid where this was not the case.[12] On the other hand, individuals below the age specified for first marriage could be regarded as sufficiently mature for marriage on the basis of moral capacity: that is, an ability to distinguish between good and evil.[13] Bracton explains that the age of majority under English common law is 'not defined in terms of time but by sense and maturity', so that a burgess's son can be regarded as being of full age 'when he knows how properly to count money, measure cloths and perform similar paternal business'.[14] The later age of majority for the heirs of knights and tenants owing military service is justified on the basis that 'Those that pertain to military service require greater strength, and greater understanding and discretion.'[15] These models of gendered and status-related youths are the product of scientific and social ideologies.

Schemes of the Ages of Man do not present a gender-neutral concept of youth, despite their claim to a universal application. Although they purport to describe and explain the life-cycle of 'man' in the sense of human-kind, in practice they delineate only the male life-cycle, a natural consequence of their focus on the male body, to the complete exclusion of the female.[16] Youth in this context is gendered as male.

The practice of making the male body stand for human kind *in toto* was a feature of the Ages of Man from its origins as a system of thought. Schemes of the Ages were first drawn up in the academic and scientific discourses of antiquity, the outcome of attempts to describe and explain the observable physical phenomenon of ageing. In this sense, the period of youth was understood primarily as a stage of bodily development. Medieval writers in the fields of natural philosophy and medicine drew on the theories of Aristotle (384–322 BC) and Galen (d. *c.* AD 200) which provided the conceptual tools for explaining ageing in terms of natural principles.[17] Schemes of the Ages did not remain confined to specialist scientific texts but became widely disseminated throughout medieval Europe in encyclopaedic literature, such as Isidore of Seville's *Etymologiae* (before 636) and the early thirteenth-century *De proprietatibus rerum* of Bartholomaeus Anglicus.[18]

The category of youth seems at first glance to be stably defined in schemes of the Ages, in texts which make authoritative statements about the

---

12 Phillips, *Medieval Maidens*, pp. 26–8.
13 Ibid.
14 *Bracton*, ed. Woodbine, II, 250.
15 Ibid., II, 251.
16 Dove, *Perfect Age*, pp. 20–5.
17 N. G. Siraisi, *Medieval and Early Renaissance Medicine: An Introduction to Knowledge and Practice* (Chicago, 1990).
18 Burrow, *Ages of Man*, pp. 82, 88.

life-course. Latin texts, for instance, develop a relatively stable set of terms for the Ages (such as *infantia, pueritia, adolescentia, iuventus, senium*) and for individuals in each Age (*infans, puer, adolescens, iuvenis, senex*).[19] There is, however, little agreement between the schemes as to precisely which periods these terms denominate, in part because different schemes divide the life-cycle into different numbers of Ages. The seven-Age scheme was perhaps the most widespread, having been popularized by Isidore of Seville, but schemes of three, four, five and six Ages were common, and indeed others are known. This variety of structure was dictated by principles other than the empirical description of bodies. Some schemes rely on numerology or analogy, such as those which draw parallels between the Ages of Man and the canonical hours, or the parable of the workers in the vineyard.[20] Four-Age schemes allowed links to be made between the Ages of Man, the four humours and the seasons of the year.[21] Some six-Age schemes, on the other hand, are founded on analogies with the six jars of water turned into wine at the wedding at Cana.[22] These structural variations mean that it is impossible to reconcile the schemes with each other to produce one unified, universal scheme of the Ages.

Moreover, when we compare scheme with scheme, we find that individual Ages are also defined very differently. The two Ages which appear to equate most readily with modern conceptions of youth are *adolescentia* and *iuventus*, which usually form the third and fourth Ages in a seven-Age scheme. As John Trevisa's Middle English translation (1389) of the encyclopaedia *De proprietatibus rerum* shows, schemes developed in different traditions produce different kinds of *adolescentia*, even if all a reader considers is what its limits in years are:

> Hereaftir comeþ the age þat hatte *adholoscencia*, þe age of a yonge stripelinge, and dureþ þe þridde seuen ӡere, þat is to þe ende of on and twenty ӡere. So it is saide *in viatico*. But Isidir seiþ þat it dureþ to þe ferþe seuen ӡere, þat is to þe ende of 28 ӡere. But ficicians strecchen þis age to þe ente of 30 ӡere or of 35 ӡere.[23]

A period of youth which only ends somewhere between 28 and 35 clearly bears little relation to modern concepts of 'adolescence'.[24] But it is also clear that there is no single concept of youth even within the Ages of Man tradition. Instead of having absolute meanings, terms for the Ages, such as *adolescentia*

---

[19] Hofmeister, '*Puer, Iuvenis, Senex*'.

[20] Burrow, *Ages of Man*, pp. 59–64; Sears, *Ages of Man*, pp. 80–9, 138–9.

[21] Burrow, *Ages of Man*, pp. 12–36; Sears, *Ages of Man*, pp. 9–37.

[22] Burrow, *Ages of Man*, pp.79–81; Sears, *Ages of Man*, pp. 54–79.

[23] Bartholomaeus Anglicus, *On the Properties of Things, A Critical Text: John Trevisa's Translation of Bartholomaeus Anglicus' De proprietatibus rerum*, ed. M. C. Seymour, 2 vols. (Oxford, 1975), I, 291–2.

[24] J. A. Schultz, 'Medieval Adolescence: The Claims of History and the Silence of German Narrative', *Speculum* 66 (1991), 519–39.

or *iuventus*, are context dependent. Indeed, in the four-Age schemes the term *adolescentia* may not appear at all, being subsumed into one long *pueritia*.[25]

When terms for the Ages are used by medieval writers in other contexts, their instability of meaning becomes even more apparent. Hofmeister, commenting on the use of such terms in medieval historical writing, was surprised to discover that their users were not really making the precise distinction between the Ages of Man that he had supposed, observing that *adolescentia* and *iuventus* were used interchangeably, or for overlapping periods of life.[26] As Burrow has concluded, 'anyone who goes to medieval discussions of the Ages of Man with the intention of ascertaining at what age youth was thought to end, or old age to begin, will find no easy answers'.[27] Individual schemes of the Ages repeatedly reconstruct periods of youth according to their own internal logic, and in ways which suggest that these concepts sometimes have only a tenuous connection to the 'reality' of men's lives and men's bodies.

Furthermore, the attempts of English writers to translate Latin terms for the Ages into Middle English reveal that the terminology often does not equate readily with what is available in English vocabulary. As we have seen above, John Trevisa defines *adolescentia* as 'þe age of a yonge stripelinge'.[28] In other contexts 'stripling' is used to refer specifically to young men in their teens.[29] Confronted with *iuventus* and *iuvenis*, Trevisa seems unable to find a Middle English equivalent, identifying the *iuvenis* simply as 'a man of that age'.[30] However, shortly before this passage, Trevisa discusses how *iuventus* related to the Middle English 'youþe' in the context of an excursus on baldness.[31] The text says that if a man's hair falls out 'in ȝouþe' then it will grow again, but it will not do so if it should fall out after this period. In order to clarify the meaning of 'ȝouþe', Trevisa interpolates the following into his translation *in propria persona*:

> *Treuisa*: here I take þis engelissch for þis latyn *iuuentus*. And *iuuentus* is here oþirwise taken þan oure comoun speche visth. For here it is itake for þe age þat duriþ from oon and twenty ȝere oþir from eiȝte and twenty ȝere, or from þritty or fyue and þritty, to fyue and fourty or fifty ȝere, as it is playnlich saide sone hereaftir in þe bigynnynge of þe sixte book.[32]

25 Burrow, *Ages of Man*, pp. 12–36.
26 Hofmeister, 'Puer, Iuvenis, Senex', p. 305.
27 Burrow, *Ages of Man*, p. 34.
28 Bartholomaeus Anglicus, *On the Properties of Things*, I, 291–2.
29 Under 'stripling', the *MED* cites *Mandeville's Travels*: 'He had . . . the faireste damyseles . . . vnder the age of xv ȝeer And the faireste ȝonge striplynges . . . of þat same age'.
30 Bartholomaeus Anglicus, *On the Properties of Things*, I, 292.
31 Ibid., I, 290.
32 Ibid.

Trevisa believes his choice of '3ouþe' for *iuventus* to be unsatisfactory, indeed potentially misleading for his readers. He does not say how '3ouþe' is understood in 'oure comoun speche', but it must denote a period widely different from that stretching anywhere from twenty-one to fifty years which *iuventus* can denominate.

Latin–English word-lists of the later Middle Ages suggest that the Middle English terms 'youthe' and 'yong' apply more generally than these Latin nouns. The *Promptorium parvulorum* (*c.* 1440) defines '3ung' as '*Iuuenis*', but '3ong man' as '*Adolescens*'.[33] Under the entry 'Agis sevyn', it explains that '*Adolescencia*' and '*Iuuentus*' denote the periods between the ages of fifteen and twenty-nine, and thirty and fifty respectively.[34] The *Catholicon anglicum* (*c.* 1483) defines a '3onge' as both an '*adolescens*' and a '*juuenis*'.[35] Thomas Elyot's *Dictionary* (1538) gives 'a yonge man' as an equivalent for '*Iuuenis*', and 'youthe' for '*Iuuentus*'.[36] As the *Middle English Dictionary* observes in its definition of 'youth', this term may apply to 'the entire period before the attainment of maturity'. Where it is used to define part of this period, it tends to be used for the older end of this age spectrum, but its boundaries are rather fuzzy.

The variety and uncertainty of the definitions of youth are reflected in the English artistic and literary depictions of the Ages of Man referred to above. These schemes show a great variety in the numbers of Ages each depicts. The Canterbury stained glass referred to earlier shows six male figures to represent six Ages, while the Longthorpe wall paintings show seven. The verse-text 'Of the seuen ages' divides the life of a representative male figure into seven Ages, while *The Parlement of the Thre Ages* depicts three personifications, Youthe, Medill Age and Elde. The De Lisle wheel of life shows ten Ages, as does the verse-text *The Mirror of the Periods of Man's Life*.

In the literary Ages of Man schemes, the term 'youth' is applied to a variety of periods. In the poem 'Of the seuen ages', '3outhe' is used for the third Age of a seven-Age scheme, called *adolescencia* in Isidore's version, though the mature man in the fourth Age is also described as '3onge'. In *The Parlement of the Thre Ages*, the figure called Youthe is in fact relatively old – 'thritty yere of elde' (l. 133). While *The Mirror of the Periods of Man's Life* does not give the Ages specific labels after 'childhood', the poem uses the word '3ouþe' liberally to describe the figure Mankind in a number of different Ages: as a 'child' of seven (l. 79); as a young man of twenty (l. 102); and as a man between forty and fifty (l. 313). When the aged Mankind repents of his misspent youth at the end of the poem, he appears to refer to more than one Age.

Early moral plays which follow in this tradition construct idiosyncratic schemes of the Ages, and as a result offer markedly different periods of male

---

[33] *Promptorium parvulorum*, ed. A. L. Mayhew, EETS ES 102 (1908), col. 550.

[34] Ibid., col. 7.

[35] *Catholicon anglicum: An English–Latin Wordbook*, ed. S. J. H. Herrtage, EETS OS 75 (1881), p. 427.

[36] T. Elyot, *Dictionary* (Menston, 1970).

youth. In *The Castle of Perseverance* (1400x1425), boundaries between stages of life are marked by the central character's entry into and exit from the Castle. When he enters, he is 'forty wynter olde' (l. 1575).[37] When he emerges, he is an aged and physically decrepit figure, and an earlier comment in the play suggests that he is now about sixty.[38]

Nature is also structured around a double fall and repentance by its central character, Man, as he makes his way from birth to death.[39] The vice Sensualyte, engaged in a battle with the figure of Reason for influence over this Man, describes his life-course in terms of that struggle:

> And standyng the nonage of thys gentylman,
> On my parell take no care therfore.
> I shall demean yt as well as I can
> Tyll he be passyd forty yerys and more,
> And, Reason, then yf ye wyll, undershore
> Hys croked old age when lusty youth ys spent;
> Than take uppon you.   (I. 323–9)[40]

Sensualyte refers first to Man's 'nonage', using the legal term which in common law normally describes the period up to the age of twenty-one. Sensualyte goes on to declare his intention to control Man until the latter is 'passyd forty yerys or more', and finally cedes a period he calls 'croked old age' to Reason's influence. Old age is constructed in opposition to 'lusty youth', which seems to cover the period from birth to forty. This extended youth, covering more than one Age, corresponds to that established in *The Castle of Perseverance*.

On the other hand, *The Worlde and the Chylde* begins in a way which suggests that it is going to describe a standard seven-Age scheme, like that popularized by Isidore of Seville.[41] From what the central character Infans says, it appears that the play is going to depict his life in stages, the first three of which last exactly seven years each.[42] Visual cues mark the boundaries of each Age for the audience, as the central character returns to his mentor in life, The Worlde, who remains seated on his throne in the playing area. With each visit, the mankind figure is given a new name, sometimes new garments, and further directions from his patron. After incarnations as 'Infans' or 'Dalyaunce', 'Wanton' and 'Lust and Lykynge', he becomes 'Manhode' at the age of twenty-one. It is less clear what the limit of this Age is in terms of years, but if we go by the speech headings in the printed edition of the play, the final

---

37 All line references are to *The Macro Plays*, ed. M. Eccles, EETS OS 262 (1969).
38 Ibid., ll. 2479–91, 416–19.
39 Medwall, *Plays of Henry Medwall*, ed. Nelson, pp. 23–4.
40 Line references are to Medwall, *Plays of Henry Medwall*, ed. Nelson.
41 *Worlde and the Chylde*, ed. Davidson and Happé, p. 12.
42 *Worlde and the Chylde*, ll. 69–70, 115–22, 129–30. All line references are to *Worlde and the Chylde*, ed. Davidson and Happé.

stage in man's life is 'Age'. Like *The Castle of Perseverance*, the play engineers the central character's absence from the stage so that he may return looking like an old man (ll. 795–801). This would mean that the play shows five Ages, rather than the seven we might have expected.[43]

In fact, a closer consideration of the text reveals that, apart from the term 'manhode', age-related terms are not used to describe the life of man. In the first speech heading, the main character is identified as 'Infans', a term familiar from academic expositions of the Ages of Man, and at the end he is identified as 'Age'. However, in the text itself he is never referred to by these names.[44] He calls himself, or is called, 'Dalyaunce', 'Wanton' and 'Lust and Lykynge'. Though the first three stages of his life neatly correspond with *infantia, pueritia*, and *adolescentia* as they would be in a seven-Age scheme, the English names refer to moral state, not age. Similarly, at the end of the play Manhode is renamed 'Shame' by Folye and then 'Repentaunce' by Reason, as he falls from and then is restored to grace. These terms clearly refer to spiritual condition rather the ageing process *per se*. In *The Worlde and the Chylde*, the moral story with its plot of fall and repentance is uppermost, though these states are pegged to particular positions in the life-cycle. As Sears has concluded, literary versions of the Ages of Man in an English context show a marked tendency to describe the moral development of a man over time, rather than the physical process of ageing, and *The Worlde and the Chylde* is a good example of this practice.[45]

The Interlude of Youth does not present an entire life-course, but seems designed to illustrate one Age. The main character is named 'Youth', and though the text does not refer directly to his age in years, this may be inferred from references to his inheritance. Youth has recently come into his father's landed property, and looks forward to spending his wealth freely (ll. 308–13),[46] so he must legally be of age. This also appears to be the case with Cornelius and Gaius from *Fulgens and Lucres* and Calisto of *Calisto and Melebea*, all of whom appear to be in full control of their lands and exempt from the authority of fathers and guardians required by the common law for minors.

For all the plays discussed, the age of twenty-one seems particularly significant. Even in *The Worlde and the Chylde*, where the Ages are presented in a more schematic way, the central character's first twenty-one years are dealt with perfunctorily in the space of 155 lines. Only at twenty-one, when he has been dubbed a knight, does the moral plot of his fall and repentance become central, as man assumes control of his own existence. This is similar to the poem *The Mirror of the Periods of Man's Life*, as the battle between the vices and virtues for Man's soul begins when he is '.xx. wyntir in age' (l. 114). The play *Nature* also moves rapidly from the end of childhood (marked by the depar-

[43] Ibid., pp. 14–15.
[44] Ibid., p. 14.
[45] Sears, *Ages of Man*, pp. 134–5.
[46] Line references are to *Two Tudor Interludes*, ed. Lancashire.

ture of the central figure's nurse Innocencye) to adulthood, marked by the setting up of a noble household for the adult man. The stress on this key moment of transition indicates that the interludes, along with other texts, are concerned not with universal concepts of youth but with gendered and status-related ones. They describe the experience of elite men for whom the age of majority meant access to property and freedom from the governance of others.[47]

Nevertheless, whether the stages of life depicted in the plays mark moral changes or changes of social status, these are still linked in fundamental ways to male bodies. The medieval disciplines of medicine and natural philosophy located youth as a stage in the physical development of the male body, following Aristotle, who first described it in *De anima* in terms of periods of growth, stasis and decline.[48] In the middle stage of life, the *acme*, man is at the height of his powers. The period of youth which precedes it is a time of developing, though incomplete powers, and forms a balance with old age, the final stage in the sequence, where the body is in decline from the optimum point. Aristotelian thinking is reflected in Trevisa's description of *adolescentia* and *iuventus* in his translation of *De proprietatibus rerum*. *Adolescentia* is the Age which is 'able to barnische [grow stout or strong] and encrece, and fonge myȝt and strenþe'.[49] The text explains that *iuventus* is 'in þe middil amonges ages, and þerfore it is strengest' and that 'a man of þat age is isette in þe ende of his ful encresinge, and þerfore he is strong to helpe at nede'.[50] In this kind of description, the stages of a man's life are understood in terms of the growth and decline of the male body's capacity for physical exertion.

Some academic texts also identify sexual maturity as a key marker of physical development. According to Isidore of Seville *adolescentia* is '*adolescentia ad gignendum adulta*' (an age mature enough for reproduction).[51] Trevisa describes *adolescentia* in similar terms, as 'ful age to gete children'.[52] Both passages imply the completion of a process, but in both cases this is not the pivotal moment in the body's development. Rather, reaching the *acme* of physical strength is the key goal of male bodies.

Medical thought explained the observable and measurable development of the body in terms of natural processes at a more fundamental level on the theoretical basis of complexion theory, first outlined by Aristotle and Galen, then elaborated by medieval writers from the late twelfth century.[53] The complexion was understood as 'the balance of the qualities of hot, wet, cold

---

[47] D. Grantley, *Wit's Pilgrimage: Drama and the Social Impact of Education in Early Modern England* (Aldershot, 2000), pp. 138–40.

[48] Burrow, *Ages of Man*, pp. 5–10.

[49] Bartholomaeus Anglicus, *On the Properties of Things*, I, 292 (ll. 4–5).

[50] Ibid., I, 292 (ll. 10–11, 14–15).

[51] Isidore of Seville, *Etymologiae*, II.ii, cited in Burrow, *Ages of Man*, pp. 200–1.

[52] Bartholomaeus Anglicus, *On the Properties of Things*, I, 292 (l. 4).

[53] Siraisi, *Medieval and Early Renaissance Medicine*, pp. 97–101.

and dry resulting from the mixture of the elements in the body'.[54] The visible differences between the bodies of young and old men were explained with reference to the invisible complexions typical of those bodies. Young men were characterized by a preponderance of heat and moisture which decrease over time as 'innate heat consumes the body's moisture over the lifespan'.[55] So the Middle English version of *De proprietatibus rerum* explains the reason for physical growth of young men on the basis that 'þe membres ben neische [soft] and tendre, and abil to strecche and growe by vertu of hete þat haþ maistrie þerinne anon to þe perfeccioun of complement'.[56] The physical development of female bodies – their outward and visible growth as well as the invisible changes to a complexion over time – was conceived as fundamentally different to that of male bodies. Women's bodies were generally held to be colder than men's, for instance, and they were set on a different developmental path from the beginning.[57]

Complexion theory also provided a way of grounding characteristics other than the physical in biology. The humours – the bodily fluids of blood, phlegm, bile and black bile – were responsible for maintaining the balance of an individual's complexion. They were, however, the cause of psychological and personality traits as well as one's purely physical characteristics. Aristotle's account of the youthful character in his *Rhetoric* set the precedent for this thinking. Young men, he claims, show traits determined by their sanguine temperament, including changeableness, hot temper, optimism, courage, idealism and sociability.[58] The logical consequence of such arguments was to associate women with widely different personal qualities from those ascribed to men, such as inactivity and inconstancy, dictated by the preponderance of cold, moist phlegm in their bodies.[59]

Medieval scholars also held that the development of male bodies affected the development of a man's reason, understood not only as cognitive ability, but as the capacity to make moral judgements. The idea that humans possessed a faculty capable of exercising control over man's competing desires was also first established by Aristotle and elaborated by medieval thinkers such as Thomas Aquinas.[60] Seven seems to have been regarded as an age at which reason was first sufficiently functional for children to take on

---

[54] Ibid., p. 101.
[55] Ibid., p. 103; P. O. Lewry, 'Study of Ageing in the Arts Faculty of the Universities of Paris and Oxford', in *Ageing and the Aged in Medieval Europe*, ed. M. M. Sheehan (Toronto, 1990), pp. 23–38.
[56] Bartholomaeus Anglicus, *On the Properties of Things*, I, 292.
[57] J. Cadden, *The Meanings of Sex Difference in the Middle Ages: Medicine, Science and Culture* (Cambridge, 1993), pp. 170–7, 183–6.
[58] Burrow, *Ages of Man*, pp. 191–4.
[59] Cadden, *Meanings of Sex Difference*, pp. 184–5.
[60] A. Kenny, *Aquinas on Mind* (London and New York, 1993), pp. 71–88; N. Kretzmann, 'Philosophy of Mind', in *The Cambridge Companion to Aquinas*, ed. N. Kretzmann and E. Stump (Cambridge, 1993), pp. 128–52.

some responsibilities.[61] For instance, it was possible to contract a marriage at the age of seven under canon law. It was not permitted that the parties consummate the marriage before twelve for girls and fourteen for boys, as much because they were regarded as incapable of giving their intellectual consent to the union before this point as that they were sexually immature.[62] Over the thirteenth and fourteenth centuries the sacraments of the eucharist, confession and extreme unction gradually became restricted to particular ages associated with the development of discernment.[63]

Works offering practical advice on the education of young men, therefore, give careful thought to the parallel development of body and mind. John Trevisa's fourteenth-century English translation of Giles of Rome's *De regimine principum* (1270s) – a work which relies heavily of Aristotelian thought – sees the characteristics of the young man as determined by the work of the humours and other aspects of his physical body, but also by his emerging capacity for reason. The young man has a relative lack of reason, and so is naturally 'inclyned to yuel maners and outrage' and to 'lecherie', and 'inclyned to folwe passions'.[64] On one hand the text sets out a regime of physical training for young princes and nobles to equip them for their military functions, but on the other it views the training of the faculties of the soul as a key objective of their education. For instance, between the ages of seven and fourteen educators should focus on the development of an 'ordinat wille', a will directed at proper objects but also indicating a faculty for order and self-control, rather than a purely intellectual understanding.[65] Moral self-discipline is necessary to moderate the great 'lust and likynge' which young men feel at this age, prompted by the body, and moreover they do not yet have the intellectual powers required to do justice to the higher branches of learning.[66]

Pictorial versions of the Ages of Man in England use depictions of the ageing male body. They distinguish infants and young children by emphasizing the small size of babies and boys.[67] Some indicate physical maturity by showing a figure wearing a beard.[68] Towards the end of life, old age is indicated through physical weakness: old men are shown with crooked backs and leaning on sticks for support.[69] Textual versions of the Ages use similar

---

61 Orme, *Medieval Children*, p. 68.
62 Ibid., pp. 334–7; Pollock and Maitland, *History of English Law*, II, 390–2.
63 Orme, *Medieval Children*, pp. 214–16; N. Orme, 'Children and the Church in Medieval England, *Journal of Ecclesiastical History* 45 (1994), 563–87 (pp. 573–6).
64 Aegidius Romanus (Giles of Rome), *The Governance of Kings and Princes: John Trevisa's Middle English Translation of the* De regimine principum *of Aegidius Romanus*, ed. D. C. Fowler, C. F. Briggs and P. G. Remley (New York and London, 1997), pp. 219 (ll. 33, 35, 40).
65 Ibid., p. 240 (ll. 9–35).
66 Ibid., pp. 240–1.
67 Sears, *Ages of Man*, p. 73.
68 Ibid.
69 Ibid., p. 147.

markers to indicate age. They usually associate childhood and youth with bodily perfection in terms of health, strength and beauty. In *The Mirror of the Periods of Man's Life* 'Liʒtnesse, strenþe, corage & bewte' (l. 33) all offer their service to the young child. The description of the thirty-year-old Youthe in *The Parlement of the Thre Ages* stresses similar physical characteristics:

> The firste was a ferse freke, fayrere than thies othire
> [. . .]
> He was balghe in the breste and brode in the scholdirs,
> His axles and his armes were iliche longe,
> And in the medill als a mayden menskfully schapen;
> Longe legges and large, and lele for to schewe.   (ll. 109–15)

Youthe represents the Aristotelian *acme* of physical health and strength, and his description makes a powerful contrast with Elde, whose decrepitude is signalled by his white beard and eyebrows, bent back, baldness and toothlessness (ll. 152–65). Similar oppositions between youth and old age are found in other English texts. The old man in *The Mirror of the Periods of Man's Life* bewails the passing of the 'strengþe, bewte & heele' of his youth, and instead has to suffer failing sight and hearing and a crooked back.[70]

These visible changes are tied to the unseen physiological processes of the ageing male body. In *The Mirror of the Periods of Man's Life*, for example, Lechery warns Mankind of the medical dangers to men of abstaining from sex:

> For if þou in ʒouþe sparist þanne þee,
> Þou maist falle in greet perille.
> Ʒouþe ful of corage wole be;
> Þou must haue helpe, or ellis spille.   (ll. 227–30)

This is a direct reference to a substantial body of medical theory which argued that a moderate level of sexual activity was actually necessary for males to maintain good health.[71] While Lechery exploits medical theory in support of his case for indulging in sex, Conscience offers a counter-argument based on humoral theory. He explains that 'Leccherie axiþ great dispense, / It distroiþe mannis kineli heete' (ll. 261–2). Conscience argues that the excess of heat, characteristic of young male bodies, will rapidly be consumed with uncontrolled sexual activity. In other words, it hastens the natural ageing process of which the old Mankind becomes aware when he later observes, 'Myn hoote blood is kelid coolde' (l. 470).

Plays also depict male ageing through key physical markers. When Humanum Genus emerges as an old man from the Castle in *The Castle of Perseverance*, the passage of time since his last appearance on stage is conveyed

---

[70] *Mirror of the Periods of Man's Life*, ll. 411, 433–8, 470.
[71] Cadden, *Meanings of Sex Difference*, pp. 273–5.

through his aged body: his hair is white, his back bent and his bones are feeble and sore (ll. 2482–91). He is also aware of his complexion changing to a colder and moister one, since he grows 'al colde' (l. 2484) and notices 'My nose is colde and gynnyth to droppe' (l. 2490). *Nature* includes a similar description of the ageing Man, which shows the same cooling process indicated by the fact that 'Hys nose droppeth' (II.945). *The Worlde and the Chylde* alludes to the physical frailty of the infant body, the vitality of the young man's body, and the decrepitude of the old man's body.[72] In *The Interlude of Youth*, the central character introduces himself to the audience with a catalogue of his body, pointing out his bushy hair and his strong, well-shaped arms and legs as signs of youthful vigour (ll. 42–54).

In this respect, the plays adopt some of the structuring principles of the Ages of Man tradition. They map the course of a man's life, from birth to death, and mark off stages in that process. Like the Ages of Man, they make characteristics of a sexed body into the markers of passing time. These characteristics may be visible ones, so that bushy hair or grey hair, strong limbs or bent backs come to stand for vigorous young bodies or decaying ageing ones. The plays also allude to the invisible processes underlying and specific to the growth and decay of male bodies: the changing complexion and interplay of bodily humours which cause the visible signs of ageing. As such, we can see that these bodies are discursively constructed, and are the product of a long tradition of scholarly thought.

Nevertheless, the plays apply this scientific knowledge in their own very particular ways. They follow Aristotelian principle in explaining behavioural and psychological characteristics of men with reference to biological facts about male bodies, but they go on to relate the biological phenomena of maleness to the social and political phenomena of different masculinities. Because of its importance for the inheritance of property and the adult rights and responsibilities which accompany it for noblemen, the age of twenty-one becomes prominent in them. The texts consistently relate the undesirable behaviour and attitudes of the young men they depict – deviant and aberrant masculinities of various kinds – to the scientifically defined period of youth. In doing so, they draw on images of and knowledge about young men from a range of later medieval sources. These are the subject of the following chapter.

---

72 *Worlde and the Chylde*, ll. 32–5, 131–4, 271, 795–801.

CHAPTER TWO

Young Masculinity
and Late Medieval Discourses of Youth

Derek Neal has recently defined a masculinity as 'a set of meanings [. . .] grounded in the male body'.[1] As argued in the previous chapter, medieval descriptions of men's development might start from the empirical observation of male bodies and attempts to account for the phenomena of ageing; but they do not end there. The interludes work from a more or less objective model of a typical male life-span (though the precise nature of the relationship between generalizing models and the 'reality' of individual bodies is open to debate); but they map onto that model other cultural and social assumptions about men, and so make them seem 'natural' and obvious. The 'set of meanings' implied in the young male characters of the interludes can only be understood in the context of late medieval discourses of youth which had already invested young male bodies with multiple significance. As the present chapter shows, not all the play-texts under discussion in this book endorse these meanings; some deliberately contest and disrupt them.

Young men and sinfulness

Late medieval devotional and morally didactic works tend to associate young men with the sinful state. Frequently used to represent the fallen state of the human race, young men are depicted as devoted to the pleasures of this world, rather than to a life of prayer and self-examination in preparation for the world to come. This association is the product of a moral discourse which refers to male bodies in order to explain human nature. Ostensibly, texts rehearse universal truths about the spiritual state of human beings in general, but in practice they frequently relate spiritual states to the physical nature of men, so that the spiritual lives they describe are thoroughly gendered.

To begin with, depicting male bodies at different points of the life-cycle is a convenient way of indicating the passing of time, and – perhaps more importantly – of showing that time is running out or counting down. Highly conscious as they are of the end of time, both as the death of individuals, and

---

[1] D. Neal, 'Masculine Identity in Late Medieval English Society and Culture', in *Writing Medieval History*, ed. N. Partner (London, 2005), pp. 171–88.

as the end of the world and the judgement to come, morally didactic works use the appearance of male bodies to represent the passing of time and to mark off stages of life.[2] The connection between life-span and historical time is made explicit in the Ages of Man window in Canterbury cathedral (*c.* 1180) which indicates the six Ages by depicting six male figures whose relative size, dress and attributes indicate their different ages.[3] This window originally formed part of a larger programme in glass, illustrating the biblical story of the Marriage at Cana in relation to its types as derived from exegetical traditions. The Ages of Man window represents the moral level of interpretation of the Biblical passage. The six jars containing the water turned into wine by Jesus are taken to represent the six Ages of man's life, in order to illustrate the possibility of repentance – of a spiritual transformation – at any stage of life.[4] The Ages of the World window, which also formed part of the programme, emphasized how the jars could be understood as representing six historical periods, up to and including the end of time. These windows remind their viewers that spiritual renewal is possible, but only up to a certain point. Either death or the Day of Judgement will mark the day at which salvation will no longer be available.

Moreover, the ageing processes characteristic of male bodies give moral writers an opportunity to expound the idea of transience. For instance, the devotional text *The Pricke of Conscience* (first half of the fourteenth century) emphasizes the attractiveness of young bodies:

> A man þat es yhung and light,
> Be he never swa stalworth and wyght,
> And comly of shap, lufly and fayre,
> Angers and yvels may hym appayre,
> And his beuté and his strength abate,
> And mak hym in ful wayk state,
> And chaunge alle fayre colour,
> Þat son fayles and fades, als dos þe flour.   (ll. 688–95)[5]

The text uses the image of the healthy and strong young male body in order to render all the more poignant the effects of disease and the passing of the years. In this context, the reference to the young body is intended to encourage meditation on 'þe wrechednes of mans kynde' (l. 351). In a world subject to decay and death, the message is to turn one's thoughts to eternal matters.

Images of old men's bodies are used for similar purposes, particularly in texts where old men reflect on their past youth, and compare their young

---

2   Burrow, *Ages of Man*, pp. 55–94.
3   Ibid., pp. 90–2; Sears, *Ages of Man*, p. 74.
4   Burrow, *Ages of Man*, p. 24; Sears, *Ages of Man*, p. 74.
5   *The Pricke of Conscience: A Northumbrian Poem by Richard Rolle de Hampole*, ed. R. Morris (Berlin, 1863).

bodies with their present, aged ones.[6] In *The Mirror of the Periods of Man Life* (*c.* 1400), the text notes the passing of the bodily 'strengþe, bewte, & heele' (l. 435) which Mankind enjoyed as a young man.[7] The speaker in the lyric 'O Vanyte off vanytes' reflects on his aged body, and ruefully declares that the young man:

> [. . .] lytell remembrys his awne febulnys;
> ho ʒouth schall pas & departe a-wey,
> And deth schall come, þat is none ney.   (ll. 59–61)[8]

The transience of mortal and male bodies is also a theme of the moral play *Everyman* (printed 1509–19). The Messenger who introduces the play explains to the audience that its aim is to remind them 'How transitory we be all daie' (l. 6).[9] He continues:

> Here shall you se how Felawshyp/and Iolyte,
> Bothe/Strengthe/Pleasure/and Beaute,
> Wyll fade from the as floure in Maye.   (ll. 16–18)

Many texts exploit these distinctions between healthy, beautiful young bodies and decrepit old ones in order to make this point. The old men of *The Parlement of the Thre Ages* and *The Mirror of the Periods of Man's Life*, for example, both paint graphic verbal pictures of their own infirm and bent bodies and similar descriptions of aged men are included in the moral plays *The Castle of Perseverance*, *Nature* and *The Worlde and the Chylde*.[10] These descriptions were probably reinforced in performance through the actors'costume, make-up and gestures. Stark contrasts between young and old bodies are intended to shock the spectator into a contemplation of their own mortality.

The artistic motif of The Three Living and the Three Dead has a similar function.[11] These images were fairly widespread in later medieval England, and survive as wall paintings in parish churches and manors, and as manuscript illuminations. The 'three living' in the images are always three young men, usually depicted as kings, who, while hawking, encounter three mouldering corpses (the 'three dead'). The corpses exhort the young men to

---

6   R. Woolf, *English Religious Lyrics in the Middle Ages* (Oxford, 1968), pp. 330–6; P. Tristram, *Figures of Life and Death in Medieval English Literature* (London, 1976), pp. 62–94; S. Shahar, 'The Old Body in Medieval Culture', in *Framing Medieval Bodies*, ed. S. Kay and M. Rubin (Manchester, 1994), pp. 160–86 (pp. 164–70).

7   *Hymns to the Virgin and Christ*, ed. Furnivall, pp. 58–78.

8   *Religious Lyrics of the Fifteenth Century*, ed. C. Brown (Oxford, 1939), pp. 238–40.

9   *Everyman*, ed. A. C. Cawley (Manchester, 1961).

10   *Parlement of the Thre Ages*, ll. 283–9, in *Wynnere and Wastoure*, ed. Ginsberg; *Mirror of the Periods of Man's Life*, ll. 485–9; *Castle of Perseverance*, ll. 2482–90; *Nature*, II.941–51; *Worlde and the Chylde*, 795–801.

11   Woolf, *English Religious Lyrics*, pp. 344–7; Tristram, *Figures of Life and Death*, pp. 162–7; P. Binsky, *Medieval Death* (London, 1996), pp. 134–8.

remember the fact that they will soon be corpses themselves. So in the De Lisle Psalter (London, British Library Arundel 83.II, *c.* 1310) the kings exclaim, 'Ich am afert', 'Lo whet ich se' and 'Me þinkeþ hit beþ deueles þre'; while the three dead ominously respond, 'Ich wes wel fair', 'Such scheltou [shalt thou] be', 'For godes loue be wer by me'.[12] The images and accompanying text powerfully delineate the contrasts between the healthy and richly attired young men and the decaying bodies of the dead, dressed in rags. Youthful health and aristocratic wealth will not avail against the common fate of all men.

In a sense, these morally didactic texts ascribe a positive value to the beauty, health and strength of young male bodies. However, their transitory nature makes them insubstantial in comparison with the solid joys and lasting treasure of eternal life, held out by the texts as altogether better. At the same time, the texts are distrustful of young male bodies, not only because they are subject to decay and death, but also because their physical attributes are represented as a potential ground of sinfulness. The very health and strength of young men leads them into the sin of the pride of life, an attitude of arrogant self-sufficiency.[13] Young men's health and strength lull them into a false sense of spiritual security, so that they believe that death and judgement will not affect them, or at least are far enough away to be no cause for immediate concern. This overconfidence in the flesh is illustrated in the early, fragmentary moral play which has come to be known as *The Pride of Life* (*c.* 1350).[14] The central character, The King of Life, is at the height of his physical powers. His implicit dependence on his body to keep him from death is symbolized by his reliance on his two knights, Streinth or *Fortidudo* (strength), and Hele or *Sanitas* (health):

> 3e, þes be kni3tis of curteisye
> And doghti men of dede;
> Of Deth ne of his maistrie
> Ne have I no drede.   (ll. 259–62)

So strong is his confidence in his body, that he refuses to listen to the advice of the Queen and Bishop to repent.[15] Only a direct encounter with Death himself destroys his trust in the youthful body.[16]

The Interlude of Youth also draws on this long tradition in linking the spiritual condition of young men to their physical characteristics.[17] When Youth first enters, he catalogues for the benefit of the audience the features of his youthful body: his 'royal' and 'thick' hair, his 'pliant' body, his 'big and strong'

---

12 Binsky, *Medieval Death*, pp. 135–7.
13 Tristram, *Figures of Life and Death*, pp. 21, 34–47.
14 *Non-Cycle Plays and Fragments*, ed. N. Davis, EETS SS 1 (1970), pp. 90–105.
15 *Pride of Life*, ll. 179–90, 199–238, 391–406.
16 Ibid., ll. 81–112.
17 T. Davenport, ' "Lusty Fresch Galaunts" ', in *Aspects of Early English Drama*, ed. P. Neuss (Cambridge, 1983), p. 125.

arms, and so on (ll. 45–54). Youth describes himself with considerable relish, and the extent of his confidence in his body becomes apparent in his exchanges with Charity, the representative of good in the play. Like the Queen and Bishop in *The Pride of Life*, Charity urges Youth to consider the prospect of death and the future judgement (ll. 65–80). Youth's contemptuous dismissal of Charity and his counsel confirms his pride of life (ll. 81–9).

Moral and didactic texts which describe the life of man by dividing it into stages also tend to incorporate narratives of fall and repentance. This has the effect of making the opening stages of man's life invariably into a period of sinfulness. The protagonists of lyrics and plays fall from grace in their infancy, a fall often represented by the child's choice of an evil counsellor rather than a good one as his guide for the life ahead. The young Humanum Genus from *The Castle of Perseverance*, the young man from the lyric 'Of the seuen ages', and the young Mankind from *The Mirror of the Periods of Man's Life* all have to choose between a Good Angel and a Bad Angel, and each selects the Bad Angel.[18] So too the young Man of the play *Nature* chooses Sensualyte over Reason as his counsellor (I.581–654). Like Infans in *The Worlde and the Chylde*, he is under the sway of 'The Worlde', a character who represents the sinful aspects of temporal existence, particularly those sins which follow from conforming to the habits of worldly life.[19] In *The Worlde and the Chylde*, The Worlde exerts even more influence over the central character as Infans remains in his household service from the age of seven to twenty-one. After this period the main character goes on to choose the advice of Folye (representing the seven deadly sins) over that of Conscyence. In this kind of structure, youth is inevitably sinful.

The structural nature of this association of youth with sinfulness is indicated when young men are performing sins marked as specific to their stage of life. In some texts, these are distinct from the sins associated with the mature or old man. For instance, in *The Parlement of the Thre Ages*, Youthe (represented as a man of thirty) is characterized by extravagant expenditure and the pursuit of love, battles, hunting and hawking, whereas Medil Age (a man of sixty) is preoccupied with his business dealings and the acquisition of property.[20]

In *The Castle of Perseverance*, Humanum Genus's youthful sinfulness is symbolized in his attendants Lust and Lykynge and Folye. These companions lead him into the pursuit of worldly and sensual pleasure, to the exclusion of thoughts of repentance. Only at the age of forty does Humanum Genus repent, spending the next twenty years protected from attack by the sins inside the Castle of Perseverance itself. When he falls for the second time, at

---

18 *Castle of Perseverance*, ll. 393–401; *Mirror of the Periods of Man's Life*, ll. 65–82.

19 Potter, *English Morality Play*, p. 61; Medwall, *Plays of Henry Medwall*, ed. Moeslein, p. 257; S. R. Westfall, *Patrons and Performance: Early Tudor Household Revels* (Oxford, 1990), p. 160; *Worlde and the Chylde*, ed. Davidson and Happé, pp. 8–9; Happé, *English Drama*, p. 85.

20 Burrow, *Ages of Man*, p. 71.

the age of sixty, he is enticed from his place of safety, not by his former companions, but by the sin Covetyse (covetousness). Humanum Genus was also covetous in his youth. As Lust and Lykynge points out, anyone who wants to live a lavish lifestyle has to be covetous in order to fund it (ll. 500–3). However, covetousness is presented as the overriding characteristic sin of the old man. As the character Covetyse shows in his temptation of Humanum Genus, this sin is the natural consequence of the fears of the old man that his final years will be poverty-stricken and miserable (ll. 2493–543).

The interludes *Nature*, *The Worlde and the Chylde* and *The Interlude of Youth* take different approaches to the depiction of the sinfulness of old age, which disrupts *The Castle of Perseverance*'s neat scheme of age-related sins. In these plays young men are still to be viewed as sinful – indeed the forms of their sinfulness are strikingly similar, as each young man makes his way into a seedy urban underworld of taverns, prostitutes, eating, drinking and gambling, which allows him full rein for his sinful inclinations.[21] But these interludes say relatively little about the sins of old age. In *The Interlude of Youth*, old age is not depicted at all since the play concludes with Youth's repentance, and though the protagonists of *Nature* and *The Worlde and the Chylde* repent both in youth and in their old age, like Humanum Genus in *The Castle of Perseverance*, the sins of their later age are given minimal representation.[22] In *The Worlde and the Chylde*, Manhode is led off to the stews of London by Folye after Manhode's second fall from grace. When the audience next sees him, only forty-seven lines later, he is already an old man, chastened by his experiences and only too ready to receive Conscyence's advice to repent (ll. 763–806). When Man in *Nature* reaches old age proper, Sensualyte reports that he will be attended by covetousness for 'a yere or twayn' (II.981), but the reference to this characteristic sin of old age is brief and dismissive. Indeed, of all the deadly sins covetousness is the only one not to be presented as a major speaking role in the play. This contrasts strongly with Covetyse's dominance in the final section of *The Castle of Perseverance* and that play's distinction between the sins of youth and those of age.[23] All three plays – *Nature*, *The Worlde and the Chylde* and *The Interlude of Youth* – deliberately minimize the sins of old age, presenting youth as the period of sinfulness *per se*, rather than just one stage of life with its own particular brand of sinfulness. They show a striking contrast between youth, as a period of sinfulness, and old age as a period of repentance and holiness, though there are subtle variations between the plays which make different effects.

---

21 Bevington, *Tudor Drama and Politics*, pp. 40–1; Potter, *English Morality Play*, p. 64; R. Southern, 'The Technique of Play Presentation', in *The Revels History of Drama in English, Vol. 2: 1500–1576*, ed. C. Leech and T. W. Craik (London and New York, 1980), pp. 72–89 (p. 153).
22 Medwall, *Plays of Henry Medwall*, ed. Nelson, pp. 23–4; *Worlde and the Chylde*, ed. Davidson and Happé, p. 10.
23 *Worlde and the Chylde*, ed. Davidson and Happé, p. 10.

In *Nature*, the decisive moment in Man's career of sin comes when old age comes upon him. The influence of Sensualyte and the seven deadly sins over Man is finally broken by the ageing of his body – when Man comes under the sway of a new character, Age. Age's ascendancy is apparent from Man's appearance, and an abrupt change in Man's companions. Sensualyte says:

> [Age] has brought in Reason
> In suche wyse that at no season
> Nothyng can be wrought
>
> But Reason must be called therto!   (II.952–5)

Since Reason has assumed charge of Man, the sins realize that their time is over and leave Man, Glutony and Bodyly Lust being the first to depart (II.958–72).[24] Men, the play implies, are simply not prone to sins in age as in youth: the changes to their bodies take away the former desires which drove them to sin.[25] In old age, men are governed solely by their intellectual powers, which, unassailed by the body, are free to direct them to repentance and holiness. *Nature*'s minimizing of covetousness, the sin of old age, is effected in this context. In *Nature*, covetousness is an inevitable sin of old age, but one which Man will simply brush off in the fullness of time. This strongly deterministic model of male sinfulness suggests that youthful sin is inevitable, even natural.[26] Indeed, *Nature* takes the model to its logical conclusion. At the end of the play, Reason assures Man that, as long as he perseveres in his repentance, 'greter reward thou shalt therfore wyn / Than he that never in hys lyfe dyd syn' (II.1404–5). This play actually ascribes a positive value to youthful sinfulness, since in overcoming it old men attain a better kind of holiness, superior even to the state of innocence Man enjoyed at the opening of the play. It may be that *The Worlde and the Chylde*'s minimizing of the sins of age seems to be predicated on a similar foundation, as its central character reappears after his foray to the London stews in the guise of Age, a much older and chastened figure, ripe for repentance. None of the sins of age is mentioned in this context. These plays imply that sinfulness is a 'natural' phenomenon of male youth, determined by physiology, and that holiness in old age is guaranteed by physical changes to the body as it ages.[27]

However, the view that sinfulness is natural to young men is attacked in other texts, including *The Castle of Perseverance*, *The Mirror of the Periods of Man's Life*, the lyric 'Of the seuen ages' and *The Interlude of Youth*. These texts counter the idea that young men cannot, or need not, repent, but may safely put off repentance to the more convenient season of old age. In each, debate

---

24 Medwall, *Plays of Henry Medwall*, ed. Moeslein, p. 263.
25 *Worlde and the Chylde*, ed. Davidson and Happé, p. 10; Medwall, *Plays of Henry Medwall*, ed. Nelson, p. 24.
26 Potter, *English Morality Play*, pp. 64–5.
27 Ibid., pp. 48, 51, 61; Altman, *Tudor Play of Mind*, pp. 16–17.

about the nature of young men and its relation to their spiritual state is articulated in arguments concerning the fate of the central male character between representatives of good and evil – good angels and bad angels, personified virtues and vices. Each participant attempts to persuade the mankind figure to embrace the way of vice or of virtue, often referring to different kinds of knowledge about young male bodies in order to strengthen his case. In *The Mirror of the Periods of Man's Life*, Lust argues that Mankind can allow himself to indulge in sex since ' "ȝouþe so muste; / ȝouþe can not kepe him chast" ' (ll. 101–2). Lust may be alluding to scientific knowledge about the sanguine complexions of young men which incline them to love and lust; but in any case his authoritative tone suggests that he refers to a commonly held belief about the nature of young men. Similar pronouncements can be seen in other moral texts, for example in a fifteenth-century sermon which declares that 'ȝonge men spare not for no drede of God, noþur þei leue not for no shame of þe world, to renne to here lechery with a like desire as a bere renneþ to ete hony'.[28] As we saw in Chapter One, competing vices and virtues in *The Mirror of the Periods of Man's Life* refer to medical theories to argue for and against sexual activity for young men (ll. 227–30, 262).[29] In this poem, Mankind himself goes on to quote age-related norms which justify his pleasures:

> '[. . .] ȝouthe axiþ delice;
> For ȝouthe þe course of kinde wole holde;
> But [unless] ȝouthe were a foole and nyce,
> How schulde wijsdom be founde in oolde'   (ll. 273–6)[30]

Mankind declares that sinfulness is natural to young men and holiness to old ones, their spiritual states produced by the 'course of kinde' or the natural process of ageing. This echoes the bad angel's earlier assertion that ' "Course of kynde is for ȝouþe to be wilde" ' (l. 79), in order to justify the child's quarrels with his peers.[31] But Mankind goes even further and implies that the wisdom of the old somehow depends on having behaved foolishly in one's youth, and that it is otherwise impossible to attain holiness in later life.

Similarly the Bad Angel in *The Castle of Perseverance* appeals to the notion that old age is the natural period for holiness, arguing that Humanum Genus can afford to postpone thoughts of repentance:

> Wyth þe Werld þou mayst be bold
> Tyl þou be sexty wyntyr hold.
> Wanne þi nose waxit cold,
> Þanne mayst þou drawe to goode.   (ll. 416–19)[32]

---

28 *Middle English Sermons*, ed. W. O. Ross, EETS OS 209 (1940), p. 236 (ll. 18–21). See also G. R. Owst, *Literature and Pulpit in Medieval England* (Cambridge, 1933), p. 461.

29 Cadden, *Meanings of Sex Difference*, pp. 273–5; Lewry, 'Study of Ageing', p. 26.

30 Burrow, *Ages of Man*, p. 148.

31 Ibid.

32 Ibid., p. 149.

The Bad Angel of the play links goodness with the physiology of the aged male body. He implies that the cooling process of the male body makes it possible to be holy, and more importantly makes it natural to be holy in old age. Conversely, the passage suggests that it is unnatural for young bodies to produce holiness. So too the vices in *The Interlude of Youth* tempt the character Youth as Pride encourages Youth to ignore the appeals of the virtue, Charity, for repentance:

> Youth, I trow that he would
> Make you holy or ye be old,
> And I swear by the rood
> It is time enough to be good
> When that ye be old.   (ll. 642–6)

Pride claims Youth has plenty of time left before he needs to turn to religion: living the holy life is appropriate to the old, not the young man. This reinforces an earlier remark by Riot, who quotes proverbial wisdom about the young:

> Hark, Youth, for God avow,
> He [Charity] would have thee a saint now!
> But Youth, I shall you tell,
> A young saint, an old devil.   (ll. 612–15)

In his study of the 'young saint, old devil' proverb, Burrow has observed that it implies powerful 'age-related norms' about what is natural to the old and the young.[33] So firmly fixed is the association between youth and sinfulness, old age and holiness in this proverb, that it represents youthful holiness as an inversion of the natural order of things.[34] Youthful holiness, unnatural in and of itself, will, it is implied, produce a further inversion of the natural order in the form of unnatural sinfulness in old age.

Yet these texts cite age-related norms, not to endorse them, but to discredit them.[35] They all attempt to combat the spiritual complacency which biologically deterministic views of men and their spiritual states threaten to engender. The arguments for postponing repentance, based on biological essentialism, are in fact put into the mouths of the representatives of evil: the bad angels and vices who seek the damnation of the central characters. In addition, *The Interlude of Youth* seems designed to show that a young man is capable of repentance, in a way which carefully distinguishes Youth's spiritual renewal from those of young men in other early moral plays. For instance, Man in *Nature* and Manhode in *The Worlde and the Chylde* both repent while young, but are quickly drawn back into sinful lifestyles. Both characters must

---

33 J. A. Burrow, ' "Young Saint, Old Devil": Reflections on a Medieval Proverb', *Review of English Studies* 30 (1979), 385–96; Burrow, *Ages of Man*, pp. 149–50.

34 Burrow, *Ages of Man*, p. 149.

35 Ibid., p. 148; Burrow, ' "Young Saint" ', p. 390.

undergo a second repentance in old age, and this is their true and lasting repentance. In contrast, *The Interlude of Youth* establishes the repentance of its young protagonist as the true and lasting one. The play reinforces this interpretation at its conclusion, as Charity equips Youth with a garment symbolizing repentance, and Humility equips him with rosary beads for his devotions (ll. 767–71). Humility also looks into Youth's future and advocates a life of prayer and the instruction of other 'misdoing men' which Youth affirms he will follow (ll. 772–82). Like other moral plays, *The Interlude of Youth* is governed by a performance convention whereby saying is the equivalent of doing.[36] Youth's words constitute a kind of speech act, and therefore tell the audience not only what he intends, but what he actually does. In this way, *The Interlude of Youth* short-circuits the pattern of a double fall and repentance which associates true repentance with old age. The play does not deny that young men are naturally inclined to sinfulness: on the contrary, it shows a young man applying himself to pride, lechery and wrath with a will. However, it refutes the suggestion that young men are incapable of repentance on the grounds of their physical development by modelling a young man's lasting repentance.

The interludes as a group, then, show considerable tension, derived from a wider medieval debate, between ideas which pull in opposite directions and result in an ambivalent attitude to young men as beings who theoretically ought to repent, but who will not, and perhaps need not, do so while they are young. The presentation of young men in *Nature*, *The Worlde and the Chylde* and *The Interlude of Youth* is determined by different views on the extent to which their spiritual state is related to their biology. These views also dictate the ways in which male life-cycles are yoked to narratives of fall and repentance.

Yet the interludes do not accommodate the full range of views on the nature of young men current in later medieval morally didactic literature. For instance, elsewhere parents are frequently exhorted to attend to the education of their children on the grounds that the young are naturally receptive to training. This trait is often mentioned by texts which advocate strict discipline and express disapproval of indulgence and the setting of bad examples by parents.[37] The penitential handbook *Ayenbite of Inwyt* (1340) compares children to the horse which must be tamed as a colt, if it is to be tamed at all; and to the new shoe which moulds itself to the wearer's foot, and then may not be reshaped.[38] *Fasciculus morum*, a fourteenth-century Latin manual on the vices and virtues, probably intended for preachers as an aid to sermon writing, quotes a similar Middle English proverb which declares that 'Woso woneþ

---

[36] J. O. Fichte, 'The Presentation of Sin as Verbal Action in the Moral Interludes', *Anglia* 103 (1985), 26–47.

[37] Owst, *Literature and Pulpit*, pp. 470–8; Orme, *Medieval Children*, pp. 84–5.

[38] *Dan Michel's Ayenbite of Inwyt, or Remorse of Conscience*, ed. R. Morris and P. Graddon, 2 vols., EETS OS 23 and 278 (1965–79), I, 220.

hym noçt to goude furst in hys youth, / Unthewes to leve were to hym in his elde wel uncoupe'.[39] The Latin text develops this idea by referring to a long-established image of children as comparable to soft wax upon which it is easy to make an impression. Adults, in contrast, are like hardened wax which will not easily take a mark. The writer extends the idea in an image of the sapling which bends easily, unlike the mature tree.[40] These figures stress that the young are particularly malleable, a concept which is also related to biological determinism, since scientific thought held that the preponderance of heat in the young rendered them physically soft and malleable. Trevisa's translation of the *De proprietatibus rerum* describes children as 'tendre and neische, quabby and gleymy' [tender and soft, moist and viscous], for example.[41] For this reason medieval thinkers held that the limbs of infants could be shaped and trained while they were young.[42] The characters of the young were by extension equally plastic. Adults, with their cooler complexions, were considered less malleable, both in body and in character. Didactic texts therefore warned that once character was set it was set for life.

In consequence, parents bear a heavy responsibility in this discourse, since they are responsible for the ways their children are formed into adults. Some *exempla* present the dreadful consequences of parental negligence in the shape of children who become fixed in their naturally wicked ways and so come to an evil end. *The Pricke of Conscience* imagines children rising up to testify against bad parents on the Day of Judgement.[43] The fourteenth-century *Alphabet of Tales* introduces us to Thais whose mother indulged her and who consequently became 'þe moste common strompyd in all þe land'.[44] Another *exemplum* in the collection features a young man who was 'tenderlie broght vp & noþing correcte nowder of fadur nor moder when he did wrong'.[45] About to be hanged as a thief, he takes the opportunity of a last embrace with his father to bite off the father's nose and to blame his faulty education for his predicament. A version of this tale also appears in the *Fasciculus morum*, where the son uses an image of flexible and inflexible rods to show his father how easy it would have been to bring him up in the right way as a boy.[46]

The absence of this kind of rhetoric from most of the interludes under discussion in this book is probably connected to the absence of parents from the texts. Only in *Calisto and Melebea* is there reference to the efficacy of education, because Melebea's father Danio is a prominent character in the play, and

---

39 *Fasciculus morum: A Fourteenth-Century Preacher's Handbook*, ed. and trans. S. Wenzel (University Park PA, 1989), p. 90 (ll. 68–9).
40 Ibid., p. 90 (ll. 71–3).
41 Bartholomaeus Anglicus, *On the Properties of Things*, I, 291 (ll. 18–19).
42 Ibid., I, 299 (ll. 21–25). See also Orme, *Medieval Children*, p. 62.
43 *Pricke of Conscience*, ed. Morris, ll. 5424–36, 5544–59, 5866–9.
44 *An Alphabet of Tales*, ed. M. M. Banks, 2 vols., EETS OS 126 and 127 (1904–5), I, 2–4 (p. 3 (ll. 3–4)).
45 Ibid., I, 152 (ll.11–12). See also Owst, *Literature and Pulpit*, pp. 467–8.
46 *Fasciculus morum*, ed. and trans. Wenzel, p. 90 (ll. 84–93).

he ascribes Melebea's resistance to Calisto's seduction to his daughter's upbringing (ll. 1025–87).[47] Melebea's virtue is thus presented as the by-product of effective paternal governance, and this gives Danio the authority to discourse on the role of parents and masters in maintaining good order in society as a whole. On the other hand, the young men of the plays may be provided with counsellors and guides, but they are not under the authority of a father figure. The emphasis is much more on their personal responsibility to regulate their own moral being.

Like other late medieval moral literature, then, the interludes hold that young men are essentially sinful. By presenting their central characters as embodied, the texts unequivocally link the spiritual states they describe with the biological and developmental characteristics of young male bodies. The interludes explore the implications of this biologically essentialist view of men. *Nature* takes biological essentialism to its logical conclusion by implying that both sin and repentance are indissolubly tied to the physical processes of ageing, so that old age produces repentance in a way that youth cannot. *The Worlde and the Chylde* also privileges old age, in that it makes no reference to old age's typical sins, but presents this period as one associated with regret for past sins, leading to a final repentance. While these plays do not exactly approve of youthful sinfulness, they appear to tolerate it as a necessary stage of existence. *Nature* even makes youthful sinfulness into the basis for a superior holiness in old men.

However, *The Interlude of Youth* takes issue with this attitude to young men. Like some moral texts, it seeks to discredit the view that sin is natural or necessary for young men. It represents such views as promoting spiritual complacency and as arising from one's own sinful desires – in short, as serving the Devil's interests, rather than God's, in enabling young men to justify their sinfulness to themselves. Instead, the play demonstrates that a true and lasting repentance is possible to young men.

In spiritual terms, the period of male youth in the interludes is a period of conflict: both the internal conflict between different parts of the young man's nature; and a wider ideological conflict over whether the spiritual condition of young men matters or not. The interludes do not present a unified view on these issues, but present different standpoints in an ongoing debate.

Young men and incivility

Biological essentialism – where character traits and behaviours are held to be produced by the male body – is a habit of thought which tends to efface distinctions between men of different status groups, ethnicities and cultures.[48]

---

[47] Line references are to *Three Rastell Plays: Four Elements, Calisto and Melebea, Gentleness and Nobility*, ed. R. Axton (Cambridge and Totowa, 1979).

[48] Shahar, 'Old Body', p. 161.

It constructs a universal masculinity, based on a male body which seems to exist outside society and culture. Yet it would not be true to say that biological essentialism alone explains the presentation of the young men of the interludes, since these men are firmly located in social terms as young noblemen and in terms of hierarchical relationships within households. Later medieval courtesy books teach young men about acceptable and unacceptable masculinities for the household context, and its methods and values are also discernible in the interludes.

Courtesy literature is in many ways an intensely practical genre as texts prescribe the minutiae of behaviour which young men should emulate, most frequently in the course of formal dining in the great hall of a noble household where they served diners or dined themselves.[49] Texts also discuss the conventions of behaviour associated with entering households,[50] going to church,[51] walking in the streets,[52] and even rising in the morning and going to bed at night.[53] The instruction offered by these works has, on one level, a very pragmatic goal. Being able to display the right forms of social behaviour at the appropriate time will help young men to get and keep jobs in household service. This is the whole thrust of Sir John Russell's 'Boke of Nurture', which opens with Russell recounting a chance encounter with an unnamed young man who laments his inability to obtain employment in a household.[54] In response, Russell obligingly draws on his own extensive experience as a household office-holder in elevated circles in order to provide the young man with the expertise he lacks.

Some courtesy texts assume a noble audience – 'The Babees Book' for example addresses young men of the 'bloode Royalle' (l. 15).[55] We know from external evidence that such books were used in great households for the instruction of young nobles.[56] The ordinances of Edward IV's household, for example, stipulate that the master of the henchmen should 'show the scoolez

---

49 J. Nicholls, *The Matter of Courtesy: Medieval Courtesy Books and the Gawain-Poet* (Cambridge, 1985), p. 14. On later medieval dining practices see C. M. Woolgar, *The Great Household in Late Medieval England* (New Haven and London, 1999), pp. 145–65; S. Wells, 'Food in the City: An Interdisciplinary Study of the Ideological and Symbolic Uses of Food in the Urban Environment in Later Medieval England' (unpublished Ph.D. Thesis, University of York, 2002), pp. 137–83.

50 'The Young Children's Book', ll. 85–96, in *The Babees Book*, ed. F. J. Furnivall, EETS OS 32 (1868), pp. 17–25; 'The Boke of Curtasye', ll. 5–31, in ibid., pp. 299–327.

51 W. Caxton, *Caxton's Book of Curtesye*, ed. F. J. Furnivall, EETS ES 3 (1868), ll. 71–98.

52 Ibid., ll. 57–70; 'Symon's Lesson of Wysdome for all Maner Chyldryn', ll. 69–76, in *Babees Book*, ed. Furnivall, pp. 399–402; 'Stans puer ad mensam', ll.195–206, in *Queene Elizabeths Achademy*, ed. F. J. Furnivall, EETS ES 8 (1869), pp. 56–64.

53 Caxton, *Caxton's Book of Curtesye*, ll. 22–56; 'Stans puer ad mensam', ll. 215–30.

54 J. Russell, 'The Boke of Nurture', ll. 1–44, in *Babees Book*, ed. Furnivall, pp. 117–239.

55 Ibid., pp. 1–9.

56 N. Orme, *From Childhood to Chivalry: The Education of the English Kings and Aristocracy, 1066–1530* (London and New York, 1984), p. 139; R. F. Green, *Poets and Princepleasers: Literature and the English Court in the Late Middle Ages* (Toronto, 1980), p. 73.

of vrbanitie and nourture of Inglond' and that he should instruct them 'after the booke of vrbanitie'.[57] The tutor employed by Edward Stafford, third duke of Buckingham purchased courtesy books among other educational materials in 1503–04, presumably for the benefit of Stafford's son and noble wards.[58] In practice, many of the surviving courtesy texts assume they are addressing readers not noble by birth, unfamiliar with the habits and manners of an aristocratic milieu, and so in need of practical advice in order to acquit themselves well in it.[59] Some declare that the codes of behaviour they advocate will help one to build a successful career in service. As 'Symon's Lesson of Wysdome' bluntly puts it, 'by fayre manerys men may þee a-vaunce' (l. 68).[60] Service in a great household offered a career structure to young men who could legitimately aspire to work their way up to an office such as steward or treasurer of the household, and so attain the status of a gentleman.[61] Courtesy texts have therefore been described as literature of social mobility, in that they teach young men 'the manners of the class to which they aspire'.[62] Indeed, the late Middle Ages seems to express a supreme confidence in the power of behaviour to assist social climbing. As the late medieval proverb puts it, 'manners maketh man'.[63] It is tempting to assume that William Wykeham, who rose from humble beginnings to be bishop of Winchester, was crediting his career success to his cultivation of good manners when he chose the proverb as his motto.[64]

However, courtesy texts are concerned with the 'making' to men in a more profound sense. They do not simply teach young men how to adopt a social persona for particular times and places, which can be put on and off at will. Rather, they aim to discipline the gestures of young men, because these proceed naturally from essentially uncivilized natures which exclude them from the civilized domain of the household. A gesture has been defined by Keith Thomas as 'any kind of bodily movement or posture (including facial

---

57 *The Household of Edward IV: The Black Book and the Ordinance of 1478*, ed. A. R. Myers (Manchester, 1959), pp. 126–7.

58 K. Mertes, *The English Noble Household, 1250–1600: Good Governance and Politic Rule* (Oxford, 1988), p. 172.

59 M. A. Amos, ' "For Manners Make Man": Bourdieu, De Certeau, and the Common Appropriation of Noble Manners in the *Book of Courtesy*', in *Medieval Conduct*, ed. K. Ashley and R. L. A. Clark, pp. 23–48 (pp. 32–3); C. Sponsler, 'Conduct Books and Good Governance', in *Drama and Resistance: Bodies, Goods and Theatricality in Late Medieval England*, by C. Sponsler (Minneapolis and London, 1997), pp. 50–74 (p. 54).

60 *Babees Book*, ed. Furnivall, pp. 399–402.

61 Mertes, *English Noble Household*, p. 71; R. Horrox, 'Service', in *Fifteenth-Century Attitudes: Perceptions of Society in Late Medieval England*, ed. R. Horrox (Cambridge, 1994), pp. 61–78 (p. 67).

62 F. Riddy, 'Mother Knows Best: Reading Social Change in a Courtesy Text', *Speculum* 71 (1996), 66–86 (p. 77). See also Amos, ' "For Manners Make Man" ', pp. 25–8.

63 'Vrbanitias', ll. 33–4, in *Babees Book*, ed. Furnivall, pp. 13–15.

64 Horrox, 'Service', p. 62.

expression) which transmits a message to the observer'.[65] Late medieval theories of gesture, developed in monastic rules governing behaviour in houses of religious, proposed that gestures transmitted messages about one's true inner self, rather than a superficial social competence.[66] This thesis implies that it is possible to read a man's invisible nature from his manners, posture and habitual gestures. Nicholls has suggested that later medieval courtesy literature developed from monastic rules.[67] In any case, it is founded on analogous principles, so that – for example – talking in church is seen not just as a breach of a social convention but is a 'token of suche as lackyth grace'.[68]

Young men's behaviour is, in this system of thought, determined by their essential nature. The significance of the bad manners of the young is made clear in Lydgate's *Testament* (c. 1448).[69] In this verse-text, Lydgate speaks of himself as old, ill and conscious of the approach of death (ll. 193–240). Like the old men of the moral works discussed in Chapter One, Lydgate feels compelled to review his young life, and (like Everyman) to give a 'rekenyng' for what he has done (l. 218): literally, an account of his life, as a household officer presents his accounts to an auditor.[70] Lydgate recounts his 'myspent tyme' (l. 248) as a novice in the Benedictine order, before a dramatic religious experience at the age of fifteen. He intends his youthful misdemeanours to be understood as determined by his young masculine nature, explicitly referring to complexion theory as a biological explanation of his behaviour, and relating his instability and changeableness of character to the volatile, hot complexion of his young, male body (ll. 290–422). Like the moral and devotional texts discussed earlier, the *Testament* characterizes Lydgate's youth as a period of sinfulness determined by his physical nature. Alongside obviously sinful deeds, such as his wrathful behaviour towards his companions (ll. 621–2), Lydgate lists apparently trivial breaches of etiquette familiar from courtesy literature, like failing to wash before dinner, talking wildly, and looking around too freely (ll. 631, 650, 664). For Lydgate, bad table manners and bad habits are much more than social *faux pas*. They, as much as overt displays of deadly sin, indicate the youthful and degenerate nature within. Listing every uncouth gesture is Lydgate's way of disclosing his secret and invisible inner self in this confessional text.

Like monastic rules, courtesy texts see the uncontrolled gestures of the young as reflecting their typical lack of self-discipline. In John Russell's

---

[65] K. Thomas, 'Introduction', in *A Cultural History of Gesture: From Antiquity to the Present Day*, ed. J. Bremmer and H. Roodenburg (Oxford, 1991), pp. 1–14 (p. 1).

[66] J. Schmitt, 'Introduction and General Introduction', *Gestures, History and Anthropology* 1 (1984), 1–23; J. Schmitt, 'The Rationale of Gestures in the West: Third to Thirteenth Centuries', in *Cultural History of Gesture*, ed. Bremmer and Roodenburg, pp. 59–70.

[67] Nicholls, *Matter of Courtesy*, pp. 22–44.

[68] Caxton, *Caxton's Book of Curtesye*, l. 82.

[69] J. Lydgate, *The Minor Poems of John Lydgate*, ed. H. N. MacCracken, 2 vols., EETS ES 107 (1911) and OS 192 (1934), I, 329–62.

[70] *Everyman*, ed. Cawley, ll. 66–71.

'Boke of Nurture', for instance, Russell's young protégé describes himself as 'wantoun & nyce, recheless & lewde / as Iangelynge as a Iay' (l. 36). 'Wantoun' connotes a lack of moral self-control and a resistance to the control of others, while 'iangelynge' designates the uncontrolled talk which proceeds from this trait, and which is deplored in several texts.[71] It is no coincidence that Russell encounters the young man alone in a wilderness, for the young man is still in a kind of natural, pre-social state. The 'Boke of Nurture' implicitly constructs the household to which the young man seeks entry as the domain of civilization. Before he may enter it, he must therefore remake himself in the image of the disciplined household servant. This is similar to the way in which monastic rules represented the novice as being trained to fit into the idealized spiritual community of a religious house.[72] Likewise, Caxton's prologue to his translation of Jacques Legrand's *Book of Good Manners* presents those of low status who do not exhibit the behaviours of the noble as something less than human. He describes 'the condicyons & maners of the comyn people whiche withoute enformacion & lernyng ben rude and not mannered lyke vnto beestis brute accordyng to an olde prouerb he that is not mannered is no man. for maners make man'.[73] Manners are, in other words, the only thing that separates men from the animals.

For the young nobleman, the discipline of gestures is doubly necessary if he is to take up his role in society. Trevisa's translation of *De regimine principum* places a similar emphasis on the way in which gestures reveal nature. In this context, the English text defines 'beryng' as the 'meuyng of membres and of lymes by þe whiche meuyng disposicion of þe soule may be know'.[74] It states unequivocally that the gestures of young men, other than purely functional ones, are the unmediated expression of their sinful nature: they 'comeþ of folye oþer of pruyde oþer of som vice'.[75] This connection between inner state and outward behaviour is not surprising given that its original writer was an Augustinian friar. However, according to the text, youthful, sinful gestures are particularly undesirable because they reveal a nature which is not suitable for governing others. Like the late medieval English courtesy texts, it selects the young man's gesture of looking around too freely as an illustration of this principle, explaining 'þat is ful vnsemelich for kynges and princes yif þei casten here eyȝen and sight nyseliche aboute, for þerby þei scholde be holde liȝt hedede and lowe and feynt herted for it wolde seme þat he wondrede of alle thinges'.[76] This gesture tells observers not only that the young ruler is in the grip of his youthful sinfulness and instability, but that he is unfit to

---

71 *MED*, *qv.* 'wantoun', 'jangeling(e)'. See also 'Lytylle Childrenes Lytil Boke', l. 90; 'Babees Book', l. 68.

72 Nicholls, *Matter of Courtesy*, pp. 23–4; Schmitt, 'Rationale of Gestures', pp. 67–8.

73 W. Caxton, *The Book of Good Manners* (London, 1500), quoted in Amos, ' "For Manners Make Man" ', p. 45.

74 Aegidius Romanus, *Governance of Kings and Princes*, p. 234 (ll. 27–8).

75 Ibid., p. 235 (ll. 6–8).

76 Ibid., pp. 229–30.

exercise his function of governance since the gesture denotes foolishness, vulgarity and a lack of courage. For this reason, the text advocates the training of noblemen and princes in 'þe maner of lokyng and closing of eiȝene so þat þei opene and close here eiȝene soberliche, for a man doþ wel in ful age þynges þat þei vsen in childhode'.[77] Young noblemen construct an identity as a ruler in part through the control of their gestures. They must adopt a particular vocabulary of gesture in order to transmit reassuring messages about their ability to rule. The control of gestures was just one bodily discipline amongst several which a young nobleman had to master. He had also to become accomplished in the arts of war and riding, in order to fulfil the military functions of his social group.[78] But his education gave equal attention to arts such as dancing, which also required a high degree of physical control, and symbolized the distinctive capacity of nobles for self-control.[79]

Like some of the morally didactic works discussed above, Trevisa's *De regimine principum* expresses confidence that young noblemen are malleable enough to be moulded into better kind of adult man. Middle English courtesy texts also assume that it is possible to learn gestures, in order to create an adult identity. Nicholls has shown that monastic rules taught bodily disciplines in order to promote a particular spiritual state. They enabled one to order one's spirit so that one would be 'receptive and acquiescent to the word of God'.[80] In other words, just as the inner state determines outward gestures, so the control of gestures is a way of reforming one's inner nature. Effectively, the young man is able to remake himself through a process of self-discipline.[81] Courtesy texts imply a similar process of self-making is possible for secular men through the discipline of gestures.

What kind of man do courtesy texts want to produce? The texts often seem to list behaviours in an apparently random way, as a list of commands to imitate or to avoid specific gestures, but it is possible to identify values important to the household masculinity they promote. To begin with, texts place a high value on gestures which express a commitment to cleanliness and personal hygiene in the context of dining. Young men are variously enjoined not to spit, or eat with their mouths full, or to splash the table cloths. Secondly, the texts promote a conscious control over or restraint of exuberant gestures. Young men should not talk wildly, or wave their arms about when they speak, or gaze about them. Rather, they are expected to show a deft touch with table implements. Thirdly, young men should strive to regulate their talk. They should endeavour to maintain stillness and silence, especially when serving dinner, but they must also be capable of using talk effectively in other situations. They should, for example, be able to converse with those they encounter

---

77 Ibid., p. 230 (ll. 5–7).
78 Orme, *From Childhood to Chivalry*, pp. 183–91.
79 Binski, *Medieval Death*, p. 155.
80 Nicholls, *Matter of Courtesy*, p. 38.
81 Amos, ' "For Manners Make Man"', p. 45.

in the street, rather than behaving like a 'dombe freke' in public.[82] This indicates the high value later medieval society placed on sociability, but also the importance of choosing the right gesture for the time and place. Finally, texts encourage men to adopt gestures of deference toward social superiors. Young men must gauge their gestures carefully in order to impress superiors and to avoid the appearance of presumption. A young man should, for instance, always stand in the presence of his lord to ensure that the lord does not think you 'bere þi-selue to hy'.[83]

These gestures were tailored to the social roles household servants were expected to perform, but they also helped the young man to construct a gendered status identity for himself. Courtesy texts often discourage behaviours by associating them with low social status. The 'Babees Book' warns young men 'Kutte nouhte youre mete eke as it were Felde men', because this will make it seem that the diner is a hungry labourer (ll. 176–9). '*Stans puer ad mensam*' warns its readers to eat slowly, 'leste þou be callyd els both cherle or gloton' (l. 84). According to 'The Boke of Curtasye', 'Þe boke hym calles a chorle of chere, / That vylany spekes be wemen sere' (ll. 261–2). In the same way, good manners are presented as a way of associating oneself with gentle status. 'The Babees Book' promises that the young man who behaves appropriately 'shalle ywys / In nurture gete a gentyl name ful sone' (ll. 115–16). 'The Lytylle Childrenes Lytil Boke' promises that when one is punctilious about table manners, 'Than men wylle say therafter / That a gentylleman was heere' (ll. 95–6).[84]

This kind of masculinity is not a 'natural' masculinity, one held to arise from one's essential maleness. It is a learned masculinity, in the form of a set of values and manners which have to be acquired. One of the tasks which young men have to achieve in order to consider themselves men in this household context is to internalize the (to them) alien values of its masculinity. Courtesy texts are remarkable for the way in which they encourage the young man to refashion himself.[85] Though the texts employ what may seem rather crude incentives for young men to conform, in the form of the promise of praise or the threat of censure by others, their strategy is much more subtle than it first appears.[86] They work first to make the young man conscious of himself as an individual, rather than an unindividuated and anonymous member of the crowd, by implying that his behaviour is constantly observed and actively commented on by a host of spectators. *Caxton's Book of Curtesye* advises:

> In euery prees and in euery company
> Dispose you to be so compenable

---

82 'Boke of Curtasye', l. 255.
83 '*Stans puer ad mensam*', ll. 171–4.
84 *Babees Book*, ed. Furnivall, pp. 16–24.
85 Sponsler, 'Conduct Books', pp. 68–72.
86 Amos, ' "For Manners Make Man" ', pp. 36–7; A. Dronzek, 'Gendered Theories of Education', in *Medieval Conduct*, ed. Ashley and Clark, pp. 135–59 (pp. 150–1).

That men may of you reporte for commendable
For trusteth wel vpon your berynge
Men wil you blame or gyue preysynge.   (ll. 150–4)

This passage wants to make young men uncomfortably aware that those around them are not only noticing their manners, but discussing and passing judgement on them. Other texts depict the censure that Caxton mentions – particularly censure of uncouth table manners – as issuing in embarrassingly audible ways, as mockery or laughter, or as status-related insults. 'The Boke of Curtasye' even imagines people passing on comments about the behaviour of the young 'be sibbe or couthe' (l. 257), suggesting that bad manners become a talking point around an extensive network of friends and relations. Courtesy texts rely on the operation of shame and embarrassment to encourage conformity to household practices.[87] As one text puts it, 'þe bigynnynge of þi worschip, is to drede schame':[88] the fear of social embarrassment is paradoxically the stimulus to the sort of behaviour which will gain respect. It may well have been that hypercritical audiences constantly monitored the behaviour of the young, as courtesy literature suggests. But whether this was the case or not, making young men think they were continually scrutinized is an effective way of causing them to modify their behaviour. As Foucault has observed in relation to the regulatory regimes of eighteenth and nineteenth-century prisons and schools, creating a consciousness of being observed effectively makes the young man into his own moral policeman.[89] Prompted by courtesy literature, he imagines how his behaviour will look to an external observer, and corrects it accordingly to avoid the censure of that imagined critic. He has, in short, thoroughly internalized the values of his courtesy texts, becoming the critical observer of his own behaviour.

Furthermore, the young man is encouraged actively to construct a masculinity for himself through the management of his gestures for the benefit of an imagined audience. In courtesy literature, meals (when the whole household is gathered together) and other public occasions become opportunities for self-representation before an audience alert to the meanings of gestures.[90] Yet the ease with which young men might adopt alternative and disturbing identities is something of a concern to courtesy texts, which warn their readers to avoid particular kinds of evil companions, on the basis that their manners are catching. The most frequently mentioned inappropriate identity mentioned is that of the gallant, a figure also familiar from morally didactic texts and early interludes and characterized by extravagant and fashionable dress, a profli-

---

87 G. K. Paster, *The Body Embarrassed: Drama and the Disciplines of Shame in Early Modern England* (Ithaca NY, 1993).
88 'Of the Manners to Bring One to Honour and Welfare', l. 9, in *Babees Book*, ed. Furnivall, pp. 34–5.
89 M. Foucault, *Discipline and Punish: The Birth of the Prison*, trans. A. Sheridan (Harmondsworth, 1979).
90 Nicholls, *Matter of Courtesy*, p. 19.

gate lifestyle, backchat and presumption.[91] *Caxton's Book of Courtesy* is particularly anxious that the aspirant young man might imitate the manners of the gallant, believing them to represent noble behaviour. It warns that the gallant represents a crude, fake and distorted image of gentility: he remains only a 'Counterfeter of vnconnyng curtoisye' (l. 452).[92] 'Of the Manners to Bring one to Honour and Welfare' warns young men to avoid 'broþels', 'boies' and the 'wastour' (ll. 25–8). The *MED* shows that the 'broþel' is associated with lechery and anti-social behaviour, whereas the term 'boie' denotes both one who indulges in reprehensible actions and one of low status – an aspect of its meaning which gives it its force as an insult. The term 'wastour' expresses moral outrage at one who is prodigal or who fails to contribute to society through hard work, and is perhaps the most familiar term of the three from the depictions of 'wastours' in moral texts like the debate poem *Wynnere and Wastour* (c. 1350).[93]

Interludes mark as problematic the same kinds of young masculinities as courtesy texts do. As Davenport has shown, several early plays, including *Nature, Fulgens and Lucres, The Worlde and the Chylde, The Interlude of Youth* and *Calisto and Melebea* take pains to depict the behaviours conventionally associated with young gallants and to mark these as inappropriate.[94] In a more general sense, interludes rely on the audience's ability to read the external appearances of characters as evidence of their true inner nature. Scholars have discussed the extravagant dress of characters as gestures which are tended to indicate their essential selves, and especially the ways in which changes of costume conventionally represent a change in spiritual state.[95] As many have noted, the first entrance of Pryde in *Nature* is built around the assumption that the audience should be able to identify the character from what he wears and the way in which he speaks – even before his name is revealed.[96] In Alford's phrase, the play establishes both a 'visual' and a 'verbal rhetoric of pride'.[97] Pryde dresses extravagantly, but also displays arrogance towards the servants in the hall, and boastfulness about his ancestry and fashionable garments. This passage is framed as a kind of 'metatheatrical game', since – though Pryde makes sly references to his name – he does not tell us directly what it is until later on.[98] The point of the game is that the audience is expected to guess his identity from the gestures he displays. This rhetoric is also exploited in

91 Davenport, ' "Lusty Fresche Galaunts" '.
92 Amos, ' "For Manners Make Man" ', pp. 43–44.
93 *Wynnere and Wastoure*, ed. Ginsberg.
94 Davenport, ' "Lusty Fresche Galaunts" '.
95 Craik, *Tudor Interlude*, pp. 73–92.
96 Bevington, *Tudor Drama and Politics*, pp. 51–2; Westfall, *Patrons and Performance*, pp. 166–7; Twycross, 'Theatricality of Medieval English Plays', pp. 72–3; Alford, ' "My Name is Worship" '.
97 Alford, ' "My Name is Worship" ', p. 156.
98 Twycross, 'Theatricality of Medieval English Plays', pp. 72–3. See also Westfall, *Patrons and Performance*, pp. 166–7; Alford, ' "My Name is Worship" ', pp. 155–8.

other plays, notably in the presentation of the noble suitor Cornelius in *Fulgens and Lucres*.[99] Cornelius dresses in the same way as Pryde and treats his rival, Lucres' low-born suitor Gaius, with a disdain reminiscent of Pryde's.[100] Lancashire has also drawn parallels between the presentation of Pryde and that of Youth in *The Interlude of Youth*.[101] Cornelius and Pryde have both been read as critiques of noble habits and lifestyles.[102] The sin of pride was traditionally associated with nobles and sermon literature routinely depicts the proud nobleman boasting about lineage and indulging in wasteful conspicuous consumption.[103] In this context, the gestures of characters like Pryde would have been understood as proceeding from their sinful inner nature.

Courtesy literature offers another way of interpreting their gestures. If the gallant is only the 'Counterfeter of vnconnyng curtoisye', then in adopting his gestures Pryde and Cornelius do not as they fondly suppose display their noble identities, but instead make do with a cheap imitation. Pryde's lack of social *savoir faire* is also revealed in his ignorance of or disregard of social conventions which govern behaviour in the great hall of the household. When Pryde makes his first entrance, he describes himself as one who 'comys in at the dorys' (I.727) – that is, the doors in the screens passage at the low end of the hall – which indicates that he is entering from outside.[104] The 'Boke of Curtasye' stipulates that upon entering a hall a stranger should salute those presiding on the dais, acknowledge the gentlemen and yeomen seated in the main body of the hall, and stand in front of the screens until the marshal or usher on duty seats him (ll. 15–31). In other words, the guest should modestly disclaim all pretensions to status by placing himself at the low end of the hall – associated with low status – and by waiting quietly until attended to.[105] Pryde, in contrast, marches right into the hall, loudly boasting about his noble connections, and abusing the servants.

Pryde's talk marks him as socially inept, in any case. Courtesy texts actively discourage boasting. For instance 'How the Wise Man Taught his Son' declares that 'Bi boostynge, men mowe foolis knowe' (l. 124).[106] In more general terms, Pryde's verbosity also jars on the ear, especially if we bear in mind the injunctions of courtesy literature, which favour concise utterances.[107] Pryde's disregard for these conventions is designed to illustrate his

99 Craik, *Tudor Interlude*, pp. 58–9; Bevington, *Tudor Drama and Politics*, pp. 51–2; Jones, 'Early Moral Plays', p. 245; Norland, *Drama in Early Tudor Britain*, p. 237.
100 R. G. Siemens, ' "As Strayght as Ony Pole": Publius Cornelius, Edmund de la Pole and Contemporary Court Satire in Henry Medwall's *Fulgens and Lucres*', *Renaissance Forum* 1.2 (1996), URL: http://www.hull.ac.uk/renforum/v1no2/siemens.htm, paragraph 27.
101 Lancashire, *Two Tudor Interludes*, p. 37.
102 Bevington, *Tudor Drama*, pp. 51–2; Westfall, *Patrons and Performance*, pp. 159–60.
103 Owst, *Literature and Pulpit*, pp. 308–12.
104 J. Grenville, *Medieval Housing* (Leicester, 1997), p. 93.
105 Ibid., pp. 89–103.
106 'How the Wise Man Taught his Son', in *Babees Book*, ed. Furnivall, pp. 48–52.
107 'Babees Book', ll. 75–6.

breath-taking arrogance: he simply does not think that they apply to him. However, it also suggests that Pryde is not perhaps as *au fait* with good manners and noble lifestyles as he would like us to think. He mistakes bluster and braggadocio for a truly noble bearing. In turn, the members of the house-hold forming the audience, who presumably appreciate these fine points, are able to congratulate themselves on their superior breeding. This further reinforces messages about what constitutes appropriate behaviour for household men.

The Worlde and the Chylde makes use of a similar breach of etiquette, both to reveal the true nature of a character representing sinfulness, and to reinforce the social norms of household masculinity. The protagonist Manhode encoun-ters the character Folye just as he has entered man's estate, and Folye asks Manhode to accept him as a servant. The humour of the scene derives from the grotesque mismatch between Folye's words and actions. Folye addresses Manhode with the utmost politeness, greeting him with 'A, syr, God gyue you good eue' (l. 525). The fact that he is simultaneously performing a particularly coarse gesture is immediately evident from Manhode's expression of revul-sion, 'Stonde vtter, felowe, where doest þou thy curtesy preue' (l. 526). He wants literally to put as much distance as possible between himself and the gross Folye. The gesture is explained when Folye replies in tones of injured innocence, 'I do but clawe myne ars' (l. 527). Courtesy literature presents scratching as an utterly uncouth gesture, particularly in the context of dining.[108] The gesture serves to confirm what the audience already knows of the character Folye. Conscyence has shortly before defined 'folye' as compre-hending the seven deadly sins (ll. 457–60). The crude gestures of the character Folye proceed from his sinful nature and confirm it. Moreover, from Folye's gesture, Manhode deduces that Folye is a social inferior, hence he calls him 'felowe' and 'þou'.[109] These contemptuous modes of address mark Folye as base. Here the ideologies of gesture, status and morality are mutually rein-forcing. Folye's outrageous breach of hall etiquette is intended to provoke laughter, shock, embarrassment and disparagement amongst the audience. This helps to stress the forms of behaviour appropriate to a household containing the socially superior and the socially aspirational. These reactions are also enlisted in the cause of moral education: the text wants the spectators to view the sins Folye represents with the same disgust as they do his gross gesture.

Interludes, like courtesy texts, are concerned with teaching young men the values of a household masculinity based on restraint, reticence, deference and the knowledge of one's place. Like them, they emphasize the ways in which men effectively construct a masculine identity through a language of gesture. Interludes reinforce the idea that what a man is on the inside will be disclosed

---

[108] 'Babees Book', ll. 78–84; 'Lytylle Childrenes Lytil Boke', ll. 141–2.
[109] *MED, qv.* 'felau(e)'.

by his external gestures. There is, however, more emphasis on uncouth gestures performed by characters who are personified sins, rather than any performed by the young and noble protagonists of the plays. Indeed, in *The Worlde and the Chylde*, it is the young gentleman Manhode who expresses such disgust at the crude gesture of another. Whatever else he has learned in the household presided over by The Worlde, he has clearly learned good manners and their relation to concepts of status – though in fact his initial disgust does not prevent him from engaging Folye as his servant. While the young noblemen of the plays are shown as being sinful, they are never shown as being overtly uncouth. At least, the texts do not draw our attention to such gestures as they do in the case of Folye and Pryde, though it seems likely that actors would deploy the typical gestures of the undisciplined young man in their performance. It appears from courtesy literature that these were so well known that they would not have required further explication.

In the play *Fulgens and Lucres* there is certainly a clear distinction between the manners of the noble and ignoble men.[110] In their competition for the hand of Lucres, Gaius and Cornelius debate which of the two of them is the more noble. Gaius and Cornelius criticize each other bluntly and Cornelius's language is at times transgressive since it threatens to stir up violence. Their servants, known as A and B, are also competing for the favours of Jone, Lucres's maid, but conduct themselves in a markedly coarser way. For instance, they play a game called 'farte prycke in cule' for Jone (I.1169). B also manages to distort Cornelius's token to Lucres into a 'lewed message' (II.309). In attempting to recount an anecdote about Cornelius and Lucres, B becomes hopelessly muddled and claims that she 'kyst hym on the noke of the ars' (II.283). This broad comedy associates coarse language with the lower orders, as B translates Cornelius's anecdote into the language of his own social group. The noblemen of *Fulgens and Lucres*, however sinful, do not use this kind of explicit language. The fact that the degenerate nobleman Cornelius is able to abide by these social conventions, even while he breaks others, is an expression of his inner nature. He may be a sinner, but he is still innately noble. Like *The Worlde and the Chylde*, *Fulgens and Lucres* reinforces status distinctions by stressing that the gentle and ungentle comport themselves in visibly or audibly different ways.

Courtesy literature, then, relies on a biologically essentialist view of young men, like that of morally didactic works, in that it sees gestures as expressing men's inner, sinful natures. However, it models a process whereby young men may reform or even recreate that essential self through the discipline of gestures. As they follow a regime to correct the uncontrolled gestures to which they are naturally prone, they construct a new masculinity for themselves. This adult masculinity is fundamentally performative, since it relies on the

[110] Grantley, *Wit's Pilgrimage*, p. 61.

literal acting out of a specific set of gestures and movements. Unlike Judith Butler's concept of performative identity, this is a thoroughly self-conscious process – in fact, as we have seen, a process which relies on self-consciousness for its efficacy.[111] In this sense the set of gestures to be acquired is closer to what Mauss called a 'technique', like the technique acquired by someone learning to swim.[112] It is also closely connected with a concept of theatricality, since it assumes an audience for its performance. Young men are acting out identity for an implied audience of friends, neighbours, peers in the household and social superiors. The audience (even if only an imagined one) takes on the vital function of affirming the young man who constructs the right kind of identity, and of censuring the young man who takes on the wrong masculinity. The early interludes rely on an audience's skills in reading gestures in the ways they present characters, and they reinforce the messages of courtesy books regarding the right kind of masculinity for young men of the household to adopt. Fifteenth-century traditions, moreover, were teaching men a self-disciplining mode which sounds remarkably like the 'self-fashioning' which Greenblatt sees as characteristic of the sixteenth century.[113]

Young men and bad government

Courtesy texts address the issue of what sort of masculinity a young man in service should adopt and how it is to be constructed through the discipline of gestures. The masculinity they promote is modelled on that of noblemen, and young men are encouraged to develop the conscious self-control of their bodies, just as nobles are supposed to. In later medieval mirrors for princes, a specifically noble masculinity is also presented as a performative identity, one constructed through the exercise of different kinds of power and authority. These texts are political literature in that they discuss the theory and practice of government, but they are also frequently framed as educational works, addressed often to specific young princes and nobles, though in fact disseminated much more widely amongst the nobility.[114] They are concerned with forming an aristocratic masculinity fitted for those whose function is to wield authority.

As Briggs has pointed out, the phrase the 'rule' or 'governance' of princes is employed so frequently as a title for princely mirrors owned in England that

---

111 J. Butler, *Gender Trouble: Feminism and the Subversion of Identity* (New York, 1990); J. Butler, 'Imitation and Gender Subordination', in *Inside/Out: Lesbian Theories, Gay Theories*, ed. D. Fuss (New York, 1992), pp. 13–31.

112 M. Mauss, 'Body Techniques', in *Sociology and Psychology*, trans. B. Brewster (London, Boston and Henley, 1979), pp. 95–123.

113 Greenblatt, *Renaissance Self-Fashioning*, 1st edn (Chicago, 1984), pp. 1–77.

114 Orme, *From Childhood to Chivalry*, pp. 88–106; Green, *Poets and Princepleasers*, pp. 135–67; J. Ferster, *Fictions of Advice: The Literature and Politics of Counsel in Late Medieval England* (Philadelphia, 1996).

when wills or inventories identify manuscripts by the term, it is impossible for modern scholars to distinguish the precise work without further evidence.[115] Such titles emphasize the centrality of concepts of rule to aristocratic masculinity, but they are also remarkably ambiguous. They refer both to the way in which aristocrats govern others, in the sense of exercising political power over their people; and to the way in which princes should be governed by others, in the sense of being guided by the counsel and advice of other men.[116] There is considerable tension between these two ideas. On the one hand, to govern successfully the ruler should seek the advice of others, since it is unwise of him to trust his own unaided judgement. On the other, he must carefully test would-be counsellors and their advice, since it is inappropriate that advice should be adopted uncritically, or that any counsellor should exercise an undue influence over his prince.

To an extent, the exercise of rule and governance was central to the identity of many if not most medieval men.[117] In the penitential handbook *Handlyng Synne*, Mannyng says that, 'A man hys manhede shal yerne, / Hymself & his meyne [household] to governe'.[118] In this definition of masculinity, a man is one who does not need to be kept under the authority of a father or husband and who is responsible only to himself, though he has others under his authority: his 'meyne', consisting of his wife, children and servants who live under his roof. In the case of noblemen, a third kind of rule comes into the equation – the exercise of political authority.

The relationships between different forms of governance characteristic of noblemen are set out systematically in Trevisa's translation of the *De regimine principum*.[119] The first book of this work, based on Aristotle's *Ethics*, deals with self-rule, or the nobleman's ability to discipline his own body and moral character. The second book, based on Aristotle's *Economics*, deals with the rule of the household, the forms of authority the nobleman exercises over his wife, his children and his servants. The final book, based on his *Politics*, deals with the rule of kingdoms. The opening remarks of Trevisa's work explain the three-book structure on the basis of the fundamental relationships between the three kinds of governance, 'For he that wol be wise and kunnynge to gouerne and rule oþer schal be wise and konnynge to gouerne and to rule

---

[115] C. F. Briggs, *Giles of Rome's* De regimine principum: *Reading and Writing Politics at Court and University, c. 1275–c. 1525* (Cambridge, 1999), p. 6.

[116] Ferster, *Fictions of Advice*, pp. 39–54.

[117] On the importance of governance to men of the urban elites see P. J. P. Goldberg, 'Masters and Men in Later Medieval England', in *Masculinity in Medieval Europe*, ed. D. M. Hadley (London and New York, 1999), pp. 56–70; S. McSheffrey, 'Men and Masculinity in Late Medieval London Civic Culture: Governance, Patriarchy and Reputation', in *Conflicted Identities and Multiple Masculinities: Men in the Medieval West*, ed. J. Murray (London and New York, 1999), pp. 243–78.

[118] R. Mannyng, *Handlyng Synne*, ed. I. Sullens (Binghampton NY, 1983), ll. 5859–60.

[119] Briggs, *Giles of Rome's* De regimine principum, pp. 11–12, 91–2.

hymself'.[120] The capacity for political authority and even for household authority depends on a noble's capacity for the discipline of his own self.

Trevisa's text understands this self-rule primarily as a moral self-discipline; that is, the ability to suppress one's tendency to vice and to develop one's capacity for virtue. Some of the virtues it promotes as necessary to noble masculinity, such as wisdom, are directly related to the business of ruling.[121] The vices to be eschewed by nobles are the fleshly and worldly pleasures familiar from moral literature, so that behaviours deplored by late medieval Christian morality dovetail neatly with the behaviours which Aristotle deplores as deviations from the moderate and rational ideal.

Other mirrors for princes understand self-rule in terms of the regulation of the body's internal economy, viewing the concept of health as a kind of governance, where the bodily humours must by kept in balance by following regimes which carefully control activities like eating, drinking, sleeping and sex.[122] The proper regulation of the body is just as vital for men in authority as the rule of their moral character, a point made by Gilbert Kymer in his *Dietarium* (c. 1414) addressed to Humphrey, duke of Gloucester.[123]

As Mary Douglas has put it, 'The body is a model which can stand for any bounded system.'[124] In late medieval political discourse, it becomes a model of the realm, and bodily discipline may be described in terms of political governance. One mirror describes how God 'hauys stabyled his [a man's] body right as a Citee, and he hauys put vnderstondyng yn hym, as a kyng sette yn þe moste noble and most souerayn stede of man, þat ys yn þe heued'.[125] In the work of John of Salisbury and Hugh of St Victor, the discipline of gestures and the discipline of one's moral character which it entails is compared to the government of the kingdom, and a man's physical body to the body politic.[126] These figures stress the interdependence of self-disciplining and political ability.

Young noblemen are not considered to be naturally inclined to this kind of self-control, since like other young men their hot complexions make them lecherous and unstable, and their under developed reasoning powers leave them unable to exercise the self-disciplining characteristic of adult noblemen.[127] They are therefore not equipped for the exercise of political authority. Ill-regulated young male bodies become images of the politically

---

120 Aegidius Romanus, *Governance of Kings and Princes*, p. 8 (ll. 9–10).

121 Ibid., p. 11 (ll. 11–17).

122 See, for example, 'The Secrete of Secretes', in *Three Prose Versions of the* Secreta secretorum, ed. R. R. Steele, EETS ES 74 (1898), pp. 1–39 (pp. 21–2).

123 G. Kymer, *Dietarium*, in *Liber Niger*, ed. T. Hearne (London, 1774).

124 M. Douglas, *Purity and Danger: An Analysis of concept of Pollution and Taboo*, 2nd edn (London and New York, 2002), p. 142.

125 'The Governance of Lordschipes' (c. 1400), in *Three Prose Versions*, ed. Steele, pp. 41–118 (p. 97 (ll. 5–10)).

126 Schmitt, 'Rationale of Gestures', pp. 67–8.

127 Aegidius Romanus, *Governance of Kings and Princes*, pp. 142–4.

unstable kingdom. In *La Male Regle* (1406), Hoccleve describes how his wild lifestyle as a young man played havoc with the internal economy of his body, leaving him diseased. He depicts his body in terms of a kingdom where the rightful ruler 'helthe' has been overthrown by youthful rebellion (ll. 9–12).[128] Young bodies symbolize badly ruled kingdoms because young bodies produce the kinds of qualities which make bad rulers, but also because young bodies are systems in chaos, representing the anarchy which ought to be the consequence of incompetent government.

The moral characteristics of the young are inimical to good rule. Hoccleve's princely mirror, *The Regement of Princes* (*c.* 1412) sets up a series of oppositions between youthful characteristics and the qualities desirable in a prince.[129] In the prologue, Hoccleve describes a meeting with an old beggar, which occurs as he wanders in the fields, like John Russell's encounter with the young man. Hoccleve is anxious about his poverty, and he and the Beggar discuss the wild youthful lifestyles which have reduced them to penury. The Beggar recites a familiar litany of youthful failures, in a lifestyle centred on the tavern, a location which he sets up in opposition to the Church and the virtuous life associated with it (ll. 596–630).[130] His activities as a young man included dicing far into the night; swearing false oaths; prodigal expenditure; and 'pryde & leccherye' (l. 648).[131] Like the old men of devotional verse, the Beggar acts as a kind of mirror to Hoccleve, showing him what he will become should he persist in his present courses.[132] In his turn, Hoccleve confesses to a misspent youth, characterized by prodigality with money (ll. 4362–89).

Together, the youthful excesses of Hoccleve and the Beggar mean that they come to stand as the antitype of the ideal prince. In the main body of the text, Hoccleve's advice to the prince, he describes the qualities which the prince should cultivate to be a good ruler. He should, for example, develop the virtue of largesse, rather than the vices of prodigality or covetousness; chastity rather than lechery; keeping faith rather than swearing false oaths.[133] The examples of Hoccleve and the Beggar also serve as a warning of the consequences of misrule in one's personal life, that is, the loss of rule in other spheres. Hoccleve and the Beggar have both lost the rule of money. As the Beggar puts it, 'O wher is now al þe wantoun moneye / That I was maister of, and gouernour' (ll. 687–8). The prince, on the other hand, has much more to lose than merely the governance of money, and this is illustrated in the text by Hoccleve's reference to the stories of Rehoboam and others who lose their positions of gover-

---

[128] A. J. Hasler, 'Hoccleve's Unregimented Body', *Paragraph* 13 (1990), 164–83.

[129] T. Hoccleve, *The Regement of Princes and Fourteen Minor Poems*, ed. F. J. Furnivall, EETS ES 72 (1897).

[130] Owst, *Literature and Pulpit*, pp. 438–41; Wells, 'Food in the City', pp. 123–30.

[131] Hoccleve, *Regement of Princes*, ll. 631–7, 645–6.

[132] Hasler, 'Hoccleve's Unregimented Body', p. 170.

[133] Ibid., pp. 166–7.

nance through the practice of youthful foolishness rather than careful self-rule.[134]

In the *De regimine principum* the qualities of young men – their lack of reason and their tendency to be ruled by their passions – make them into the type of the bad ruler:

> For no man cheseth ȝungelynges to be dukes, for it is vnworthy þat a childe be a prince. Bote as it is iseide, primo Ethicorum, no differens is bytwene a child of ȝong age and one with maneres of ȝong age, for on þat vseth soche likyng. For thei he be olde of tyme and of age, for a is a child in maneres, he [is] vnworthi to be a prince.[135]

So closely are the qualities of the bad ruler associated with the young, that the older man who demonstrates them is considered to be a child. Conversely, it is possible for the young man to qualify for the position of ruler, but he must conquer his youthful nature and demonstrate the qualities associated with age. In other words, 'A childe of age and olde of maneres is worth to be a prince'.[136]

The good ruler exemplifies his political competence not only in the way he rules himself, but in the way he conducts his household. *De regimine principum* understands household rule in terms of the management of different kinds of relationships: those between husband and wife, those between father and son, and those between master and servant.[137] They represent different kinds of political rule and are founded on different principles. For example, the rule of servants is solely for the profit of the master, whereas the rule of sons is intended for the sons' profit rather than the father's.[138] Dealings with servants are an opportunity for the noble master to demonstrate a political ability in a display of his prudence. He is advised to test a servant's trustworthiness over a long period, by placing him first in a lesser office, and then advancing him gradually as he proves his merit. He should, moreover, avoid overfamiliarity with servants, only entrusting private business to the one who has proved a selfless attachment to his master over many years.[139] These prescriptions are designed to help the noble preserve the right balance of power between himself and his servants, to ensure that status distinctions are observed and that no servant gains an undue influence over him.

This advice closely parallels that offered to princes concerning the business of government of a kingdom. Here the political competence of the prince is figured, not through his relationships with his subjects *per se*, but through his

---

134 Ferster, *Fictions of Advice*, pp. 148, 154–7.
135 Aegidius Romanus, *Governance of Kings and Princes*, p. 18 (ll. 5–10).
136 Ibid., p. 18 (l. 13).
137 Ibid., p. 175.
138 Ibid., p. 213.
139 Ibid., p. 283.

relationships with counsellors.[140] Middle English versions of the *Secretum secretorum* frequently list the characteristics of good counsellors and suggest a test for them, so that the prince can be sure he selects the proper person as counsellor in the first place.[141] In the test, the prince is told to pretend he is in financial difficulties. The evil counsellor will suggest acquiring more money from the populace, while the good counsellor will respond by putting his own wealth at the prince's disposal. Princely mirrors express anxiety about kingship and absolute power by discussing the influence of evil counsellors. Bad kings are those susceptible to all kinds of evil speech issuing from bad advisers. As the Middle English *De proprietatibus rerum* puts it, evil kings 'louyth lyers and priue and iuel taletellers and bacbiters and bowiþ þe eres to here counsailes'.[142] The way a prince deals with his good and bad counsellors is crucial to how he is perceived.

In the rhetoric of counsel, young men – both as princes and as counsellors – are symbolic of bad government. Old men are associated with good counsel, partly because of their greater experience, and partly because they are no longer controlled by passions and so are free to exercise reason.[143] The counsel of young men is by the same token suspect, because of their intellectual immaturity. As Judith Ferster has shown, the political ineptitude of the young was frequently illustrated with reference to the biblical *exemplum* of Rehoboam in I Kings 12:1–24.[144] According to this account, Rehoboam, who acceded to the throne of Israel upon the death of his father Solomon, was petitioned by his subjects for a less exacting regime. His father's counsellors, old and experienced men, advised him to agree to the request. His own young companions counselled him to impose an even harsher regime. Rehoboam took the advice of the young counsellors, and thereby sealed his own fate. A popular uprising followed which led to the division of the kingdom. This story sets up a stark opposition between the old and the young, associating the former with political *savoir faire* and the latter with its lack. Furthermore, it demonstrates Rehoboam's political incompetence solely through his choice of the wrong counsel. Ferster demonstrates how this *exemplum* came to be used as a 'political code' in later medieval England, particularly by those criticizing the kingship of Richard II.[145] Indeed it continued to be cited well into the sixteenth century to illustrate the susceptibility of young kings to evil counsellors.[146]

---

140 Green, *Poets and Princepleasers*, pp. 161–7; Ferster, *Fictions of Advice*, pp. 39–54; J. A. Guy, 'The Rhetoric of Counsel in Early Modern England', in *Tudor Political Culture*, ed. D. Hoak (Cambridge, 1995), pp. 292–310.

141 For example, 'The Secrete of Secretes' (fifteenth century), in *Secretum secretorum: Nine English Versions*, ed. M. A. Manzalaoui, EETS OS 76 (1977), pp. 29–113 (pp. 77–9).

142 Bartholomaeus Anglicus, *On the Properties of Things*, I, 319–20.

143 Ibid., I, 293 (ll. 1–4); Aegidius Romanus, *Governance of Kings and Princes*, p. 51. See also Shahar, 'Old Body'.

144 Ferster, *Fictions of Advice*, pp. 122–6.

145 Ibid., pp. 125–6.

146 R. Edgeworth, *Sermons Very Fruitfull Godly and Learned by Roger Edgeworth: Preaching in*

The story of Rehoboam had become a kind of political shorthand for the bad kingship associated with young princes.

The web of ideas connecting young men, bad government, households and counsel is apparent in the alliterative poem *Richard the Redeless* (c. 1400).[147] This work offers criticism of the kingship of Richard II, a kingship compromised from the beginning by Richard's youth on his accession to the throne. Richard's youthful incapacity for kingship is signalled in the work by his failure to listen to the right counsellors. The speaker, who addresses his words to Richard directly as a form of counsel, laments his choice of young counsellors:

> Whane ye were sette in youre se as a sir aughte,
> Ther carpinge comynliche of conceill arisith,
> The chevyteyns cheef that ye chesse evere,
> Weren all to yonge of yeris to yeme swyche a rewme.   (I.86–9)

Richard makes the mistake of Rehoboam in listening to the advice of the young – that is, the wrong advice. Not only has Richard selected the wrong counsellors, but he is also incapable of appreciating the good advice offered by worthy counsellors – in the text, the counsellor Wit (also referred to as Wisdom), whom he utterly rejects (II.206–38).

Richard is, however, never directly depicted in the poem. Instead his incapacity for good government is figured through the actions of the members of and hangers-on within his royal household.[148] These individuals are also in an informal sense the king's counsellors. The speaker deplores their youth, and solely on the basis of their lack of years he contemptuously denigrates the guidance they offer, 'For it fallith as well to fodis of twenty four yeris, / Or yonge men of yistirday to geve good redis, / As becometh a kow to hoppe in a cage!' (III.260–63). The young men also appear to be in control of the royal household. Richard's rejection of good counsel is represented in terms of the ejection of Wit from the physical space of Richard's household, though it is not Richard himself who effects it. Instead, Wit is hounded out by the fashionably dressed and idle young courtiers around Richard, and then barred from re-entering by the porter at the gate (III.207–38). This episode shows how the household can come to stand for the person of the king, since the actions of the evil young courtiers stand for the king's actions, and their domination of the household represents their domination of Richard. Furthermore, the household also stands for the kingdom. Through their control of the king and his household the text implies that the evil young men control the kingdom.

the *Reformation*, ed. J. Wilson (Cambridge, 1993), pp. 354–6; F. Greville, *A Treatise of Monarchy*, ll. 980–5, in *Fulke Greville: The Remains*, ed. G. A. Wilkes (Oxford, 1965).

147 *Richard the Redeless and Mum and the Sothsegger*, ed. J. M. Dean (Kalamazoo, 2000).

148 J. Nuttal, 'Household Narratives and Lancastrian Poetics', in *The Medieval Household in Christian Europe, c. 850–1550: Managing Power, Wealth and the Body*, ed. C. Beattie, A. Maslakovic and S. Rees Jones (Turnhout, 2003), pp. 91–106 (pp. 99–104).

The alliterative poem *Mum and the Sothsegger* also equates the effective exercise of political power with effective household rule and the acceptance of good counsel.[149] Though the opening of the poem is lost, it seems from remarks within the text that it described the household of Henry IV, and in glowing terms:

> Now is Henryis hous holsumly ymade
> And a meritable meyny of the moste greet,
> And next I have ynamed as nygh as I couthe,
> And the condicions declarid of alle,
> Rehershing no rascaille ne riders aboute.   (ll. 206–10)

In contrast with Richard's household, Henry's is a model because it is composed only of worthy members – a 'meritable meyny' instead of Richard's arrogant young courtiers.[150] This well-ordered household is a reflection of Henry's kingly virtues of wisdom, faith and knightly prowess (ll. 211–20). However, Henry's household is not altogether perfect since it lacks members who are prepared to tell Henry the truth about what is really going on in the realm (ll. 156–70). The problem with the household is its silence, rather than its evil counsel, since individuals prefer to avoid the potentially unpleasant consequences of being a truth-teller. The main body of the work concerns the narrator's attempts to find a truth-telling counsellor who will complete this model household. As it proceeds, the poem seems to cast doubt on the welcome which such a one would receive at the court, since the truth-teller figure, Sothsegger, is rejected by every other institution in the land (ll. 788–99).[151] Henry's orderly household offers a picture in little of his successful rule of the kingdom, which stands in sharp contrast to Richard's failures as illustrated in *Richard the Redeless*. At the same time, anxieties about Henry's kingship are expressed in the form of concerns over the composition of his household. Nuttall points out the parallels with political events of time. The Long Parliament of 1406 attempted to reduce Henry's household expenditure, which resulted in the expulsion of various members of the household, some of whom the Commons suspected of attempting to exert undue influence over king and queen.[152]

In the political discourse of the later Middle Ages, noble masculinity is predicated on the ability to govern: to govern one's own body; to govern one's household; and to govern a kingdom. For noblemen, the cultivation of moral

---

[149] *Richard the Redeless and Mum and the Sothsegger*, ed. Dean; H. Barr and K. Ward-Perkins, ' "Spekyng for one's sustenance": The Rhetoric of Counsel in *Mum and the Sothsegger*, Skelton's *Bowge of Court*, and Elyot's *Pasquil and Playne*', in *The Long Fifteenth-Century: Essays for Douglas Gray*, ed. H. Cooper and S. Mapstone (Oxford, 1997), pp. 249–72; P. Strohm, 'Hoccleve, Lydgate and the Lancastrian Court', in *Cambridge History of Medieval Literature*, ed. Wallace, pp. 640–61 (p. 648).

[150] Nuttall, 'Household Narratives', p. 102.

[151] Ibid., p. 103.

[152] Ibid., pp. 100–1.

virtue is not simply an end in itself, but has to do with demonstrating the kind of self-discipline characteristic of the good ruler. An orderly household testifies in a more direct way to a man's practical abilities as a governor, but in addition it acts on a symbolic level as a figure of the well-regulated aristocratic body and as a sign of a wider political competence. The way a nobleman conducts himself and his household is a kind of political statement about his capacity to rule. In this discourse, the young ruler is emblematic of a lack. He is the type of the man who cannot discipline his naturally unruly nature, a nature which can be read off the body by the corporeal signs of gestures and postures. By extension, the young man is the type of the bad governor: the man who is unable to regulate his relationships with servants and counsellors; who is readily manipulated; who presides over unruly households and kingdoms. The young man exemplifies a threatening and dangerous masculinity, because his body both represents and produces social and political disorder, and that threat becomes multiplied when the young man is placed in a position of social and political authority. The following chapter will show how the troubling associations which young male figures carry are exploited in the interludes to create sophisticated discussions of noble masculinity.

CHAPTER THREE

Noble Masculinity in the Interludes

The young noblemen of the interludes *Nature, Fulgens and Lucres, The Worlde and the Chylde, The Interlude of Youth* and *Calisto and Melebea* are mature in physical terms – not only sexually mature, but they have clearly reached the end of their 'ful incresing', in the words of John Trevisa, and have attained the height of their physical powers.[1] Some of these plays also mark characters' transitions to an adult aristocratic masculinity with decisive change in their circumstances, as they engage servants and enlarge households. These young men are socially mature, since they no longer have to live under the authority of others, unlike the young noblewomen of the plays who remain under the governance of their fathers. Instead, young men exercise an authority of their own, usually as the masters of servants. Yet they remain socially immature to an extent, in the sense that few have experienced all of what Mark Ormrod has called the 'life-events' and 'career firsts' typical of later medieval English aristocrats.[2] None are yet married. Only Gaius in *Fulgens and Lucres* has taken part in military campaigns and is actively involved in the exercise of political authority (I.97, II.681). The young noblemen are located in a liminal period between childhood and fully realized noble adulthood. They are in the process of negotiating for themselves an adult masculinity which will determine the tenor of their adult lives.

The plays are not purely descriptive of young noblemen at this interesting stage of their lives. As we have seen in Chapter Two, they have a didactic emphasis, for instance marking particular kinds of adult masculinity as wrong. They tend to focus on young noblemen as problems, as negative *exempla* of men who fail to make the proper transitions to the right kind of noble masculinity. In *The Worlde and the Chylde*, the central figure suffers a miserable and destitute old age as a result of his youthful choices. In *Nature*, Man is full of regret at his failure to direct his courses in a fitting way as a younger man. Youth of *The Interlude of Youth* only repents and changes after a period of sometimes violent resistance to the forces of good. Cornelius in *Fulgens and Lucres* and Calisto in *Calisto and Melebea* are presented in stark opposition to the old noblemen, Fulgens and Danio – and in the case of

---

[1] Bartholomaeus Anglicus, *On the Properties of Things*, I, 292.
[2] W. M. Ormrod, 'Coming to Kingship: Boy Kings and the Passage to Power in Fourteenth-Century England', in *Rites of Passage: Cultures of Transition in the Fourteenth Century*, ed. N. F. McDonald and W. M. Ormrod (York, 2004), pp. 31–49.

Cornelius, to the younger man Gaius – all of whom represent an aristocratic masculinity they seem unlikely ever to attain. Even in *Nature*, which reassures men about their ultimate salvation, the acquisition of masculine and noble adult identities means the negotiation of a difficult pathway. The major obstacle to the successful transition to male adulthood is the young men themselves, naturally inclined to deviant masculinities.

One of the key problems facing the young nobleman is the successful use of gestures to communicate a disciplined noble nature to a watching world. As we saw in the previous chapter, Pryde from *Nature* and Cornelius from *Fulgens and Lucres* may be seen as figures who fail to transmit the right messages about status. Westfall has called Pryde's opening speeches in *Nature* 'a lesson in signification'.[3] In her reading, the figures of Pryde and Cornelius represent an inadequate traditional noble masculinity, which contrasts with the new noble masculinities of a body of 'rising men' under the early Tudor kings, who valued intellectual ability, hard work and moral virtue. In this chapter I want to reconsider the problems of noble signification, particularly in relation to a positive *exemplum* of the effective deployment of signs by Gaius in *Fulgens and Lucres*. Moreover, though many scholars have noted that the young noblemen of the plays are accompanied by servants, few have considered the wider significance of the servant–master relationship for noble identities.[4] The second part of this chapter will explore the ways in which the introduction of household servants makes the noble household and the practice of householding central to noble masculinity. By understanding the young male protagonists in the context of the household and its ideologies, it is possible to see the interludes as participating in a much more wide-ranging discussion of what it means to be a noble man than if one considers bodies and gestures in isolation.

Noble masculinity and noble male bodies

In the interludes, the male body is the place where the construction of aristocratic masculinity begins. As we have seen, Pryde in *Nature* and Cornelius in *Fulgens and Lucres* expressly design their clothes, gestures and speech to declare their status, so that the visible body transmits messages about the innate but invisible nobility within. This is an utterly self-conscious process. In *Nature*, Pryde assures us that his expensive and fashionable dress is an unequivocal sign of the aristocratic status he claims. He defines himself as 'A gentylman [. . .] / That all hys dayes hath worn gylt sporys'(I.727–8), implying

---

3 Westfall, *Patrons and Performance*, pp. 155–6. See also Alford, ' "My Name is Worship" ', p. 156; Twycross, 'Theatricality of Medieval English Plays', p. 72.

4 Rossiter, *English Drama From Early Times*, p. 104; Potter, *English Morality Play*, p. 64; Medwall, *Plays of Henry Medwall*, ed. Moeslein, p. 90; Westfall, *Patrons and Performance*, pp. 160, 171–73, 190; Grantley, *Wit's Pilgrimage*, p. 150.

that it is the wearing of spurs which guarantees his nobility. His investment in expensive clothing is designed to display the noble wealth derived from his estates (I.731–70). In turn, one of Pryde's first pieces of counsel to Man is to adopt a more fashionable style of dress (I.1022–34). In *Fulgens and Lucres*, Cornelius also seeks to display the wealth which he sees as central to his nobility in his own dress and that of his servants (I.717–70). The leisured, noble lifestyle of 'ease and plesaunt idelnesse' which he promises Lucres is also designed to mark aristocratic status, through noble pursuits such as the wearing of luxurious dress, hunting, hawking and music (II.543–63). These Cornelius presents as the defining activities of a nobleman or woman. In a similar way, Youth in *The Interlude of Youth* is determined to build himself a reputation through extravagant conspicuous consumption, since he believes that, 'he is not set by / Without he be unthrifty' (ll. 63–4). Hence the vice Pride also advises Youth to adopt a specific visual rhetoric of status. Pride commands:

> Be in company with gentlemen.
> Jet up and down in the way,
> And your clothes – look they be gay.
> The pretty wenches will say then,
> 'Yonder goeth a gentleman,'
> And every poor fellow that goeth you by
> Will do off his cap and make you courtesy.   (ll. 346–52.)

These gestures are designed to articulate noble status and depend on Youth making himself highly visible by associating with other nobles, strutting in the streets, and wearing eye-catching, bright clothing. Dress is also a satisfying marker of high status for Manhode in *The Worlde and the Chylde*. He describes himself as 'ryall arayde' and as clothed in the fabrics of high status, being 'proudely aparelde in purpure and byse' (ll. 268–9). Like the gestures taught in courtesy books, these gestures of nobility rely for their effect on an audience who, it is assumed, will be watching and passing judgement on the performer. Pride claims that self-conscious display of the right signs will elicit the spontaneous tribute of respect from observers, in this case those of lower status who are also out on the public streets.

Many characters also use language to construct themselves as noble. They deploy pronouns which are marked for status as a way of emphasizing the social distance between themselves and their servants. In *The Worlde and the Chylde*, Manhode, when confronted by the base Folye, positions himself as superior by addressing him with the familiar 'þou' and by calling him 'felowe' (l. 526). In *The Interlude of Youth*, Youth addresses his prospective servant Pride as 'thou' and as 'fellow', while Pride addresses Youth as 'sir'.[5] In *Fulgens and Lucres*, Cornelius makes a deliberate attempt to disparage Gaius, his rival for Lucres' hand, by addressing him as 'thou' (II.529–35). In fact, he is being so

---

5   *Interlude of Youth*, ll. 327–8, 331.

offensive and provocative to Gaius in this strategy that Lucres has to reprove him (II.536–8). In *The Interlude of Youth*, Pride encourages Youth to adopt the sort of verbal rhetoric which has the object of debasing others in order to exalt oneself. According to Pride, Youth should, 'Put down the poor, and set nought by them' (l. 345). Young men are also quick to make their own nobility the theme of much they say. In *The Interlude of Youth*, Youth claims his superiority to every other lord (ll. 589–96). Manhode boasts of his military exploits in *The Worlde and the Chylde* (ll. 237–66). Cornelius in *Fulgens and Lucres* and Pryde in *Nature* vaunt their noble ancestry.[6]

The problem for the young noblemen of these plays is that the system of signs they adopt to express their innate nobility is an unreliable one. To begin with, it is possible for the observer to put a different interpretation on their gestures, as the verbal and visual rhetoric, not of nobility, but of sinfulness. Indeed some plays make it impossible to avoid this reading of their gestures since they are advocated by characters called pride. Even where this is not the case, the audience's knowledge of the visual and verbal rhetoric of pride from moral and religious texts will ensure that they see these gestures in a very negative light. The point is that the young bodies of the aristocrats effectively disrupt even conscious attempts to construct an adult noble masculinity through the performance of gestures. Gestures express in an unmediated way the true nature within. In the case of these characters, the nature which makes itself seen is not a noble nature but the youthful, inherently sinful nature dictated by male bodies. The interludes warn that constructing a noble masculinity through gestures is problematic because gestures may reveal more about the performer's true inner self than that person intends.

However, the interludes regard other kinds of gestures as problematic for the opposite reason – that they are *not* an unmediated expression of an essential nature. *Nature* and *Fulgens and Lucres* show a particular concern about the unreliability of dress as a signifier of noble status. In these plays, apparel is not necessarily an involuntary expression of inner nature, since this sign of nobleness may be purchased by anyone with enough cash to spend. The correspondence, or lack of correspondence, between inner nature and outer garb was a particular concern to the elites of the late fifteenth and early sixteenth centuries. Sumptuary legislation was repeatedly enacted in order to control the consumption of particular styles of dress and fabrics, and so to preserve visual distinctions between different status groups.[7] In the 1509–10 legislation, for example, only servants of noble birth were permitted to wear 'eny goune or coote or suche lyke apparrell of more clothe then two brode yerdes and a halfe in a shorte gowne and thre brode yerdes in a longe gowne'.[8] The legislation

---

6 *Fulgens and Lucres*, II.455–514; *Nature*, I.731–4.

7 J. Scattergood, 'Fashion and Morality in the Late Middle Ages', in *England in the Fifteenth Century*, ed. D. Williams (Woodbridge, 1987), pp. 255–72; Sponsler, *Drama and Resistance*, pp. 1–23.

8 Record Commission, *Statutes of the Realm*, 11 vols. (London, 1963), III, 8–9.

wanted a man's dress to be a reliable index of his inborn nature.[9] One should be able to look at the amount of cloth a servant has on his back and be able to tell whether that servant is noble or not. This kind of concern was also expressed by Edmund Dudley, who warned the mercantile elites not to 'presume aboue ther own degree, nor any of them pretend or conterfete the state of his Better, nor lett any of them in anywise excede in ther apparell or diet'.[10] The implication of such exhortations is that dress had become an unreliable sign of nobility, and that distinctions between status groups were being effaced as the low-born adopted styles of dress previously the preserve of the noble.[11] Indeed, these texts evince a concern that the lower orders are actively deploying dress to construct noble identities for themselves which do not correspond to any nobility within. There is some evidence to show that rising levels of disposable income at the end of the fifteenth century left ordinary people with an increased amount of money to spend on material goods, and that social elites changed their patterns of consumption to more exclusive fabrics in response to this new social competition from relatively low-status consumers.[12]

In *Fulgens and Lucres*, a concern about the significance of dress first becomes apparent in the opening section of the play, where the two servants known as A and B set up the action to follow. A and B are presented as acquaintances who have encountered each other by chance while they wait in the great hall to see the play. A apologizes for assuming that B is one of the actors:

> Nay, I mok not, wot ye well,
> For I thought verely by your apparell
> That ye had bene a player
> [. . .]
> Lo, therfor, I say
> Ther is so myche nyce aray
> Amonges these galandis now aday
> That a man shall not lightly
>
> Know a player from a nother man.   (I.48–56)

In contemporary sumptuary legislation, players were frequently exempted from regulations regarding apparel because of their professional obligations to dress like people of other status groups.[13] The exchange between A and B indicates that B is comparatively richly dressed – more richly dressed than his status in fact strictly entitles him to be. A does not make the mistake of

---

9   Scattergood, 'Fashion and Morality', pp. 259–60, 269–70; Sponsler, *Drama and Resistance*, pp. 12, 20.

10   E. Dudley, *The Tree of Commonwealth*, ed. D. M. Brodie (Cambridge, 1948), pp. 45–6.

11   Alford, ' "My Name is Worship" ', pp. 167–8.

12   C. Dyer, *Making a Living in the Middle Ages: The People of Britain, 850–1520* (New Haven and London, 2002), p. 322.

13   Record Commission, *Statutes of the Realm*, II, 402, 469; III, 8–9.

assuming B is noble, because of his previous acquaintance with B. Instead he assumes that B is wearing his fine clothing because he is a player. In apologizing for his error, A hardly improves matters since he implies that B's dress constructs him as a gallant, one deliberately making a false claim to a noble identity. As Westfall has observed, this is potentially a telling side-swipe at any extravagantly dressed men of lower status in the audience of the play.[14] The episode reveals the difficulties of distinguishing between different kinds of men on the basis of their appearance. In turn, it calls into question whether we are able to read the extravagant dress of Cornelius, described later in the play, as a marker of nobility, as he wishes us to do.

The problematic nature of Cornelius's dress is explicitly discussed at the moment when the servant B boasts about his master's fashionable and expensive clothes (I.713–70). B admits that deploying dress as a sign of nobility is not without its difficulties:

> A gentylman shall not were it a daye,
> But every man wyll hym self araye
> Of the same fascyon even by and by
> On the morow after!   (I.754–7)

Cornelius's dress only works to mark his superiority as long as lesser men do not dress in the same way. Fashionable dress can only ever be a provisional sign of nobility for young men because fashions are soon taken up by the ignoble. In *Nature*, Pryde also remarks on this, as he comments unfavourably on Man's appearance: 'It ys now two dayes agon / Syth that men bygan thys fassyon, / And every knave had yt anon!' (I.1026–8). The currency of Man's style of dress among low-status men has, in Pryde's eyes, debased it as a sign of nobility. His solution is to devise a new fashion for Man, more outrageous than the last (I.1053–81). Fashionable dress must continually be renewed if it is to remain effective as a gesture revealing nobility, especially when others of lower status constantly seek to appropriate it.

Since adopting the exterior signs of nobility is relatively easy, the benefit of making aristocratic identity contingent on abstract qualities like modesty and truthfulness is that these cannot be counterfeited, or at least not with such ease. Such virtues can be seen as proceeding more directly from an essentially noble nature, and not merely as the purchase of wealth which anyone might acquire. An alternative way of constructing a noble masculinity through gestures which indicate virtuous qualities is suggested in the presentation of Gaius in *Fulgens and Lucres*. Gaius is not noble by birth, and apparently does not enjoy the inherited wealth which allows Cornelius to indulge in conspicuous consumption. However, Gaius is, like Cornelius, self-consciously engaged in constructing a noble identity, not only for himself, but for his descendants:

---

[14] Westfall, *Patrons and Performance*, pp. 108–9.

By these wayes, lo, I do aryse
Unto grete honoure fro low degre,
And yf myn heires will do likewyse
Thay shal be brought to nobles by me.   (II.686–9)

Although Gaius does not make it explicit, marriage to Lucres is part of his long-term dynastic strategy. Marriage was an important matter to all later medieval nobles, since producing legitimate heirs was crucial for the preservation of family lines and family estates.[15] As for Gaius, Lucres' wealth and status will help to produce nobleness in his descendants – as it has in the case of Cornelius.

Bevington and others have argued that Gaius is intended to represent a new kind of noble: an emergent social group of the late fifteenth and early sixteenth centuries of individuals who owed their advancement to talent and ability rather than to birth.[16] Since Gaius has obtained 'office and fee', and devotes himself to study and to a virtuous life, scholars have tended to see him as a type of the competent Tudor administrator.[17] Gaius modestly disclaims noble status for himself in the passage quoted above, and Cornelius bluntly insists on Gaius's low birth.[18] However, these are tactical moves in a rhetorical contest between the two men, and as Grantley has suggested, the play-text presents them as on more of a par than their choice of epithets might suggest.[19] Whatever their personal antipathy, Cornelius and Gaius clearly have much more in common with each other than either has with their servants A and B. In other words, *Fulgens and Lucres* may be less of a debate about who is and who is not noble, and more of a debate about how to be noble, how to construct the noble masculinity which will set one apart from other status groups, and indeed from other nobles, in the competition for scarce resources – like the marriageable heiress, Lucres, for whom Cornelius and Gaius are rivals.

As a theoretical model, the figure of Gaius has as much to say to the established nobility as to emergent nobles, concerning the ways in which aristocrats might express their essentially noble nature without recourse to ambiguous or unreliable material signs. Gaius performs nobility in a different way to Cornelius, but in some senses he is a resolutely traditional noble. While Cornelius is indulging in aristocratic leisured pastimes, Gaius has made a

---

15 K. B. McFarlane, *The Nobility of Later Medieval England* (Oxford, 1973), pp. 10–11, 151–3; K. Mertes, 'Aristocracy', in *Fifteenth-Century Attitudes*, ed. Horrox, pp. 42–60 (pp. 45–7); D. Starkey, 'The Age of the Household', in *The Later Middle Ages*, ed. S. Medcalf (London, 1981), pp. 225–90 (pp. 232–43).

16 Bevington, *Tudor Drama and Politics*, pp. 42–53; Westfall, *Patrons and Performance*, pp. 161, 181–2; Norland, *Drama in Early Tudor Britain*, pp. 234–5; Watkins, 'Allegorical Theatre', pp. 774–6.

17 *Fulgens and Lucres*, II.568, 679–70.

18 Ibid., II.530–5, 564–70.

19 Grantley, *Wit's Pilgrimage*, pp. 61, 88.

name for himself through military exploits (II.681–5). In this sense Gaius is not offering a radically new kind of nobility at all, but fulfilling the traditional aristocratic function. The one innovative aspect to Gaius's noble activities is his devotion to 'study', which was not an uncontested marker of noble masculinity. Paul Strohm has argued, for example, that Hoccleve's fifteenth-century works mark 'practices of reading and introspection' as female.[20] Gaius realigns the activity of study with the aid of long-standing concepts of noble masculinity, and is able to make it central to his noble masculinity because it prevents 'idleness' and so discourages vice (II.680). Study is significant not just because it produces virtue, but because it is a disciplining activity, a way of training the unruly young body, just as military exploit requires the training of the physical body. As I have discussed in Chapter Two, it is the very act of disciplining oneself which is so politically significant, as the marker of the noble and indeed the king.[21] Gaius shows in the way that he trains and rules himself the capacity he has for ruling others, which Cornelius is unable to display in his lifestyle of leisure and pleasure.

Gaius may also be using the visual rhetoric of status to transmit messages about his nobility. There is no description of Gaius's appearance in the play-text, and therefore no direct reference to any of the ways in which Gaius uses dress to express his noble nature. This in itself suggests that Gaius's external appearance is completely unremarkable, and by extension that he forms a striking visual contrast with Cornelius – particularly if Cornelius is wearing a gown made of seven 'brode yerdis' of cloth, which B claims he usually wears (I.740–2). In theatrical terms, Gaius's unremarkable dress makes a powerful statement about his restraint if it forms a visual antithesis to Cornelius's extravagance.

Such a visual contrast also reflects the way in which Gaius presents himself as the antithesis of Cornelius in his speech, a strategy which requires careful negotiation to avoid transmitting the wrong messages about himself. Gaius claims to embody the virtues of continence, industry and moderation, setting his good qualities in opposition to Cornelius's vices of incontinence, idleness and prodigality.[22] On the basis of such moral virtues he claims to have a superior kind of nobility. His virtues can be seen as noble, because they are identified as characteristics of noblemen and princes in mirrors for princes.[23] However, they are difficult to represent in a visual way, so Gaius demonstrates his possession of them by employing what we might describe, after Alford, as a verbal rhetoric of virtue.[24] Gaius frequently calls attention to or comments on his own manner of speaking. For instance, in his early exchanges with

---

[20] Strohm, 'Hoccleve, Lydgate', p. 648.
[21] Ferster, *Fictions of Advice*, p. 44.
[22] *Fulgens and Lucres*, II.627–55, 670–99.
[23] O. Horner, '*Fulgens and Lucres*: An Historical Perspective', *METh* 15 (1993), 49–86 (pp. 55–9).
[24] Alford, ' "My Name is Worship" '.

Lucres, Gaius declares his refusal to employ 'flatering wordis' (I.521) normally employed by lovers, which he describes as a way of winning people's love by guile. He is determined to 'be short and playne' (I.526), and he cites his proposal of marriage to Lucres in 'wordis expresse' as example of this directness (I.530). He urges Lucres to use the same kind of language (I.526–8) and to reply to his proposal with 'a playne ye or nay' (I.538). In the nobility debate with Cornelius before Lucres, he declares his intention to tell 'the veray trouth' (II.598). Gaius's plain speaking and directness are gestures which express his sincerity and honest dealing. Like the courtesy texts discussed in Chapter Two, he puts a high value on brevity, and implies that verbosity is a negative trait. His suspicion of flattery echoes political literature, where flattery is associated with evil counsellors and a desire to manipulate; whereas plain speaking is a characteristic of the truth-telling, good counsellor.[25]

Gaius's decision to be a truth-teller in the nobility debate means that he has to speak plainly about himself and Cornelius. Even before the debate itself, he has drawn attention to his reluctance to impugn Cornelius. When Gaius's new servant A tells him that he has seen Lucres in Cornelius's company, Gaius declares, 'He shall not be dispraysid for me / Withoute that I be compellid therto' (I.667–8). In the debate with Cornelius, Gaius claims that he is 'loth . . . to make ony reportur / Of this mans foly or hym to dispice' (II.594–5). This seems to echo Lucres's dislike of 'all suche wordis as may gyve occasion / Of brallynge or other ongodely condycion' (II.373–74). Lucres and Gaius's values contrast with those of Cornelius, who speaks so disparagingly to Gaius in the nobility debate (II.529–35). Indeed, Gaius takes advantage of Cornelius's outburst to point out that Cornelius 'spekyth after his lernyng' in scorning him (II.539). Rather than hurting Gaius, Cornelius's words disclose Cornelius's true nature, and provide an implicit contrast with Gaius's measured tones.

In order to press his claim to nobility, Gaius has to describe his own virtues and this is uncomfortably close to the kind of boasting which characterizes the proud Cornelius. Gaius is only able to exhibit his lack of pride by expressing reluctance to talk about himself. He declares that he is 'lothe [. . .] / To boste of myne own dedis – it was never my gyse' (II.592–3). He denies that he is mentioning his own virtues 'for myne one prayse' (II.670), anxiously making clear that his words in this instance do not arise from a sinful state, but are compelled by circumstances over which he has no control.

Gaius demonstrates how to perform a noble masculinity without recourse to material displays which, as earlier noted, will frequently fail to transmit messages about nobility effectively. Instead, he makes use of a rhetoric of virtue, where he displays honesty, sincerity, lack of contentiousness, and modesty through the way in which he speaks. By this strategy, he seeks to display his noble nature, though perhaps paradoxically this involves

---

25 Barr and Ward-Perkins, ' "Spekyng for one's sustenance" '; Strohm, 'Hoccleve, Lydgate', p. 648.

cataloguing the features of his own speech, in a way reminiscent of Pryde's exhibition of his fashionable dress in *Nature*. The positive example of Gaius is constructed in opposition to those young noblemen in other early interludes who project the wrong messages about their inner natures.

In *The Worlde and the Chylde* the debate about nobility and the construction of a noble masculinity centres on the concept of knighthood, which is explicitly discussed by Conscyence, in response to Manhode's evident pride in his status as knight when they first meet. Manhode demands to know Conscyence's business, calls him offensive names, and promises that he shall be taught who Manhode is (ll. 317–23). He boasts of his relationship with the King of Pride whom he serves and claims this makes him 'as gentyll as iay on tre' (l. 327). Conscyence therefore seeks to re-educate Manhode about what 'longeth to a knyght' (l. 331). He constructs an image of a knighthood based on Christian virtue, rather than that associated in the play with vice. In dubbing Manhode a knight, The Worlde has taught Manhode to seek pre-eminence through the use of arms. He gives him 'a swerde and also strength and myght' for battle (l. 210), and Manhode proceeds to conquer many nations, defeat many individuals in battle and to boast about it at length (ll. 237–74). Conscyence criticizes Manhode's education since he was never taught 'To mayntayne maner' (l. 329) or pursue an ideal of moderation, and to keep a 'Conscyence clere' (ll. 328–31). Conscyence begins by arguing against Manhode's allegiance to each of the deadly sins (ll. 340–447). He proposes a new set of activities for Manhode the knight: the service of God, the observance of the commandments, attendance at matins and mass, and the protection of the Church.[26] He also indicates how Manhode should manage his life in the world, without becoming worldly. Manhode does not have to abjure an aristocratic lifestyle: he should however exercise moderation and 'good gouernance' or self-discipline over himself in his pleasures.[27] Moreover, Conscyence confirms that Manhode may dress 'honestly' and 'In all maner of degre' (ll. 465–8). In other words, he claims it is entirely possible for a knight to dress in a way that expresses his status, without it becoming an outlet for his pride, though Conscyence does not specify how this is to be achieved.[28] Conscyence attempts to reinterpret knighthood, to discourage Manhode from behaviour which he sees as proceeding from a worldly, and therefore sinful, set of values. He seeks to reorientate knighthood back to long-standing concepts of knighthood as Christian service.[29] Like Paul, Conscyence acknowledges that though the individual should not be 'of the world', he still has to live 'in the world'. In this account moderation and self-control are key to living a life in the world without becoming prey to sin, just as they are

---

26 *Worlde and the Chylde*, ll. 356–9, 424–39, 441–7.
27 Ibid., ll. 448–51, 469–72.
28 Craik, *Tudor Interlude*, pp. 82–3.
29 M. Keen, *Chivalry* (New Haven and London, 1984), pp. 4–6, 44–63.

presented as crucial virtues for nobles and princes in later medieval political literature.

A noble masculinity dependent on moral virtues may conflict with other conceptions of masculinity. When Youth of *The Interlude of Youth* is first urged to amend his ways by Charity, he does not see the life of virtue as consonant with his noble status. When Charity quotes scripture to Youth, he recoils in horror and hostility, exclaiming 'What! methink ye be clerkish, / For ye speak good gibb'rish' (ll. 113–14). His anger seems in part motivated by a rejection of a 'clerkish' identity.[30] Youth perhaps associates the clergy not only with learning but with a lifestyle which rejects many kinds of aristocratic activity.[31] Clergy were forbidden to carry arms, and were discouraged from conspicuous consumption and aristocratic pursuits like hunting and hawking. Youth's forceful rejection of Charity stems from his fear that Charity is trying to deprive him of the noble identity which means so much to him.

The act of constructing a gendered status identity on the body appears to be a particularly complex one for the young men of these interludes. Man in *Nature*, Cornelius in *Fulgens and Lucres*, Manhode in *The Worlde and the Chylde*, and Youth of *The Interlude of Youth* attempt to live up to concepts of adult, noble masculinity which are false. Instead of demonstrating their nobility through gestures, they reveal only sinfulness dictated by their young natures. Adult male identities are problematic for many of these young men precisely because of their male bodies. The idea that young men are ruled by the powerful natural forces inherent in their physical development underpins *Nature*, *The Worlde and the Chylde* and *The Interlude of Youth*. Young men are susceptible to sensuality, weakness in their capacity for reason, and the interplay of the humours in determining their complexion. However hard they try to construct their own social identities, the biological essentialism of male developmental models assures us that their natural selves will out. On the other hand, *Fulgens and Lucres* presents Gaius as a young man who has managed to transcend his youthful, male nature through the self-conscious discipline of his body. Attaining an appropriate aristocratic manhood may be difficult, but Gaius demonstrates that it is possible, and that self-disciplining nobleman enjoys as a result a substantial advantage over his noble rivals.

---

30 Grantley, *Wit's Pilgrimage*, p. 141.
31 P. H. Cullum, 'Clergy, Masculinity and Transgression in late Medieval England', in *Masculinity in Medieval Europe*, ed. Hadley, pp. 178–96. For a wider discussion of attitudes to Latin, see J. Dillon, *Language and Stage in Medieval and Renaissance England* (Cambridge, 1998).

Noble masculinity and the noble household

In the late medieval and early Tudor periods, noble households were central to noble identities in a number of ways.[32] The physical household – the castle or manor which housed the noble and his *familia* – was not just concerned with supplying the practical needs of a nobleman or woman, and was not just a centre for the administration of estates. Such places were also sites of conspicuous consumption, where nobles displayed their status through their investment in architecture, material goods and a particular style of living.[33] This investment was not just for the satisfaction of personal tastes, but had a practical political value. It was incumbent on nobles to display the quality of liberality in their mode of living, and those who did not do so not only lost face, but lost political power as a result.[34] Through the tactical deployment of liberality, nobles attracted the service of gentry and others, who were interested both in the material rewards to be won from a magnificent noble and the prestige of being associated with such an individual.[35] For this reason, the building and rebuilding of manors have often been seen as strategic, political acts. The alterations to the manor of Collyweston by Lady Margaret Beaufort can be read in the context of her role in the administration of the Midlands and as an assertion of her status as the king's mother.[36] The construction of Westhorpe by Charles Brandon has been seen as an attempt to bolster his position as Duke of Suffolk, to which title he had been somewhat precipitately elevated by Henry VIII.[37] The duke of Buckingham's household at Thornbury and the earl of Northumberland's manors at Wressil and Leconfield have both been interpreted as tools in the political strategies of these nobles.[38]

The performance of interludes and the provision of other entertainments at festive occasions formed part of the magnificent lifestyles of great nobles.[39]

---

[32] Girouard, *Life in the English Country House*, pp. 14–80; Starkey, 'Age of the Household', pp. 225–90; Mertes, *English Noble Household*; Woolgar, *Great Household*.

[33] Girouard, *Life in the English Country House*, p. 15; Starkey, 'Age of the Household', pp. 224, 253–61; Mertes, *English Noble Household*, pp. 102–3; C. M. Barron, 'Centres of Conspicuous Consumption: The Aristocratic Town House in London 1200–1550', *The London Journal* 20 (1995), 1–16; Woolgar, *Great Household*, p. 1.

[34] Starkey, 'Age of the Household', pp. 255–6.

[35] Mertes, 'Aristocracy', p. 50.

[36] M. K. Jones, 'Collyweston – An Early Tudor Palace', in *England in the Fifteenth Century*, ed. Williams, pp. 129–41.

[37] S. J. Gunn and P. G. Lindley, 'Charles Brandon's Westhorpe: An Early Tudor Courtyard House in Suffolk', *Archaeological Journal* 145 (1988), 272–89.

[38] B. J. Harris, *Edward Stafford, Third Duke of Buckingham, 1478–1521* (Stanford, 1986), pp. 76–103; R. Larsen, 'Expressions of Nobility: Conspicuous Consumption and Segregation in the Household of the Fifth Earl of Northumberland' (unpublished M.A. dissertation, University of York, 1998).

[39] Westfall, *Patrons and Performance*; P. H. Greenfield, 'Festive Drama at Christmas in Aristocratic Households', in *Festive Drama*, ed. M. Twycross (Cambridge, 1996), pp. 34–40; S. R.

Nobles were prepared to invest the financial and human resources of their households in festivity because these occasions were an opportunity to manage political relationships. The Duke of Buckingham, for example, entertained a large number of the local gentry at the feast held at Thornbury on Twelfth Night, 1508.[40] Buckingham intended such gentlemen to be impressed by his magnificence and honoured to be invited to such an occasion; and hence be all the more ready to repay their obligations to him by expediting his business in the locality.[41] The touring of players patronized by a nobleman was also a way of reinforcing his political relationships with towns, religious houses and other nobles.[42] Rewarding a lord's players was a tangible means by which to recognize an alliance with or an allegiance to that lord. Those who hosted touring companies often operated a sliding scale of payments to companies, depending on the closeness of their relationship with their patron.[43]

The later medieval noble household was not just a group of buildings or a physical space. Kate Mertes has defined it as a 'collection of servants, friends and other retainers around a noble and possibly his immediate family', living 'as a single community, for the purpose of creating the mode of life desired by the noble master and providing suitably for his needs'.[44] This collection of people, or *familia*, helped the aristocrat to construct a noble identity in a number of ways. To begin with, employing a large number of servants was also a kind of conspicuous consumption, a way of making visible one's wealth and power in terms of sheer manpower.[45] Evidence available for later medieval great households suggests that their size in terms of the numbers of staff employed was related to status and wealth.[46] It is probable that most noble households numbered between thirty and seventy persons, though there are considerable difficulties in generalizing about household sizes.[47] The households of great aristocrats, however, were much larger. On the basis of records of the numbers of portions served at meals in the manor of Edward Stafford, duke of Buckingham, at Thornbury in November 1508 to January 1509, the duke's household numbered 157 people.[48]

Westfall, ' "A Commonty a Christmas gambold or a tumbling trick": Household Theater', in *A New History of Early English Drama*, ed. J. D. Cox and D. S. Kastan (New York, 1997), pp. 39–58.

[40] Harris, *Edward Stafford*, p. 92.

[41] Westfall, *Patrons and Performance*, pp. 2–3, 11.

[42] Ibid., pp. 122–7.

[43] Ibid., pp. 132, 143; J. Wasson, 'Professional Actors in the Middle Ages and Early Renaissance', *Medieval and Renaissance Drama in England* 1 (1984), 1–11.

[44] Mertes, *English Noble Household*, p. 5.

[45] Ibid., pp. 132–3; Girouard, *Life in the English Country House*, p. 19.

[46] Starkey, 'Age of the Household', pp. 243–4; Woolgar, *Great Household*, pp. 8–24.

[47] Mertes, *English Noble Household*, p. 18. On the problems inherent in calculating the size of households, see Woolgar, *Great Household*, pp. 8–24.

[48] Woolgar, *Great Household*, pp. 12–13; Harris, *Edward Stafford*, p. 77.

Those with large landed estates needed a large administrative staff to manage them. But as Mertes' definition implies, with its reference to the 'creation of a mode of life', the function of many of the servants who resided in this 'single community' was as much symbolic as purely practical.[49] The *familia* participated in a continual round of ceremony and ritual centred on the person of the noble, which served constantly to reinscribe his or her status.[50] When the noble was present in the hall, for example, his or her status was marked in terms of physical space by the noble's being seated on a dais at the 'high' end of the hall, elevated above the other diners, and with a celure or canopy overhead.[51] The supreme authority of the lord was emphasized by the careful gradations in rank which were observed in the seating plan of the hall, where the status of diners was signalled by their proximity to the dais.[52] The rituals of dining, performed by the attendant staff, were also designed to produce the aristocrat as noble.[53] So, for example, those serving the lord performed a series of gestures of deference to this figure as they set up the tables for dining, even though the lord was not present.[54] As they served the food, they knelt to offer him or her bowls for washing, and utensils for eating.[55] Even where nobles customarily dined in separate chambers, their food was still ceremonially paraded along the length of the hall before the diners within the hall were served, as a way of making visible the invisible lord.[56] Whenever the noble entered the hall, he or she would do so as part of a formal procession, an entrance heralded by musicians, usually trumpeters.[57] As the Northumberland Orders for Twelfth Night indicate, the first part of the performance on this festive occasion was not the interlude, but the procession of the earl, his officers and family into the hall.[58] The earl was placed in the middle of the procession, and the rest of the participants were arranged in order of importance around him, so that the least important in status were positioned at the very beginning or the very end of the procession. The status of all the other participants, whether the earl's family or household officials, was made to depend on the earl. Conversely, this arrangement also served to stress the earl's pre-eminence over all the others.

[49] Woolgar, *Great Household*, p. 16.

[50] Girouard, *Life in the English Country House*, pp. 46–51.

[51] Ibid., p. 34. On the architectural layout and fabric of the great hall, see M. Wood, *The English Mediaeval House* (London, 1965); and Grenville, *Medieval Housing*, pp. 89–120. On hall furnishings, see Woolgar, *Great Household*, pp. 147–57.

[52] Woolgar, *Great Household*, p. 103.

[53] Girouard, *Life in the English Country House*, pp. 47–51; Westfall, ' "A Commonty" ', pp. 46–7.

[54] Girouard, *Life in the English Country House*, p. 47.

[55] Ibid., p. 49; M. Camille, *Mirror in Parchment: The Luttrell Psalter and the Making of Medieval England* (Chicago, 1998), pp. 84–5.

[56] Girouard, *Life in the English Country House*, p. 48.

[57] Westfall, *Patrons and Performance*, pp. 64–74.

[58] I. Lancashire, 'Orders for Twelfth Day and Night circa 1515 in the Second Northumberland Household Book', *ELR* 10 (1980), 7–45 (pp. 15–16).

Nobles were at the centre of a performance designed to transmit messages about power and status. In part, as we have seen, they were obliged to construct their noble identity through their gestures, on and through bodies, to draw attention to their essential noble natures. Daily household practices were also a kind of performance designed to disclose nobility, but these relied on the gestures and behaviour of household servants to signify the nobility of their master. Paradoxically, then, servants were fundamental to constructing noble identity within the household. In the earl of Northumberland's procession on Twelfth Night, the earl gives meaning to his inferiors, but by the same token they are necessary to demonstrate his superior status.

In the interludes we are considering, the importance of householding to noble masculinity is suggested by the fact that all the young male protagonists are provided with servants. Each is, in other words, represented in the context of a *familia*. Man in *Nature* employs Pryde and the other deadly sins, as well as the competing counsellors in the form of Reason and Sensualyte. In *Fulgens and Lucres*, Gaius employs A as a servant, while Cornelius employs B. We learn from B that Cornelius already has a larger household, and he claims to be rich enough to support a household of 'an hundred or twayne' if Lucres should marry him.[59] Manhode in *The Worlde and the Chylde* begins his career as a servant of The Worlde, and as a young adult employs Folye in his own service. Youth in *The Interlude of Youth* engages Pride as his servant, though Youth suggests he has other servants, by speaking of his desire to have 'one man more / To wait me upon' (ll. 312–13). Calisto has two servants, Sempronio and Parmeno. These plays tend not to depict *familiae* as consisting of kin, though Riot in *The Interlude of Youth*, who is called Youth's companion or 'compeer' (l. 216) rather than his servant, also seems to be a member of his *familia*.

In the interludes, relationships of service are sometimes used to mark transitions to adulthood by the young nobles. This is particularly clear in *The Worlde and the Chylde*, where the protagonist's life-cycle is defined in terms of different kinds of service – his own service of noble lords as a child and adult, and his engaging of his own servant as a mature man.[60] The play shows the variety of forms of service that the late medieval noble might experience in relation to other men of a range of status groups. As the child Infans, the central character enters The Worlde's household as a servant. Life-cycle service of this kind was a common stage in the education of many of the lesser and the greater nobility. Young men of noble status routinely spent some of their formative years in the service of a noble patron, though many were not intended for permanent careers in household service.[61] Rather they and their families expected household service to help them acquire the manners and polish of a gentleman, and to make useful contacts for later life. The childhood

---

[59] *Fulgens and Lucres*, I.760–4, II.561–3.

[60] Westfall, *Patrons and Performance*, p. 172.

[61] Orme, *From Childhood to Chivalry*, pp. 45–65; Girouard, *Life in the English Country House*, pp. 16–18; Mertes, *English Noble Household*, pp. 30–1, 60; Woolgar, *Great Household*, p. 37.

of Infans in *The Worlde and the Chylde* conforms to this model, though this character does not seem to come from a particularly privileged background. He first seeks service with The Worlde as a child of seven, because he cannot provide for himself. He requests 'Mete and clothe my lyfe to saue' (l. 62), offering loyal service in return (ll. 61–3). This may not be intended to indicate the typical social background of a life-cycle servant: Infans's desperation for the necessities of life is a familiar trait of the newborn figures of moral literature, and emphasizes human weakness and vulnerability in a hostile world.[62] By the age of fourteen, the young man, as 'Wanton', describes himself as The Worlde's 'page' and is now able to base his claim to The Worlde's favour on the fact that 'This seuen yere I haue serued you in hall and boure / With all my trewe entent'.[63] Rather than being a menial servant, Wanton has been involved in personal service to his lord, usually referred to as chamber-service or body-service, of the type which the well-born life-cycle servant would undertake.[64] In this context, The Worlde's gift of clothes to his servant signifies not only the moral status of the young man, but also his status as a household servant, since the gift of garments was a familiar form of payment for service.[65]

At the age of twenty-one the young protagonist, now called Manhode, is dubbed a knight by The Worlde and leaves his household service, but this does not mean that he is beyond the influence of or excluded from the patronage of his former master. Manhode goes on to enter other relationships of service at the instigation of The Worlde, as he becomes the retainer of the seven kings (the seven deadly sins). Manhode is not permanently resident in their households, but is at the service of these lords in return for the benefits they can bestow on him.[66] Manhode boasts of the 'letters' he gains from the King of Lechery, presumably letters patent confirming the grant of offices or lands (l. 276). Manhode also receives livery from four of the other kings (ll. 279–81), and is now able to call on their 'mayne' and 'myght' to help him expedite his own business (l. 278). He owes his advancement to his early household career and to the patronage of his lord, The Worlde, since it is he who dubs Manhode a knight – one able to render the kings the military service they require – and he who recommends Man to the seven kings (ll. 168–203). The prospect of this kind of patronage in later life made household service in youth particularly attractive for young nobles.

For Manhode in *The Worlde and the Chylde*, and Youth in *The Interlude of Youth* the engaging of a servant is also a life-cycle marker. Both texts show the

---

62 See for example *Mirror of the Periods of Man's Life*, ll. 1–24, in *Hymns to the Virgin and Christ*, ed. Furnivall, pp. 58–78; *Castle of Perseverance*, ll. 275–300, in *Macro Plays*, ed. Eccles.

63 *Worlde and the Chylde*, ll. 117, 121–2.

64 Starkey, 'Age of the Household', pp. 250–1; Mertes, *English Noble Household*, pp. 42–6; Woolgar, *Great Household*, pp. 41–2.

65 Woolgar, *Great Household*, pp. 31–2.

66 McFarlane, *Nobility of the Later Middle Ages*, pp. 102–21; Starkey, 'Age of the Household', pp. 264–76; M. A. Hicks, *Bastard Feudalism* (London, 1995).

young men, having attained their majority, acting as noble masters by negotiating terms of service with new servants, though servants of different status.
In each case, the terminology employed indicates that it is specifically household service. In *The Worlde and the Chylde*, Folye seeks service with Manhode
after Manhode is dubbed a knight at the age of twenty-one. Folye requests the
most basic kind of remuneration, simply 'mete and drynke' for one resident in
the household, without wages of any kind (ll. 636–8). Rather than reflecting
extreme youth, as in the case of Infans, Folye's request reflects his low status.
Manhode, for example, assumes Folye is of ungentle birth by asking him if he
is a 'craftes man' (l. 537). Folye is probably to be thought of as occupying a
menial position within Manhode's household.[67] In *The Interlude of Youth*,
Youth engages Pride as his servant upon inheritance of his father's property.
He requires an extra servant 'To wait me upon', that is to provide day-to-day
service to Youth in the household context (l. 313). However, Pride seems
superior in status to someone like Folye, since Youth offers Pride 'gold and
fee', and not just food and lodgings (ll. 329–30).[68]

Nature depicts a more complex process of the formation and re-formation
of a noble household as the young noble Man grows up. At the beginning of
the play, Nature appoints a small number of servants to act as Man's household from birth, comprising Innocencye (Man's nurse), Sensualyte and
Reason, whom Nature makes pre-eminent amongst the others (I.101–5).
Sensualyte describes Reason as Man's 'chyef counseyller', and this is also how
Man introduces Reason to The Worlde.[69] Like all noblemen, Man has the
benefit of a council of advisors, whose expertise and experience will serve to
expedite his business, whether in estate administration, political action, or
familial business, such as the negotiation of marriages.[70] This arrangement for
the young Man reflects the royal practice of establishing a separate household
for heirs to the throne, run by a council while the prince was a minor.[71] Man
soon reconstitutes his household on the advice of The Worlde, relying on The
Worlde's protegés, Sensualyte and Worldly Affeccyon, for counsel, rather than
Reason, and appointing more servants to reflect his status.[72] The re-formation
and the enlargement of Man's establishment reflect the actions of one who has
just come of age. The Worlde has inducted Man into his rule of 'thys empyry',
and on a cosmic level this represents the role of humanity in ruling the secular
world (I.421–7). However, Worldly Affeccyon describes this event in terms of

---

[67] Mertes, *English Noble Household*, pp. 23–8.
[68] For this formula, see *MED*, qv.'fe' (n.(2)), 3 a and b; Mertes, *English Noble Household*, p. 60.
[69] *Nature*, I.205, 533.
[70] C. Rawcliffe, 'Baronial Councils in the Later Middle Ages', in *Patronage, Pedigree and Power*, ed. Ross, pp. 87–108; C. Rawcliffe and S. Flower, 'English Noblemen and their Advisers: Consultation and Collaboration in the Later Middle Ages', *Journal of British Studies* 25 (1986), 157–77; Mertes, *English Noble Household*, pp. 126–31.
[71] N. Orme, 'The Education of Edward V', *BIHR* 57 (1984), 119–30; F. Hepburn, 'Arthur, Prince of Wales and his Training for Kingship', *The Historian* 55 (1997), 4–9.
[72] *Nature*, I.526–32, 706–8.

a young nobleman inheriting his lands at the age of twenty-one. He urges Man to live like a nobleman, 'Syth that ye be come to your own' (I.689), and asks:

> Wyll yt lyke you therfore that I survey
> And se thextent of all your land
> And theruppon in all the hast purvey
> Both for you and yours all maner of vyand,
> Wyth other utensylls redy at your hand,
> So that ye be purveyd all tymes erely and late
> Of eche thyng that belongeth to your estate?   (I.695–701)

Worldly Affeccyon is offering to hold a view or valor of Man's estates, in order to determine what his income is, so that he can decide the scale on which Man can afford to live, and then provide all the practical necessities for household life on that scale.[73] His concern about 'vyand' reflects the fact that the provision of food and drink took up a large proportion of a noble's income, and much of the household organization was devoted to the supplying, preparation and serving of food.[74]

Man's transition to legal adulthood at the age of twenty-one is marked by the establishing of a great household, and the employing of new servants. His exalted noble status is underscored by the fact that he employs Pryde, who himself claims to be noble and a landowner in his own right (I.727–36). Pryde's aim is to obtain an office with Man, which will carry a fee, rather than to become a menial servant (I.834), in this case the substantial annual fee of twenty pounds (I.887). Envy later refers to the 'office', 'fees' and 'wagys' which Pryde holds from Man (II.848–9). Pryde's much-vaunted noble status works to the benefit of Man, since the employing of gentlemen servants carried considerable social cachet for the greater nobility, and also was a form of patronage deployed to gain influence amongst the local gentry.[75] In order to secure the service of such men, the fifth earl of Northumberland operated a kind of rota system for his most important gentlemen servants, who were thus able to spend part of their time in attendance on Northumberland, and devote the rest to their own affairs as landowners.[76] Man's other new servants, the remaining deadly sins, are introduced to Man's service through Pryde, and these figures are clearly also members of the *familia*, since Pryde urges each of them to 'gyve contynuall attendaunce, [. . .] / After the propertye of hys offyce' at one point (I.1099–101). At another, Man complains about the bad service rendered by Slouth, who comes and goes as he pleases, and Man is also angry with Bodely Lust and Pryde for neglecting their household

---

73 Mertes, *English Noble Household*, pp. 77–8.
74 Ibid., pp. 104–20; Woolgar, *Great Household*, pp. 111–35 (p. 111).
75 Horrox, 'Service', pp. 63–5; Mertes, *English Noble Household*, p. 59; Woolgar, *Great Household*, p. 37.
76 Mertes, *English Noble Household*, p. 59.

duties.[77] This reflects contemporary concerns of noble masters over the absences of members of the *familia* without official leave.[78]

The engaging of servants has less significance as a life-cycle marker in *Fulgens and Lucres* and *Calisto and Melebea*. These texts do not present male life-cycles in their entirety in any case. In *Fulgens and Lucres*, Cornelius's desire for an extra servant is occasional: he needs another servant to help him expedite his suit to Lucres, though he already has a large establishment.[79] In the case of Gaius, it is the masterless man A who applies to Gaius for employment, though he specifically offers to aid Gaius in his suit to Lucres (I.613–20). The structure of the play implies that servants are a marker of nobility, for the introduction of A and B ensures that each of the main characters has a servant. Lucres is already provided with her servant Jone. In *Calisto and Melebea*, Calisto's two servants, Sempronio and Parmeno both seem to have been in Calisto's service for some time. Both are conversant with his plans with regard to Melebea, and both offer their counsel to him on how to proceed with the affair.

The importance of households for the construction of an adult masculinity is indicated in the attempts of young characters to use the *familia* as way of self-consciously reinforcing a noble identity. The protagonists of *The Interlude of Youth* and *Nature* both use their servants as a form of conspicuous consumption, to advertise their wealth and status by the number of servants in their train. Youth, for example, is spurred by the acquisition of his lands to engage an extra servant (ll. 308–13). For Youth, his new source of income not only allows him to enlarge his *familia*, but almost obliges him to do so in order to make a public display of it. In *Nature*, the young Man is all too ready to listen to the advice of The Worlde, who urges him to acquire more servants since he is 'nothyng accompanyde / Accordyng to a man of your degre' (I.528–9). The Worlde implies that there ought to be a strict correlation between rank and the numbers of servants in one's train. Man is soon anxiously exclaiming, 'I must have mo servauntys what so ever chaunce!' (I.708). What is perhaps surprising about these passages is that they are clearly working to mark the practice of keeping a large household as (at least potentially) sinful and undesirable. The young men are prompted to engage more servants by the evil parts of their natures – by their pride and their desire to do as everyone else in the world does. *Nature* and *The Interlude of Youth*, at any rate, do not want us to believe that status ultimately rests on how many servants one has.

Although it might be tempting to regard such passages as a critique of large noble households by those outside the secular nobility, there were in the late fifteenth and early sixteenth centuries sound political reasons why the noble patrons of interludes might use them to decry unnecessarily large households. Henry VII had enacted legislation in 1504 to limit the numbers of retainers

---

[77] Ibid., II.166–7, 416–18, 431–4. See also Slouth's ironic comment at II.388.

[78] Starkey, 'Age of the Household', pp. 251–2.

[79] *Fulgens and Lucres*, I.347–53, 760–4.

maintained by great nobles, and was all too ready to levy substantial fines on aristocrats for having excessive numbers of followers.[80] Strictly speaking this legislation did not apply to those servants directly employed in the household, but to retainers who were only paid during actual periods of service, usually military service.[81] Retaining was necessary to the king, since he relied on his own retinue and those of great nobles in any military action, so the legislation was designed rather to restrict the ability of nobles to buy political and military support which might pose a threat to the crown.[82] However, in practice it was probably less easy to draw a hard and fast line between household servants and retainers, since some individuals might be bound by rather loose ties to the household where they served, like the earl of Northumberland's gentlemen of the chamber. Given these sorts of uncertainties, it was probably wise to voice a commitment to a small and strictly functional body of household servants. If it is right to associate *The Interlude of Youth* with the Northumberland household, the Percies may have had an additional reason for taking such a position: the fifth earl was indicted for illegal retaining in 1504, and his imprisonment in the Fleet in 1516 may have been on this score.[83]

If *Nature* and *The Interlude of Youth* mark the inflation in household size as undesirable, they and other interludes also show their young protagonists failing to perform noble masculinity effectively through relationships with their *familiae*. As we have seen in Chapter Two, mirrors for princes and other political texts imply that the 'rule' or 'governance' of a household was a crucial way of signifying noble status, since it enabled nobles to demonstrate the qualities which justified their enjoyment of noble status and its attendant privileges.[84] The ongoing management of servants by a noble master contributed to maintaining of such a status identity, and this is why so many of the mirrors are concerned with intensely practical advice on how to deal with households and servants.

Noble status depended in part on the maintenance of unequal power relations with inferiors, especially those of non-noble status. In the plays considered here, the ineffective management of servants endangers status identities because it results in the inversion of power relations.[85] Even servants of noble birth can pose a threat to their aristocratic masters if they set themselves to undermine their noble authority. Young men in *Nature*, *The Worlde and the Chylde*, *The Interlude of Youth* and *Calisto and Melebea* cease to be noble in an

---

80 Record Commission, *Statutes of the Realm*, II, 658–60. On Henry VII's use of indictments for retaining, see S. B. Chrimes, *Henry VII* (London, 1972), pp. 188–90; D. Loades, *Tudor Government: Structures of Authority in the Sixteenth Century* (Oxford, 1997), p. 238.

81 Starkey, 'Age of the Household', pp. 267–8.

82 Ibid., pp. 268–71; G. W. Bernard, *The Power of the Early Tudor Nobility: A Study of the Fourth and Fifth Earls of Shrewsbury* (Brighton, 1985); Loades, *Tudor Government*, p. 238.

83 T. B. Pugh, 'Henry VII and the English Nobility', in *The Tudor Nobility*, ed. G. W. Bernard (Manchester, 1992), pp. 49–110 (p. 75).

84 Starkey, 'Age of the Household', pp. 253–6.

85 Alford, ' "My Name is Worship" ', p. 160.

important sense, because they end up effectively under the control of their servants, rather than exercising their proper and natural authority as nobles over their social inferiors. In the moral scheme of these plays, this role reversal stands for the ways in which sin acts progressively on the soul. This implies that while the exercise of authority over inferiors was seen as the noble's natural right, the exercise of that authority was understood as far from unproblematic. In the context of these relationships of service, noble status is not something automatically ascribed to a passive recipient, but an identity which must worked out in a continuous power struggle with unruly inferiors.

Relationships of service in later medieval England were potentially a site of contest for power between those of different status, because of the nature of the contracts on which they were based.[86] These were personal contracts (most frequently oral) between individuals which set out the mutual obligations of master and servant, as agreed by both parties.[87] Though noble masters may be assumed to be the more powerful party at the moment of entering a contract, nevertheless this was a point at which a servant was able to exercise independent 'bargaining power'.[88] In other words, it was potentially a levelling moment in terms of power relations, and likely to set the tone for the subsequent interaction between master and servant.[89] Relationships of service were *ongoing* relationships between the master and the servant, and this meant that they were open to renegotiation over time. Servants and masters would both have had opportunities over time to develop mutual affection and trust, or to become antagonistic, or to exploit the other party to their own advantage.[90]

Nature, Fulgens and Lucres, The Worlde and the Chylde and *The Interlude of Youth* all depict this crucial moment, where noble masters bargain with new servants over the terms of their contract. In the interludes, this is frequently a moment where one party establishes an ascendancy over another. Of these plays, *The Worlde and the Chylde* is the only interlude to show its young nobleman first as a relatively powerless household servant in relation to a powerful noble master (The Worlde). Right from the beginning the balance of power in this relationship is tilted in favour of The Worlde, a king, secure and confident in his wealth and power (ll. 1–24). As Infans, the central character first seeks service with The Worlde in order to supply his own bodily needs, offering loyal service as a 'true seruaunt' in return for food and clothing

---

[86] On contracts, formal and informal, between noble masters and gentleman servants, see Horrox 'Service'. On great household service more generally, see Woolgar, *Great Household*, pp. 30–45. On contracts between masters, male apprentices and servants, see Goldberg, 'Masters and Men in Later Medieval England'; and P. J. P. Goldberg, 'What was a Servant?', in *Concepts and Patterns of Service in the Later Middle Ages*, ed. A. Curry and E. Matthew (Woodbridge, 2000), pp. 1–20.

[87] Horrox, 'Service', p. 63.

[88] Ibid., p. 65; Goldberg, 'What Was A Servant?', pp. 9–10.

[89] Goldberg, 'What Was A Servant?', p. 10.

[90] Ibid.

(ll. 61–3). The Worlde promises Infans that 'I wyll the fynde whyle thou art yinge', but he demands in return that Infans 'be obeyent to my byddynge' (ll. 65–6). Obedience in any case was a fundamental requirement (implicit if not explicit) of a relationship that demanded the servant acknowledge the authority of the master.[91] However, the pressing nature of the body's needs and Infans's inability to provide for himself otherwise mean that he is not bargaining from a position of strength.

In this context, The Worlde's gifts of clothes to Infans take on a multiple signification.[92] On the moral level, they represent the spiritual state of man. As in other moral plays, the change of costume reflects a change in spiritual state, in this case Infans's succumbing to the lures of the worldly life.[93] In terms of relationships of service, they refer to familiar household practices of the giving of cloth and clothing as part of a servant's liveries.[94] They are also an aspect of the power relations between The Worlde and his servant. They remind the latter of the contract into which he has entered, but more importantly The Worlde's gifts call for a reciprocal gesture. Since Infans in his poverty is unable to match the gift, he remains in the debt of his master, a debt he can only repay through allegiance to The Worlde.

Infans depends on The Worlde completely for all his subsequent advancement, and as time passes he accrues ever more obligations to his master, though as he grows older he can make these requests on the basis of a history of faithful service which calls for a reward. At fourteen years, for example, man as Wanton reminds The Worlde that 'This seuen yere I haue serued you in hall and in boure / With all my trewe entent' (ll. 121–2). Between the ages of fourteen and twenty-one, man as Lust and Lykynge affirms his commitment to The Worlde's service, declaring 'For the Worlde wyll me auaunce, / I wyll kepe his gouernaunce' (ll. 148–9). As an ambitious young man, Lust and Lykynge is bound to The Worlde not only out of obligation for past benefits, but in the hopes of future ones, and so he voluntarily submits to his authority. At the age of twenty-one, the substantial material benefits of his service become ever more evident, as The Worlde dubs Manhode a knight and introduces him to the service of seven kings – the seven deadly sins (ll. 168–83). Service with one lord was a means of obtaining service with others. It was quite usual for gentlemen of independent standing to enter relationships of service with more than one noble master.[95]

The ongoing exchange of worldly benefits in return for service in *The Worlde and the Chylde* binds the central figure ever more closely to The Worlde. Given this long history of relations with The Worlde, the adult Manhode is

---

91 Ibid.
92 *Worlde and the Chylde*, ll. 67, 96–7.
93 Craik, *Tudor Interlude*, p. 82.
94 Twycross, 'Theatricality of Medieval English Plays', p. 81; Woolgar, *Great Household*, pp. 31–2.
95 Horrox, 'Service', pp. 71–3.

most reluctant to take any step which would displease him, even once he has left his household service. When Manhode meets Conscyence, for example, he at first appears to follow his dictates, and accepts that 'Conscyence techynge is trewe' (l. 505). However, when Manhode remembers his long association with The Worlde and what he has obtained through it, he is unwilling to abandon The Worlde's principles. As he observes, 'The Worlde fyndeth me all thynge / And dothe me grete seruyse' (ll. 516–17). Manhode is reluctant to dismiss Folye outright, in part because Folye is 'felowe with the Worlde' (l. 618). On one level this demonstrates how entanglement in worldly life makes it increasingly difficult to repent. However, on another it demonstrates how household service might secure for a powerful nobleman a life-long influence over an individual who was obliged to him for his patronage early in life.

Some of the plays show young noblemen engaging servants and this gives the audience an opportunity to judge their effectiveness in exercising aristocratic authority over lower-status men. In *The Worlde and the Chylde*, Folye seeks service with the twenty-one-year-old Manhode. Since Folye appears to be impoverished (ll. 636–8), Manhode ought to be the more powerful party of the two, and these power relations seem to be reflected with Manhode addressing Folye by the familiar 'thou',[96] while Folye deferentially addresses Manhode as 'you' and as 'syr'.[97] However, Manhode first cedes ground to Folye when he accepts his service despite his own better judgement. He correctly reads Folye's base nature from his crude gestures; but despite this, and despite Conscyence's warnings, he takes him into his service anyway.[98]

Manhode attempts to follow the example of The Worlde in establishing ascendancy over a powerless servant. Like him, he requires Folye to be his 'trewe seruaunt' (l. 643). However, he is soon treating Folye as an equal, rather than an inferior of not much moment. The Worlde's attitude to his servant was always characterized by a calm confidence in his own superiority, an air of aloof condescension which Starkey has described as characteristic of the nobleman.[99] Manhode, however, is easily goaded by Folye's insinuations of cowardice into a wrestling match with him (ll. 551–63). This is a levelling moment, where Manhode forgoes any sense of social distance in order to respond to a taunt about his courage. Finally, Folye consolidates his influence over Manhode by pandering to his baser desires: he offers Manhode an entrée into the world of London vice, of drinking, lechery and gambling (ll. 652–80). By accepting Folye as his guide to this milieu, Manhode cedes his advantage to Folye, and gives him the means of gaining a greater influence over him, since it is through drunkenness that Folye expects to be able to counter the influence of Conscyence's reasoned arguments over Manhode (ll. 649–51).

Folye's complete ascendancy over man is represented by his renaming of

---

96 *Worlde and the Chylde*, ll. 526, 529, 537.
97 Ibid., ll. 525, 527–8.
98 Ibid., ll. 456–60, 526, 529.
99 Starkey, 'Age of the Household', pp. 523–55.

Manhode as Shame (in fact, part of Folye's own name).[100] It is probably also represented in spatial terms: the text suggests that as the pair exit, Folye literally leads the way (ll. 697–8). By this point, Manhode, who began by regarding the low-status Folye with horror and disgust, has come to regard him affectionately as 'my felowe in fere' (l. 683). The regarding of such a vile companion as an intimate friend represents both a moral and a social degradation. Here Folye exercises power over his master, in that he has ensured that Manhode conforms to his values and emulates his lifestyle, rather than the other way round. In allowing himself to be manipulated by his servant, Manhode risks the gradual erosion of his noble identity.

Similar inversions of power are apparent in *Nature*. As in *The Worlde and the Chylde*, the action of the play describes the internal conflict within the young man, as different parts of his nature attempt to determine his actions, and this is shown in terms of the conflict between household servants and counsellors for influence over a noble master. The language of household dispute is introduced by Sensualyte, who complains about Nature's appointment of Reason to govern the young Man's actions. Nature describes Reason as Man's 'chyef gyde' (I.97) for the 'great and longe vyage' of life (I.103), using the metaphor of a journey or pilgrimage, familiar from other moral texts.[101] In contrast, Sensualyte uses terms which make the confrontation between Reason and Sensualyte sound like rivalry between members of a *familia*. Sensualyte claims that Reason and Innocencye are 'avaunced and I let go by' (I.172). He objects that Nature has 'put me out of hys [Man's] servyce' (I.187), and refers to Reason's role as the position of 'chyef counseyller' (I.205). This comparison of Man's interior life to a household naturally introduces a discourse of rule and governance, and these terms are used throughout the opening section of the play.[102] The household established by Nature is there to ensure that Man is ruled by others, in this case Reason. At this point, such an arrangement is quite proper because he is still a child and by definition not responsible for himself. For instance, the counsellors of princes like the heirs of Edward IV and Henry VII had the responsibility of enforcing the educational regime laid down for the prince, as well as conducting the business of the prince's household on his behalf.[103]

The good household order established by Nature is disrupted under the influence of The Worlde. The Worlde advises Man to conform to the habits of other nobles in keeping a household which will reflect his status (I.526–636), and to reject Innocencye and Reason in favour of Sensualyte and Worldly

---

100 *Worlde and the Chylde*, ll. 681–2. See also l. 607.

101 See for example *The Mirror of the Periods of Man's Life*, ll. 29–30; *Castle of Perseverance*, l. 277. See also S. C. Chew, *The Pilgrimage of Life* (Port Washington and London, 1962); E. T. Schell, 'On the Imitation of Life's Pilgrimage in *The Castle of Perseverance*', *JEGP* 87 (1968), 235–48; A. Forstater and J. L. Baird, ' "Walking and Wending": Mankind's Opening Speech', *Theatre Notebook* 26 (1971–72), 60–4.

102 *Nature*, I.101, 159–61, 259–61, 538.

103 Orme, 'Education of Edward V'; Hepburn, 'Arthur, Prince of Wales'.

Affeccyon. Man reforms his household according to this advice, but in doing so he ensures that his authority over his servants is compromised from the beginning. Man has accepted as his chief counsellors men who are closely bound to The Worlde. The Worlde describes Sensualyte as one who 'hath ben longe of myne acquayntaunce' (I.606); while Sensualyte describes The Worlde as 'my good mayster meny a day' (I.244). On the basis of this long-standing relationship, he appeals to The Worlde for help in obtaining Reason's place in the household. Serving more than one noble master was not in and of itself problematic,[104] but Man unquestioningly accepts Sensualyte and Worldly Affeccyon without ascertaining their obligations to other lords, or indeed requiring them to make the usual pledges of loyalty to him.[105] In accepting their service, Man illustrates both human susceptibility to the sins of the world and the flesh, and a naive reliance on new and untested counsellors, which in princely mirrors is the mark of an incompetent nobleman.[106] Man's incompetence is a function of his youth and inexperience. As The Worlde puts it, he is like a stranger in a strange land, who must rely totally on 'some syngler person that can shew hym the way / Of all the behaviour and gyse in that contray' (I.565–6).

Man's ignorance and reliance on counsellors puts him at a distinct disadvantage in his relationship with them. In this context, Sensualyte's intention to be a 'ruler' over Man takes on rather sinister connotations.[107] In one sense this term refers to the practice of offering advice, which is Sensualyte's office as Man's counsellor.[108] In another, it refers to the inverted power relations between Man and Sensualyte where the counsellor is able to exercise (undue) domination and control over his master. The remainder of the play illustrates the consequences of Man's fatal decision. Man's fall into ever greater sin is represented by the hiring of a number of servants. In effect Sensualyte and Wordly Affeccyon govern Man's household and pack it with their own allies. When Pryde enters, seeking a household office, he turns first, not to Man, but to Sensualyte, since he reckons that winning Sensualyte's support is the key to obtaining the position (I.811–18). Sensualyte is virtually able to hire and fire at will, and promises Pryde that 'I shall bryng the in servyce for twaynty pound' before Pryde has even met Man (I.887). The negotiation of the contract of service is not primarily between Pryde and Man, but between Pryde and Sensualyte. Instead, two servants agree to help each other, in order that both may profit at their noble master's expense. Pryde will gain his office with its substantial annual fee and the prospect of further material benefits; Sensualyte will gain Pryde's assistance in maintaining the estrangement between Man and Reason (I.862–85). This negotiation reveals the relative

---

104 Horrox, 'Service', pp. 71–3.
105 Woolgar, *Great Household*, pp. 30–1.
106 Ferster, *Fictions of Advice*, pp. 39–54.
107 *Nature*, I.323–36, 816; II.316–17.
108 See *MED*, *qv.* 'reulen', 1(f)

powerlessness of Man: he has little control over the people employed in his household and keeps his servants ultimately to their profit rather than to his own.

Man's first meeting with Pryde further demonstrates his lack of that acumen which princely mirrors see as so important to noblemen, since he is unable to judge Pryde's true identity as one of the deadly sins from his dress and gestures, as the audience has been able to do.[109] He is fully deceived by Pryde's adoption of the pseudonym 'Worshyp' (I.836–40) and immediately compounds his error by soliciting Pryde's 'counsel', rather than prudently testing his new servant over a long period as princely mirrors advise (I.942–5). Man gives Pryde the opportunity to manipulate him, which Pryde is ready to exploit. Pryde has planned that, once in Man's service, he would employ the powerful tool of flattery to combat Reason's influence. His plan is to inflate Man's opinion of his own intellectual abilities, so that he believes he may dispense with Reason's counsels (I.862–85). Pryde proceeds with his plan, and Man responds exactly as desired (I.922–1017), succumbing to Pryde's flattery and arrogantly dispensing with Reason's good counsel, unaware that he is uncritically accepting evil counsel. This passage reveals the power of advising, and the way in which contemporaries feared that advice might slip into flattery, a means of manipulation and control.

Finally, Pryde seeks to extend his influence over Man by influencing the composition of Man's *familia*. Pryde advises Worldly Affeccyon, 'To bryng hym [Man] shortly in acquayntaunce / Wyth all the company of myne affyaunce' (I.1097–8). Pryde manages to fill the household with members of his own affinity, individuals who owe him obligations of service. These individuals turn out to be the remaining seven deadly sins, who, like Pryde, serve under pseudonyms (I.1192–9). Sensualyte also describes the sins as Worldly Affeccyon's 'kynnesnen' (I.1195). This means that Man's household is full of servants who owe an allegiance not only (perhaps not even primarily) to him, and who will form further channels through which Pryde will control Man. Their influence is based on their intimacy and familiarity with their master. Pryde intends that they should give 'contynuall attendaunce' on Man (I.1098), that is, actively exploit their constant access to him, so that he is continually exposed to their counsel. They also gain power from the fact that they control access to the nobleman by others. In the royal household, the right of access to the king was what conferred power on royal servants, and it was for this reason that they were courted and retained by other noblemen, who expected that royal servants would help them to further their business with the king.[110]

---

109 Twycross, 'Theatricality of Medieval English Plays', pp. 72–3.

110 On early Tudor royal servants, see M. M. Condon, 'Ruling Elites in the Reign of Henry VII', in *Patronage, Pedigree and Power in Later Medieval England*, ed. C. Ross (Gloucester, 1979), pp. 109–42 (p. 123); D. Starkey, 'Intimacy and Innovation: The Rise of the Privy Chamber, 1485–1547', in *The English Court From the Wars of the Roses to the Civil War*, ed. D. Starkey (London, 1987), pp. 71–118.

In *Nature*, the servants' skilful exercise of their power means that in effect it is they who control both Man and his household. In consequence, the natural dependence of the young man on the counsel of others becomes unnaturally extended into Man's later life, so that he only attains the condition of a mature nobleman, purging the evil influences from his household, with the advent of old age.

A similar inversion of power relations is implied in *The Interlude of Youth*, as the nobleman Youth engages Pride as his servant. Pride effects this despite the fact that Youth is very conscious of his social superiority. Pride seems content to accept the inferior position allotted to him when Youth addresses him as 'good fellow', since he addresses Youth as 'Sir' and employs the respectful 'you' towards him (ll. 327–33). The true power relations of their connection are revealed in Pride's use of the word 'rule'. As Pride is being engaged as a servant, he promises Youth that 'If ye will be ruled by me, / I shall you bring to high degree'.[111] As he negotiates the terms of their relationship, Pride is aware that he has something which Youth wants: the knowledge about how social climbing is to be achieved. Pride's 'counsel', the advice he offers on how to be noble (ll. 354–7), confers on Pride the power to govern Youth. In this way Pride ensures that Youth exchanges the true basis of noble status – the right to rule others – for the fake signs of nobility, like the extravagant dress and arrogant manners which Pride recommends.

The climactic scene of the play is a debate for the soul of Youth, conducted in terms of a struggle by good and evil counsellors for influence over their master.[112] The text uses the rhetoric of counsel to evoke this context. Charity and Humility offer 'our counsel and our rede' (1.607). Pride and Riot repeatedly urge Youth to be 'ruled' by their 'counsel' instead.[113] The turning point of the play comes when Youth agrees to 'be ruled after you [Charity]', rather than Riot and Pride (ll.727–9). Youth eventually makes the correct distinction between good and evil counsel, and rejects the evil counsellors, despite having followed their advice for much of the play. The play therefore seems to show the transition of Youth, not just from sinner to repentant, but from immature to mature nobleman, able to exercise the judgement which is a mark of noble masculinity.

Youth's ultimate success stands in contrast to the failure of the knight Calisto in *Calisto and Melebea* to act like a nobleman. As the master of two servants, Parmeno and Sempronio, Calisto illustrates his own foolishness and viciousness by accepting the counsel of the evil servant Sempronio and the offices of Celestina, the bawd to whom Sempronio introduces him, rather than that of Parmeno, the good servant. As is clear to the audience, Sempronio and Celestina are ready to facilitate Calisto's seduction of Melebea, neither out of loyalty to nor out of sympathy for Calisto, but because doing so will earn them

---

111   *Interlude of Youth*, ll. 336–8, 620–3.
112   Grantley, *Wit's Pilgrimage*, p. 150.
113   *Interlude of Youth*, ll.620–3, 635–6, 673–6, 690–1.

the material rewards they desire. Both make broad hints about the rich rewards which they expect from Calisto. When Calisto gives Sempronio his gold chain as a reward for his help, Sempronio comments that 'wythout rewardes it is hard to work well' (l. 276), and advises Calisto that in his dealings with Celestina he must 'let rewardis go' (l. 292). When Calisto addresses Celestina with high-flown rhetoric, she tells Sempronio to 'Byd hym close his mouth and to his purse get' (l. 447). Observing their manoeuvres, Parmeno cites them as an example of 'How servauntis be dissaytfull in theyr maisters foly' (l. 470). It is not so much that Calisto is employing these individuals in his own business, but they are pandering to his base nature in order to further their own designs.

Calisto shows his lack of noble prudence, as well as his lack of moral virtue, in his wilful blindness to the way he is being manipulated and his inability to appreciate the disinterested advice of Parmeno. Parmeno goes out of his way to warn Calisto against his bad servants and acts purely out of loyalty to his master. He refuses Celestina's bribes to make him cooperate with Sempronio (ll. 528–53), and declares, 'I love to lyfe in joyfull poverte / And to serve my mayster with trewth and honeste' (ll. 540–1). Parmeno at this point represents the kind of faithful service which princely mirrors value. He is the servant who should be rewarded with advancement and entrusted with the important business of his lord. However, Calisto repays Parmeno only with insults (ll. 609–11). In doing so, Calisto is instrumental in creating another bad servant, who will consider his own advantage before that of his master. Embittered by Calisto's treatment, Parmeno resolves in future only to tell Calisto what he wants to hear, a form of 'flatery' which will ensure his pecuniary gain (ll. 619–32). It is clear that honest dealing is not going to win the approval of Calisto, let alone the proper rewards which should accompany loyal service. Calisto is the antitype of the effective noble, in that he consciously chooses to be swayed by bawds and flatterers, rather than accept the plain speaking of his truth-telling counsellor.

This episode of incompetent rule stands in stark contrast to the successful governance practised by the older nobleman of the play, Danio, father to Melebea. Danio's competence as a governor is illustrated not by the way he deals with his servants, but by the way he has dealt with his daughter. Danio has taken seriously his obligation to train his daughter (or to have her trained) in her devotional habits when she was young, and this education has saved her from succumbing to Calisto's seduction in deed, if not in thought. Danio is one who has thought carefully about the theory and practice of governing others, as his closing speech reveals.

The connection between the competent management of servants and noble identity also suggests a further reason why *Fulgens and Lucres* features parallel scenes where Gaius and Cornelius engage the servants A and B. These reinforce the distinctions between the effective and ineffective noble in the play. Cornelius's careless attitude toward the governance of his servants is clear from his general invitation to the 'gode felowes' who are watching the play to come and work for him (I.354–9). Yet he proposes to engage a servant 'To gyve me counseile and assistence' in the delicate and personal matter of his suit to Lucres (I.350). Cornelius is apparently all too ready to allow a comparative stranger intimate access to him and his affairs. The inappropriateness of B, the servant whom Cornelius employs, for the delicate business of negotiating a noble marriage is immediately clear when B explains that he is fitted to the task, 'For there is not in this hondred myle / A feter bawde than I am one' (I.367–8). B's unsuitability as a messenger is also apparent when he garbles Cornelius's story about Lucres into a crude 'lewed message' (II.175–315). This episode reflects the consequences of employing a base servant in sensitive personal matters, business which in a noble household would normally be conducted by high-status chamber servants or officers of the household.[114]

Gaius deals with A, who seeks service with him, in a much more cautious manner than Cornelius. Before he engages A, he requests a 'surete', someone who will act as a guarantor of A's good behaviour (I.623). The practice of obtaining sureties seems to have been used, for example, in the royal household for those household staff in sensitive or important offices.[115] When A is only able to produce B as his surety, Gaius, though still rather doubtful about A, agrees to employ him (I.624–8). He is, however, careful to maintain proper power relations in the contract he enters into with A. Gaius stipulates that 'after thi gode deservynge, / So shall I thy wagys pay' (I.652–3). Gaius makes A's remuneration completely dependent on A's conduct in his service, and reserves for himself the right not to pay A any wages at all, if he finds him wanting. A is in truth not a very efficient messenger. He garbles his greeting to Lucres, though not in the crude way which B does; he loses the letter he was supposed to deliver to Lucres; and forgets his master's and then his own name (II.316–55). Gaius's shrewdness, however, has ensured him some power of redress for this bad service.

The link between an inability to govern oneself and an inability to govern others is made in *Nature*, *The Worlde and the Chylde* and *The Interlude of Youth*, where the servants whom the young men fail to govern are at one and the same time the sins to which young men are particularly prone, as a function of their physical and mental development. The sins/servants are not external to man's being, not supernatural forces of good and evil, but traits of his own being.[116] This device confirms that a capacity for rule is contingent on male biology. However, it also suggests that the noble household is a metaphor for the noble body: that the way a nobleman rules his household makes visible and concrete the invisible conflicts taking place in his physical, spiritual and intellectual being. In these plays, therefore, the household is not just an arena wherein the nobleman can act out his nobility and construct his noble masculinity through what he does. Nor are the servants merely foils against which to

---

114 Mertes, *English Noble Household*, pp. 123–4.
115 Woolgar, *Great Household*, pp. 30–1.
116 Alford, ' "My Name is Worship" ', p. 160; Crupi, 'Christian Doctrine'.

construct a noble identity. In a real sense the households of Man, Manhode and Youth stand as a visual representation of their essential selves.

This endows the noble household with considerable symbolic power. The early part of this chapter discussed the ways in which a nobleman's gestures worked to construct a masculinity. These gestures were signs which expressed his inner nature, interpretable by audiences as evidence of his essential self. *Nature, The Worlde and the Chylde* and *The Interlude of Youth*, however, also present the conduct of the young man's *familia* as a sign from which his inner nature may be read. The conduct of the *familia* is significant in a double sense. First of all, the way in which individual servants behave in these plays can be attributed to their master. In the case of *Nature*, for example, the boastfulness, and arrogance of Pryde in *Nature* can be attributed to his master Man, because this relationship is a way of showing how the sin of pride is part of Man's fallen nature. But secondly, the way in which the noble master governs, or attempts to govern his servant, reveals the extent to which he is successful in disciplining himself. Man's failure to judge Pryde and his counsel effectively shows that he is self-deluding, unable to recognize his own sin for what it is, instead believing it to be wisdom. The progressive manipulation of Man by his servants shows how he becomes progressively compromised by his sins.

As we saw in Chapter Two, the close identification between household and nobleman is apparent in political literature, where the households of kings are used to illustrate their moral characters and their capacity or incapacity for rule. It is also implied in later medieval ordinances for royal households and households of the greater nobility. Like mirrors for princes, household ordinances appear at first to have a ruthlessly practical bent. They specify guidelines for the conduct of household life, sometimes in painstaking detail.[117] Many set the numbers of servants to be employed, their precise functions and duties, and their remuneration. Others give detailed instructions for the execution of household ceremonial and ritual, down to the smallest gestures of the participants.[118] This attention to detail was driven in part by financial prudence and the desire to keep expenditure under control. Great households were sites for extravagant conspicuous consumption, but that consumption was rigorously managed.[119] The management of money was also an aspect of good rule with an important message about a nobleman's competence. Prodigality was not just a moral vice, but a mark of the ineffective ruler.

Household ordinances were nevertheless important as much for their ideological impact as for their practical application.[120] Extant manuscript copies of the Northumberland household books, for example, do not appear to be

---

117 Mertes, *English Noble Household*, pp. 6–7.
118 Girouard, *Life in the English Country House*, p. 47; Lancashire, 'Orders for Twelfth Day and Night'; Woolgar, *Great Household*, p. 1.
119 Mertes, *English Noble Household*, pp. 75–120.
120 Ibid., p. 7.

well-thumbed exemplars, carrying the physical evidence of day-to-day use.[121] Rather, they are large volumes, written in a decorative script which indicates that they were probably intended for display.[122] More practical and less expensive copies may have been in everyday use, but nobles' investment in display copies indicates that they were also a means of projecting an image of good order and careful regulation. The act of categorizing, labelling and defining is itself a way of asserting authority and power.[123] Through the compilation and display of such documents, nobles were making statements about their capacity to govern, and hence reinforcing their own noble identities, just as chief executives and managers project an image of professional competence by the use of convincing-looking diagrams in their annual reports.

Royal household ordinances and rules drawn up in the later fifteenth and early sixteenth centuries suggest that the way a royal household was conducted would be observed and commented on, and that its conduct would reflect for good or ill on the king at its head. Ordinances of the household of Henry VI (*c.* 1455) state that a 'sadde and substantiall reule in the king's houshold' will ensure him 'not oonly greet honour and worship in this his reaulme, and comfort to his people; but also it shold be to his singuler renoume, fame and laude in other lands and countrees'.[124] The *Ordinances of Eltham* (1526) are particularly conscious that 'the king's house [. . .] is requisite to be the myrrour and example of all others within this realme' in its governance and therefore requires 'mynisters and offices, elect, tryed, and picked, for the King's honour'.[125] The conduct of the king's household is particularly important because here so much political power is at stake.

Royal ordinances often stipulate that household staff and their personal servants should exhibit certain qualities, because they will reflect on the king.[126] In the Black Book of Edward IV (1478) the ordinances state that if courtiers employ their own young servants, these should be 'comyn of clene blood; good of condycions, vertuouse, and of person lykely, that if it fortune them to growe to the kinges seruice, the worship of the courte to continue by suche chosen people'.[127] The 'worship' of the court – its public reputation, and hence the reputation of the king at its head – depends on the qualities shown by those in the king's service. The quality of the court – and by extension the quality of the king – will be judged from the quality of the individual servant. Thus, in such ordinances as well as in the interludes earlier discussed, the

121 Larsen, 'Expressions of Nobility', p. 58.
122 Lancashire, 'Orders for Twelfth Day and Night'; D. M. Barratt, 'A Second Northumberland Household Book', *Bodleian Library Record* 8 (1968), 93–8.
123 M. Foucault, *The Archaeology of Knowledge*, trans. A. M. Sheridan Smith (London, 1972).
124 Society of Antiquaries of London, *A Collection of Ordinances and Regulations for the Government of the Royal Household* (London, 1790), p. 15.
125 Ibid., p. 146.
126 Mertes, *English Noble Household*, pp. 177–9.
127 *Household of Edward IV*, ed. Myers, p. 163.

servant is a living sign of his master. The *Ordinances of Eltham* (1526) draw attention to the necessity of advancing only those who are 'of good towardnesse, liklyhood, behaviour, demeanour, and conversation' and are 'personages of good gesture, contenance, fashion and stature'.[128] These directions regard not only the moral character of servants but their physical appearance and the way in which they use gestures. They sound not unlike the fifteenth-century courtesy literature described in Chapter Two, but here the concern is that gestures of servants will be read as evidence of their master's character as much as their own.

The royal servant's behaviour is regarded as reflecting on his master, whether the servant is physically within household space or not. The Black Book carefully delineates punishments for the officer who is a 'theof or outrageous royatour in much haunting sclaunderous places, companyes, and other'.[129] The ordinances for the household of George, duke of Clarence (*c.* 1469) say that household servants should be 'of wurshipfull, honeste, vertuouse conversation, absteyninge themselves from suspected places; and also restrayning them from seditious language, varyaunces, discentions, debates and frayes, as well within the seide Duke's courte as withoute'.[130] Both texts clearly refer to the behaviour of the individual outside the physical space of the household and away from the presence of the king or noble lord, conscious that the servant's allegiance could be identified by his livery. Household service created a situation where masters and servants gained signification from each other. The service of a noble master carried social cachet for the servant, especially one in Royal service.[131] But in turn the servant was a kind of living sign representing his master, a gesture transmitting messages about him for good or ill.

Ordinances also show a particular concern for the orderly conduct of day-to-day household activity. The Black Book of Edward IV urges officers to ensure that there is 'good and sad rule within theyre offyces'.[132] It also says that the controller of the household should literally supervise the behaviour of its members and should be 'sytting dayley at metes and soupers in the hall after the syght that he takyth, furst of the seruyce of alle hoole court, or ellez then he syttythe in other place or office with in the court to see the good gouernaunces thereof and the dylygence of offycers and theyre conueyaunce in worship and profitt to the king'.[133] The proper execution of daily duties is presented as an opportunity to enhance the king's reputation. On the other hand, violence and quarrelling offend against the standards of order and

---

128 Society of Antiquaries, *Collection of Ordinances*, p. 146.
129 *Household of Edward IV*, ed. Myers, p. 163.
130 Society of Antiquaries, *Collection of Ordinances*, p. 89.
131 D. Starkey, 'Representation Through Intimacy: A Study of the Symbolism of Monarchy and Court Office in Early Modern England', in *Symbols and Sentiments*, ed. I. M. Lewis (London, 1977), pp. 187–224.
132 *Household of Edward IV*, ed. Myers, p. 161.
133 Ibid., pp. 147–8.

harmony which the writers of ordinances associate with the ideal household. Robert Grosseteste's rules for the governance of a noblewoman's household, drawn up in Latin *c.* 1241, advise that there should be no 'strife, discord or divisions within the household, but all shall be of one accord'.[134] The Black Book also commands that there should be no fighting or 'perrturbance [. . .] nyghe to the hyghe presence and hys famous houshold'.[135] The deft service rendered by members of the *familia* and a peaceable atmosphere are valuable in that they are understood to spring from the effective governance of the noble head of the household.

In comparison with these ideal households, the households of the young men of the interludes begin to look dystopic. Far from excluding the base, the violent and the unmannerly, the young nobleman often actively employs these types in his household. This rejection of household values is first figured in *Nature* and *The Worlde and the Chylde* through the employment of servants (such as Pryde and Folye) who consciously violate the customs of the household space in which their interludes are being performed, as we have seen in Chapter Two. However, as *Nature*, *The Worlde and the Chylde* and *The Interlude of Youth* proceed, it becomes clear that the young noblemen themselves are being transformed into such types. In *The Interlude of Youth*, for example, Youth adopts the violent behaviour of Riot, which the audience is able to see directly as Youth threatens Charity with his dagger, and assists Riot as he stocks Charity.[136] This kind of violent affray is exactly the sort of disorder which later medieval household ordinances want to exclude from household space.

The Worlde and the Chylde and *Nature* seem particularly anxious about young nobles adopting particular kinds of hyper-masculine identities which rely on the exhibition of physical strength and aggressive competition with other men. In *The Worlde and the Chylde*, for instance, the labelling of the protagonist as 'Manhode' in his third stage of life plays on the double meaning of the word as a developmental term for the attaining of male adulthood, and a term for a concept of masculinity.[137] In the context of *The Worlde and the Chylde*, 'manhode' refers in part to a physical prowess which has to be displayed in competition with other men. In the play, Folye goads Manhode into a wrestling match by accusing him of cowardice (ll. 541–65). As Manhode puts it, 'Manhode wyll not that I saye naye' (l. 555). Here, it is Manhode's wounded masculine pride and his fear of Folye's insult being broadcast which spurs him into action. Having agreed to the fight, it is crucial to both Manhode and Folye that they win the fight, and that the by-standers recognise their victory. Both appeal to the audience to bear testimony to their supremacy

---

134 *Women of the English Nobility and Gentry, 1066–1500* (Manchester, 1995), ed. and trans. J. Ward, p. 159.

135 *Household of Edward IV*, ed. Myers, p. 162.

136 *Interlude of Youth*, ll. 83–4, 130–2, 158–61,173–4, 520–46.

137 *MED*, qv. 'manhed(e)' (n.).

(ll. 560–3). The text is seeking to undermine this masculine competitiveness by representing it as the product of a kind of moral stupidity.

Nature and *Fulgens and Lucres* also make direct references to forms of masculinity based on violence and antisocial behaviour. When Sensualyte first gains influence over Man in *Nature*, he urges him to 'play the man' and 'play the boy' (I.660–3). Nelson glosses 'play the man' as 'act the part of a swaggering man'.[138] As this remark follows directly from the dismissal of Innocencye (I.637–54), it appears in the context of Man's response to the promptings of his sensual nature which will lead to his commission of all the deadly sins. Sensualyte represents the sinful lifestyle as an attractive form of masculinity. Other uses of this phrase in the play suggest a more restricted significance. It is used by the vicious characters as they describe Man's violent attack on Reason. Reason remonstrates with Man, after finding him in the company of prostitutes at the tavern, and in response Man strikes Reason on the head with his sword (I.1146–70). Sensualyte describes this incident as one where Man 'played the man' (I.1153), and Worldly Affeccyon asks, 'But can our master play the man now / And fare wyth thys gere?' (I.1169–70). Worldly Affeccyon refers to Man's facility with the weapons of war. These contexts associate an adult masculinity with a readiness to resort to physical violence to resolve grievances. This association is confirmed by the inclusion of the sin of wrath in Man's 'retynue' of servants (I.1200), a figure who adopts the pseudonym Manhode, as Sensualyte explains, 'bycause he ys somwat hasty' (I.1217–18). In *Fulgens and Lucres*, Cornelius also evinces these characteristics. His servant B expects him to react violently to Lucres' choice of Gaius as husband. B is so afraid that Cornelius will 'with hym self fare / Evyn as it were a lade', that he fails to deliver the news to Cornelius (II.823–4). This kind of masculinity, associated with physical violence and contention between men, is exactly the sort of identity which both courtesy texts and household ordinances mark as inappropriate to a household context.

Indeed, so strong are the associations of household space with good order, that as the moral corruption of the young nobleman proceeds, he is lured away to other kinds of spaces, where he will be able to indulge in his sinful pastimes more freely. As the ordinances cited above indicate, the undesirable servingman is associated with 'sclaunderous places',[139] while the desirable servitor is one capable of 'absteyninge themselves from suspected places'.[140] Frequenting of these locations is presented as a threat to the household and its master because they foster behaviours like drunkenness, whoring, violence and gambling and so attract disrepute. In *Nature*, *The Worlde and the Chylde* and *The Interlude of Youth* the young nobleman and his evil servants forsake the household space, and the values associated with it, for places of illrepute. In *Nature*, for example, the sins/servants whom Man employs entice him away

---

138 Medwall, *Plays of Henry Medwall*, ed. Nelson, n. to I.660.
139 *Household of Edward IV*, ed. Myers, p. 163.
140 Society of Antiquaries, *Collection of Ordinances*, p. 89.

from the household space of the great hall where he begins the play, off to the tavern where he meets the prostitute Margery and where he assaults Reason (I.1112–57). Man's second fall is also marked by his return to this milieu (II.165–302). In *The Worlde and the Chylde*, Folye leads Manhode off to explore the stews of London, and the drinking and gambling associated with them (ll. 652–708). In *The Interlude of Youth*, after the assault on Charity, Youth and his followers all exit for the tavern, which is presented as the proper place both for drinking and consorting with Lechery (ll.520–46). The departure of the young men from household space is significant because it indicates the young nobleman's implicit abdication from his responsibilities to rule. The hierarchical structure of the household was designed to place the members of the *familia* under the ultimate authority of the nobleman; but by decamping to the tavern the young noblemen threaten this arrangement. Late medieval towns expressed considerable anxiety about the fact that taverns hosted a transient population who were not under the authority of any respectable person.[141] Urban legislation attempted to make tavern-keepers responsible for the conduct of guests who stayed for more than two nights. That is, it attempted to construct a hierarchy to govern a group of people who found themselves, at least temporarily, outside the social structures designed to produce good order. In effect, when the young men of the interludes depart from household space they call their own authority into question. The means which the noble household offers to construct a noble masculinity is lost to them, and all that is left is the spurious signs of nobility in the form of wealth, dress, boasting and so on, which – as we have seen – are inadequate for the purpose.

The interludes therefore reveal the ways in which noble householding offers opportunities and threats in terms of noble signification. Households are crucial to noble masculinities in these plays, as places where nobility is constantly reinscribed through the act of governing others. The orderly implementation of routines and the demeanour of servants testified to observers about the political competence of the noble master. The aristocratic governor was also one who could maintain appropriate power relations with his followers over time: who could establish an ascendancy over them at the outset of their relationship, and who would be alert to attempts to manipulate and control him by those he allowed to have day-to-day contact with him. The effective rule of a *familia* is symbolic of the mature capacity for self-discipline of mind, body and soul which the true nobleman is also able to convey by the careful control of speech and gestures. In the context of a royal household, the household also stands as a model of the kingdom and its rule exemplifies the effective of ineffective deployment of political power.

In his natural state, the young aristocrat of the plays stands as the antithesis of these values. According to the interludes, adult noble masculinity had to be

---

141 Wells, 'Food in the City', pp. 154–7.

learned and then practised on a daily basis, a process which seems sometimes painfully difficult for the young protagonists. The threat of an unregulated young masculinity to noble identity is suggested in *Nature, The Worlde and the Chylde* and *The Interlude of Youth*, where the progressive sinfulness of the young nobles is inextricably linked to a progressive loss of aristocratic control over the *familia* and an alienation from household spaces. This means that young men are deprived of the signifying power of the household. They fail to make use of household structures and spaces which are designed to produce them as nobles, and finally are persuaded to abandon them, in favour of extra-household spaces which are dangerously free of hierarchies and the good order these promote. These interludes raise the spectre of the dissolution of noble masculinity, as young men fail to acquire this adult identity, becoming instead generic 'boyes', 'brothels', and gallants.

CHAPTER FOUR

Interludes and the Politics of Youth

The anxiety expressed in these interlude texts about young masculinity is an anxiety about political power, since noble masculinity is predicated on an ability to rule and govern others. The lack of moral self-discipline displayed by many of the young male characters is symptomatic of a wider political incompetence, further illustrated in the interludes by the failure of young men to govern their own household servants, and to evaluate counsel and counsellors effectively. The question of how to become an adult nobleman is therefore closely bound up with questions of good and bad government. The figures of young noblemen are a convenient means for the texts to introduce a political discussion, which draws on familiar assumptions in late medieval political texts.

The connection between noble masculinity and the ability to govern in these plays is to be expected, given that the later medieval nobility constituted a ruling class. Many noblemen were active at the political centre through their roles as members of parliament and privy councillors.[1] Others were appointed to offices at the disposition of the king which conferred power and status, since the holders were deputized to act on behalf of the king.[2] Nobles exercised political authority at a local level by serving on commissions of the peace in their counties, as well as contributing to the maintenance of good order through their households.[3] For many noblemen, to govern was to be noble, and the interludes reflect this by making the government of others the defining test of noble masculinity. Indeed, Greg Walker has argued that the act of watching an interlude was also part of noble image-making, since the noble patron thereby showed he or she was capable of listening to and accepting the political counsel which it contained.[4]

The interlude is a political genre in the sense that it makes the exercise of political authority into a theme. It was also frequently used throughout the sixteenth century as a vehicle for commenting on the personalities and controversies of high political life.[5] For instance, *Magnyfycence* (1519?) is a political

---

1 Miller, *Henry VIII and the English Nobility*, pp. 102–33.
2 Ibid., pp. 164–206.
3 Loades, *Tudor Government*, pp. 236–46.
4 G. Walker, 'Household Drama and the Art of Good Counsel', in *Politics of Performance*, pp. 51–75.
5 Bevington, *Tudor Drama and Politics*; N. Sanders, 'The Social and Historical Context', in *The Revels History of Drama in English, Vol. 2*, ed. Leech and Craik, pp. 3–67 (pp. 12–23).

play in this double sense. It is set in the court of the prince Magnyfycence, whose moral fall is the result of the influence of his evil courtiers, and the play's depiction of the royal household is a discussion of the theory and practice of royal government.[6] The virtue of magnificence was, after all, not a moral virtue which is to be imitated universally by all men, like humility or charity, but a status-specific virtue – the open-handedness characteristic of kings, rather than the less lavish liberality which characterizes other virtuous men.[7] It was seen as one of the markers of a good king and derives from Aristotelian traditions of political virtues. The interlude *Magnyfycence* also comments directly on personalities and topical events at the court of Henry VIII, in this case probably the so-called 'Purge of the Minions' in 1519, when a group of young courtiers were expelled from the court, on the grounds of their evil influence over the king.[8]

While internal evidence in *Magnyfycence* makes it clear that the play is closely engaged with the politics of the royal household, it is sometimes more difficult to make a connection between other interlude texts and topical events. Interlude texts are clearly very allusive in nature and are texts designed for performance at particular times and places. However, the oblique allusions within the plays, and the lack of information about times and places of their first performance sometimes make them difficult to interpret as topical plays.

Critics have been ready to see some of the interludes which are the subject of this book as politically engaged. Many have read *Fulgens and Lucres* as the product of the London political culture in which the author Henry Medwall and his patron John Morton lived and moved. The text's first modern editors, Boas and Reed, suggested that *Fulgens and Lucres* should be understood in the context of the negotiations between England and Spain regarding the proposed marriage of Prince Arthur to Katherine of Aragon. They suggested that the play was first performed in Morton's household for the Spanish and Flemish ambassadors present in London in 1497.[9] Bevington saw *Fulgens and Lucres* as a play supporting Henry VII's policy of employing men of relatively undistinguished birth in his administration, rather than members of the greater aristocracy.[10] In this reading, the young Gaius represents a new class of rising men, while the young nobleman Cornelius represents a decadent aris-

---

6 G. Walker, 'A Domestic Drama: John Skelton's *Magnyfycence* and the Royal Household', in *Plays of Persuasion: Drama and Politics at the Court of Henry VIII* (Cambridge, 1991), pp. 60–101; J. Scattergood, 'Skelton's *Magnyfycence* and the Tudor Royal Household', *METh* 15 (1993), 21–48.

7 Scattergood, 'Skelton's *Magnyfycence*', pp. 23, 25–7.

8 Ibid.; Walker, 'Domestic Drama'; A. Fox, *Politics and Literature in the Reigns of Henry VII and Henry VIII* (Oxford, 1989), pp. 237–9.

9 H. Medwall, *Fulgens & Lucres: A Fifteenth-Century Secular Play by Henry Medwall*, ed. F. S. Boas and A. W. Reed (Oxford, 1926).

10 Bevington, *Tudor Drama and Politics*, pp. 123–32.

tocracy who fail to fulfil the functions of their estate.[11] Lucres' choice of Gaius over Cornelius therefore stands for the triumph of the rising men over the scions of noble houses in the quest for political offices under Henry VII. Other scholars have read the depiction of Cornelius as an attack on specific enemies of the Tudor dynasty.[12]

The Interlude of Youth has been associated with the household of Henry Algernon Percy, the fifth earl of Northumberland, and this has encouraged a reading of the play both as a work of noble education and as a satire on the young Henry VIII. As Lancashire pointed out, Henry indulged in many of the same pastimes as Youth, and was also associated through his own songs with a courtly cult of youth.[13] Lancashire also suggested that the inclusion of Riot is a topical reference to the political situation in the north in the early years of Henry VIII's reign.[14] Northumberland was not appointed as Lieutenant of the North, an office he appears to have considered his due. In this reading, the play insinuates that, by not appointing Northumberland, Henry VIII is allowing civil disorder to reign unchecked, just as Youth allows himself to be governed by Riot.

In the case of *Nature, The Worlde and the Chylde* and *Calisto and Melebea*, recent readings have concentrated on their general, rather than specific, political significance, as texts which, like *Fulgens and Lucres* and *The Interlude of Youth*, develop an ideology of nobility.[15] Westfall, following Bevington, viewed these interludes as commenting on the rise of a new nobility who achieved their noble status though administrative ability, rather than through inherited wealth and status. Lancashire has associated *The Worlde and the Chylde* with the household of Richard Grey, earl of Kent, and identified Folye with Henry VII's officials Empson and Dudley, but this has not been widely accepted.[16] *Nature* has been surprisingly neglected, even though there is a general consensus that it, like *Fulgens and Lucres*, was first performed in John Morton's household. *Nature* seems to be viewed as an apolitical play, perhaps because of its classification as a 'morality', or relatively unsophisticated and naive drama.[17] In the minds of scholars, its overt moral and religious didacticism appears to preclude it from topicality, in terms of comment on or participation in high political life.[18] But as Potter has pointed out, if we are to

---

11 Westfall, *Patrons and Performance*, pp. 182–3.

12 Medwall, *Plays of Henry Medwall*, ed. Moeslein, pp. 60–8; Siemens, ' "As Strayght as Ony Pole" '; R. A. Godfrey, 'Nervous Laughter in Henry Medwall's *Fulgens and Lucres*', *Tudor Theatre* 3 (1996), 81–96.

13 *Two Tudor Interludes*, ed. Lancashire, pp. 54–6.

14 Ibid., pp. 56–8.

15 Westfall, *Patrons and Performance*, pp. 180–99; Grantley, *Wit's Pilgrimage*.

16 I. Lancashire, 'The Auspices of *The World and the Child*', *Renaissance and Reformation* 12 (1976), 96–105; *Worlde and the Chylde*, ed. Davidson and Happé, pp. 3–5.

17 Medwall, *Plays of Henry Medwall*, ed. Moeslein, p. 5.

18 Altman, *Tudor Play of Mind*, pp. 13–30; Jones, 'Early Moral Plays', pp. 213–91.

associate *Nature* with John Morton's household, the play is a 'courtly enter-tainment' squarely placed in a high political context.[19]

It is difficult to see the political specificity of many of the plays, since their political sub-texts – their allusion to political issues and personalities – would have been more apparent in performance. The performance of a play in a high political context and in the presence of political figures almost immediately reconfigures its meanings. Hall's well-known anecdote concerning Wolsey's reaction to the play directed by John Roo at Gray's Inn in 1526–27 illustrates this effectively.[20] Wolsey was the guest of honour at a performance of a now lost interlude, a political allegory telling the story of how 'lord gouernance was ruled by dissipacion and negligence' to the ruin of 'lay Publike wele'.[21] Wolsey, interpreting the play as a satire on his own role in government, imprisoned Roo and gave the young actors a severe dressing-down. It is perfectly possible that Roo was using the occasion to make such criticisms, though he seems to have argued that, because the play was fifty years old, it could not possibly have been written with Wolsey in mind. This may have been a disingenuous strategy, since it is perfectly possible to perform old plays in such a way that they make political points about current regimes. Wolsey's touchiness about the play may equally well have been a symptom of his own paranoia. However, the episode reveals the powerful effect of staging an inter-lude before a person with a high political profile. In the case of Roo's produc-tion, parallels between Wolsey and the play – whether intended or not – are almost unavoidable, since Wolsey stood in relation to the king almost exactly as the characters 'dissipacion' and 'negligence' seem to have stood in relation to 'lord governance' in the play, as trusted advisors, whose counsel was powerfully influential. The simple fact of Wolsey's presence in a place of honour on the dais in Gray's Inn hall may have been enough to generate the political sub-text, without any further effort from the players, though the identification of Wolsey with 'dissipacion' and 'negligence' might also have been encouraged through the gestures and movements of the actors.

The arrangement of space in later medieval great halls would have rein-forced this identification. The play itself was performed on the floor of the hall, while Wolsey would have been seated in his place of honour on the dais.[22] Wolsey's position on this raised platform meant that he was peculiarly

---

[19] Potter, *English Morality Play*, p. 58.

[20] E. Hall, *The Union of the Two Noble and Illustre Families of Lancaster and Yorke* (London, 1809), p. 719.

[21] Ibid.

[22] Twycross, 'Theatricality of Medieval English Plays', pp. 66–83. On the manipulations of space in interludes, see J. Debax, ' "God Gyve You Tyme and Space": Toward a Definition of Theatrical Space in the Tudor Interludes', in *French Essays on Shakespeare and His Contemporaries: 'What Would France With Us?'*, ed. J. Maguin and M. Willems (Newark and London, 1995), pp. 50–65; A. Lascombes, 'Time and Place in Tudor Theatre: Two Remark-able Achievements – *Fulgens and Lucres* and *Gorboduc*', in *French Essays on Shakespeare*, ed. Maguin and Willems, pp. 66–80.

visible. Indeed, the dais of the great hall was designed to mark high status and to make nobles visible, by raising them above the level of the hall floor, and by the deployment of decorative and architectural features turned toward or positioned beside the dais.[23] At the performance of John Roo's play, it was in effect Wolsey on the stage, rather than the actors.[24] For one standing at the low end of the hall, the action of the play would have been framed by the backdrop of Wolsey seated in state. This visual association was probably enough in and of itself to have encouraged an identification of the counsellor in the play with the counsellor on the dais.

Accounts of performances in the later sixteenth and early seventeenth centuries attended by Elizabeth I and James I suggest that the incorporation of the royal guest of honour in the spectacle of a performance was by that point a common affair.[25] For the performance of a Terentian comedy in the chapel of King's College, Cambridge, in 1564, Elizabeth's officials constructed the staging so that the queen was seated on the stage directly facing the players, while the main body of the audience sat at right angles to both the play and the queen.[26] The audience was not watching the performance of a play, but was watching the queen watching a play.[27] At Christ Church, Oxford, in 1605, James I insisted that his seat be moved from amongst the audience, though it had been carefully placed to give him the optimum view of the new perspective scenery.[28] James preferred to sit on the stage, since he saw himself as an important part of the spectacle. Hall's rather gleeful account of Wolsey's reaction to Roo's play suggests that the responses of the great to plays were an important part of their enjoyment, enough to make this performance remembered when many others had been forgotten. As Walker has suggested, the spectacle of a great lord viewing an interlude was one itself fraught with political significance.[29] By watching the play, the lord implicitly accepted the advice and even the criticism which it offered, and so he displayed his ability to accept unpalatable counsel, so often the mark of the good ruler in political literature.

Performances of interludes within noble households were framed both temporally and spatially by other kinds of performance on the part of the noble and his or her *familia*. As we saw in Chapter Three, the noble household, both as a body of people and as a physical space, was engaged in the business of producing its lord as noble. The occasion of the performance of an interlude, like much of the household routine, served as an opportunity for demonstrating and enacting aristocratic status. As we have seen, The

---

23 Grenville, *Medieval Housing*, pp. 111–13.
24 Twycross, 'Theatricality of Medieval English Plays', p. 67.
25 S. Orgel, *The Illusion of Power: Political Theater in the English Renaissance* (Berkeley and London, 1975).
26 *Records of Early English Drama: Cambridge*, ed. A. H. Nelson, 2 vols. (Toronto, 1989), II, 718.
27 Orgel, *Illusion of Power*, pp. 9–10.
28 Ibid., pp. 14–16.
29 Walker, 'Household Drama'.

Northumberland Orders for Twelfth Night envisage the entertainments of the evening beginning with the formal procession of the earl, his family and his household officers into the great hall.[30] As Lancashire has pointed out, the orders are not an account of any one festive occasion, but a set of detailed instructions for the benefit of the ushers on duty in the hall.[31] The ushers were responsible for the practical oversight of the hall during the evening's entertainments. They arranged the furnishings of the dais and the hall, they seated the guests in their proper places, and managed the entrances and exits of the performers – both the earl and his procession, as well as the entertainers. The ushers' 'performance' – the swift and efficient dispatch of their duties – would also help to emphasize that this was a well governed household.

Just as these forms of performance were centred on the person of the lord on the dais, so it is likely that the performance of the interlude was intended to be understood in relation to that figure. The images of power and authority being developed in the 'real' household are the backdrop against which the story of the fictional young nobleman is told, and the context in which his exploits and those of his household are understood.

As the previous chapter suggested, noble masculinity in the interludes is closely bound up with the exercise of power. The first part of the present chapter will examine how the anxiety about noble masculinity apparent in these texts might relate to the social and political position of the nobility at the end of the fifteenth century. The second part of the chapter will consider how age-related masculinities of the plays offered a flexible political code for transmitting individualized messages about political competence and incompetence in relation to specific nobles and their households. The depiction of young men and their households gave opportunities for patrons, writers and performers to deploy such codes in order to speak to the political situations in which they found themselves.

The politics of noble masculinity

In his study of early modern masculinity, Mark Breitenberg points out that masculinities are 'inherently anxious', even paranoid, in that they constantly anticipate threats and dangers which may or may not exist.[32] This anxiety about identity is closely related to an anxiety about power:

> Anxiety and masculinity: the terms must be wed if only for the obvious reason that any social system whose premise is the unequal distribution of power and authority always and only sustains itself in constant defense of the privileges of some of its members and by the constraint of others [. . .]

---

[30] Lancashire, 'Orders for Twelfth Day and Night', p. 18.
[31] Ibid., pp. 16–19.
[32] M. Breitenberg, *Anxious Masculinity in Early Modern England* (Cambridge, 1996).

> those individuals whose identities are formed by the assumption of their own privilege must also have incorporated varying degrees of anxiety about the preservation or potential loss of that privilege.[33]

Far from indicating that social structures are about to disintegrate, this anxiety performs an important function, because it ensures that men of elite standing work to defend their privileges, and to fend off the encroachments of others.

The interludes discussed in this book are to a greater or lesser extent trying to induce a level of anxiety about noble masculinity, under threat from the youthful natures of young men. As we have seen in Chapter Three, *Nature, The Interlude of Youth* and *The Worlde and the Chylde* show that, if unchecked, young men are driven by their unruly bodies into anti-noble forms of masculinity. Seduced by the fake signs of nobility, in lifestyles of conspicuous consumption, they fail to govern households in an orderly way, and allow themselves to be governed by their own servants. They abandon their households for the tavern life of drinking, violence, sex with prostitutes, and gambling. Youth in *The Interlude of Youth*, Man in *Nature*, and Calisto of *Calisto and Melebea* spend their time pursuing illicit sexual relationships instead of getting married and producing heirs. Manhode in *The Worlde and the Chylde* reduces himself to penury. Though Cornelius of *Fulgens and Lucres* attempts to marry Lucres, he is rejected in favour of a low-born man.

Noble masculinity is threatened, quite literally, from within – threatened by the perverseness of young nobles themselves. However, the plays also indicate the existence of external threats to noble privilege. In *Fulgens and Lucres* the rising, low-born man Gaius enters directly into competition with the established nobleman Cornelius. In several plays, men of lower status, even within noble households, are constantly seeking to manipulate their masters to their own advantage. These characters represent the enemy within, both the sinful aspects of young masculinity, and the manipulative servants of the *familia*. Viewed in this light, these texts deliberately play on the anxieties of mature noblemen, who are attempting to make alliances through marriage, preserve family estates, and to show their skill as governors. As Grantley has pointed out, figures such as Youth and Manhode represent every noble father's nightmare, precisely because their antics threaten the continuation of noble lines.[34] Gaius makes a similar point when he criticizes Cornelius for his complacent reliance on his inherited privileges, rather than carefully constructing a noble masculinity which will justify his possession of those privileges. Cornelius runs the risk that 'nobles of thyn auncetours everycheon / Shall utterly starve and die in the alone' (II.691–2). Gaius raises the spectre not just of the dishonour of a noble family through the behaviour of one of their number, but also of the family losing their noble status over time, or their noble line becoming extinct with Cornelius.

---

[33] Ibid., p. 3.
[34] Grantley, *Wit's Pilgrimage*, p. 138.

This implies that these texts were written in the interests of the established nobility, not of any class of rising men, such as was proposed by Bevington and Westfall. Their anxieties are those of men who have much to lose. There is evidence to suggest that in the socially competitive fifteenth and sixteenth centuries, nobles felt under pressure. They switched their patterns of consumption in the later fifteenth century to more exclusive items, as a response to the increasing buying power of other social groups.[35] Jane Grenville has drawn attention to the significant numbers of longer and thinner halls constructed in noble houses in the early sixteenth century, and the increasingly elaborate features which marked the high end of the hall, as ways of putting a greater emphasis on the social distance between the noble and the ignoble.[36]

The element of social competition is strongest in *Fulgens and Lucres*, though only because the nobleman Cornelius fails to enact his nobility effectively. As critics have noticed, this interlude expresses a great deal of anxiety about Lucres' choice of the low-born Gaius as husband, rather than the well-born Cornelius.[37] The servants A and B, who outline the action at the beginning of the play, take a rather ambivalent attitude toward her decision, expressing outrage that a 'gentilman born' should be considered less noble than a 'chorles son' one minute, and then disclaiming their ability to pass judgement the next (I.126–46). Lucres is, moreover, reluctant to act as a judge between her two suitors to decide which of them is the more noble, wishing to refer the case to the senate or a disinterested party (II.414–33). She only agrees to do so if her judgement is not taken as a precedent. After she has chosen Gaius as the more noble man, she takes pains to justify her decision to B and hence to the audience (II.752–807).[38]

Such careful explanation reveals a high level of sensitivity about Lucres' judgement. Usually critics have accounted for this nervousness by seeing it as a tactful form of back-pedalling from a triumphant celebration of the rise of new men, in order to respect the sensibilities of nobles from old-established families.[39] However, far from allaying noble fears, *Fulgens and Lucres* is trying to incite them, as the play deliberately calls attention to the disturbing implications of the action for nobles. The play's opening exaggerates Lucres' final judgement, as the servant A expresses his horror that performance will 'afferme that a chorles son / Sholde be more noble than a gentilman born' (I.130–1). Apart from the fact that there does not seem to be such a stark disparity between Gaius and Cornelius as A declares,[40] this is a deliberate misrepresentation of Lucres' words. Indeed the 'nervous' sections of the play

35 Dyer, *Making a Living in the Middle Ages*, p. 322.
36 Grenville, *Medieval Housing*, pp. 107–13.
37 Colley, '*Fulgens and Lucres*: Politics and Aesthetics'; Godfrey, 'Nervous Laughter'.
38 Godfrey, 'Nervous Laughter', pp. 89–90.
39 Colley, '*Fulgens and Lucres*: Politics and Aesthetics', pp. 323–4.
40 Grantley, *Wit's Pilgrimage*, p. 61.

carefully qualify and clarify its message with regard to nobility, and stress that the best kind of noble is not actually represented in it at all. If Cornelius does not stand for the ideal of nobility, then neither does Gaius. When Lucres' choice is discussed towards the end of the play, B asks her to consider the case of a 'gentilman bore' with 'godely maners to his birth accordyng' (II.780–1). Lucres replies that:

> Suche one is worthy more lawde and praysyng
> Than many of them that hath their begynnyng
> Of low kynred, ellis God forbede! –
> I wyll not afferme the contrary for my hede,
>
> For in that case ther may be no comparyson!   (II.783–7)

At the end of the play, B concludes that its aim is to incite 'gentilmen of name [. . .] to eschew / The wey of vyce and favour vertue' (II.891–94). The text uses anxiety about noble status as a way of encouraging noblemen to work out their noble masculinity, as Gaius does, rather than to take their noble status for granted, as Cornelius does. It raises the threat of a loss of noble privileges in competition with other nobles in order to lend urgency to this task.

Like other interludes, *Fulgens and Lucres* is ultimately reassuring, in that it points to ways in which noble power may be preserved. In *Nature* and *The Worlde and the Chylde*, the operations of male nature ensure that the male characters repent in time to be saved.[41] In *The Worlde and the Chylde*, man in the person of Age suffers penury in old age as the result of his youthful wastefulness, but in *Nature*, Man's property and status never seem to be in serious jeopardy. *The Interlude of Youth* indicates the possibility of repentance and reform at a relatively early stage of life.[42] There is no indication that Calisto in *Calisto and Melebea* and Cornelius in *Fulgens and Lucres* are reformed, but these texts do offer positive role-models of noble masculinity in the form of Gaius in *Fulgens and Lucres*, and the older nobles, Danio in *Calisto and Melebea* and Fulgens in *Fulgens and Lucres*.

The renegotiation of what noble masculinity means, apparent in an interlude like *Fulgens and Lucres*, may also relate to the anxieties and uncertainties of individual nobles, in their continual work to consolidate and extend the noble power enjoyed by themselves and their noble line. The remainder of this section will discuss how *Fulgens and Lucres* might reflect the strategies of a noble, and will discuss the interlude in relation to Lady Margaret Beaufort,

---

41 Potter, *English Morality Play*, pp. 48, 51, 61, 65–6.

42 Grantley interprets Pride's references to Youth's 'thin' clothing as evidence that Youth has been brought to penury through his tavern life. See Grantley, *Wit's Pilgrimage*, p. 147. This may be an ironic reference: Youth has had no opportunity in the play to don the 'gay' garments which Pride sees as an essential marker of noble status at l. 348. Youth's clothes are not particularly poor, but they appear so in Pride's mind in comparison with the splendid garments Pride prefers.

Countess of Richmond and Derby, and mother of Henry VII. Olga Horner first suggested that the play should be read in connection with the figure of Lady Margaret.[43] Horner noted the way in which the figure of Lucres dominates the closing section of the play, and showed how Lucres' role as an arbitrator between Gaius and Cornelius parallels Lady Margaret's role in arbitration and the administration of justice in the Midlands and East Anglia.[44] The motif of a young noblewoman's choice between two suitors may also be intended as a reference to a tale regarding Lady Margaret's personal history, and her choice between two suitors as a girl.[45] While making persuasive parallels between the play and Lady Margaret's circumstances, Horner did not suggest how the noble ideologies of the play might be addressing the case of Lady Margaret. How might the question of anxious masculinity be relevant to her?

As many scholars have indicated, *Fulgens and Lucres* is a play closely engaged with the issue of marital politics of such vital interest to nobles.[46] Successful marriages ensured the continuation of family lines and the preservation of estates. For great nobles they were also almost inevitably a political decision, a means of making or cementing alliances with other families, to the advantage of all. Several readings of the play have focused on the political ramifications of marriage in suggesting their relevance to topical events. Following Boas and Reed's suggestion that *Fulgens and Lucres* was performed for the Spanish ambassadors to London in 1497, Kipling saw the play as addressing the negotiations for a marriage between Prince Arthur and Katherine of Aragon.[47] In Kipling's reading, the play is an *apologia* for the relatively obscure origins of Arthur, the scion of a newly established royal house. This of course depends on the audience reading the low-born but virtuous Gaius in the play as representing Arthur. It is perhaps unlikely that Henry VII would have approved of his son and heir being portrayed in such a disparaging light, even indirectly. Godfrey, on the other hand, explains the high degree of tension about the issues of nobility and marriage in the play with reference to the marriage in 1515 of Charles Brandon, the newly created duke of Suffolk, to Mary Tudor, the recently widowed queen of France and sister to Henry VIII.[48] In his reading the play acts as a justification for Brandon's presumption in marrying Mary, given the disparity between them, and more particularly given the fact that they married without Henry's permission.

Lady Margaret Beaufort was also a figure closely engaged in the business of marital politics. She took a leading role in the festivities for royal marriages. She gave a dinner for Katherine of Aragon's entourage at the Coldharbour in

---

43 Horner, '*Fulgens and Lucres*'.
44 Ibid., pp. 67–71.
45 Ibid., p. 71.
46 Mertes, 'Aristocracy', pp. 45–7.
47 G. Kipling, *The Triumph of Honour: Burgundian Origins of the Elizabethan Renaissance* (Leiden, 1977), pp. 20–1.
48 Godfrey, 'Nervous Laughter', pp. 91–5.

London following Katherine's arrival in England in 1501, where the entertainments included performances by two companies of actors.[49] The celebrations for Margaret Tudor's marriage at Lady Margaret's manor at Collyweston in 1503 also included dramatic performances.[50] A performance of a play like *Fulgens and Lucres* in Lady Margaret's festivities for Katherine and Margaret might therefore function in as a celebration of a noble woman who had made (in terms of Tudor policy) the right choice in marriage, and had thereby contributed towards notable foreign policy successes.

Lady Margaret was, however, also a key player in the making of other marriages, particularly of high-born aristocratic women to her more modest kin. Jones and Underwood have suggested that Margaret was the driving force behind the marriage of her kinsman John Welles to Cecily of York, daughter of Edward IV, in 1487.[51] There is direct evidence of Margaret's involvement in the aftermath of Cecily's next marriage to Thomas Kyme of Friskney in 1502.[52] Not only did Cecily arouse the king's displeasure by marrying without permission, but she chose to marry a gentleman of low degree. Kyme was only an esquire. Margaret protected the couple by allowing them to live at Collyweston, and negotiated an agreement with the king which secured Cecily and her husband both an exemption from the fines which would otherwise have been imposed, and property on which to live.[53] In another case, Margaret helped to organize what Jones and Underwood described as the 'extraordinarily advantageous match' between her relative Richard Pole and Margaret Plantagenet, daughter of the duke of Clarence.[54] These marriages certainly seem to illustrate Margaret's promotion of suitors of relatively undistinguished birth, and support for an aristocratic woman who has made an independent choice of such a suitor. *Fulgens and Lucres* may in other words represent a justification of what might otherwise look like Margaret's practice of advancing her kinsmen through ambitious marriages to aristocratic women.

While is clear that *Fulgens and Lucres* would speak to Lady Margaret's role in marital politics, it is perhaps less obvious that she would feel the painful interest in the problems of noble masculinity evident in *Fulgens and Lucres*. Quite apart from the fact that she was not a man, there were no doubts about her nobility. However, as we have seen above, noble masculinity is bound up with questions of power and the exercise of power; and anxieties about noble masculinity may be regarded as anxieties about the maintenance of power. Again, it might seem that Lady Margaret had little cause for concern since she

[49] M. K. Jones and M. G. Underwood, *The King's Mother: Lady Margaret Beaufort, Countess of Richmond and Derby* (Cambridge, 1992), p. 166.
[50] Ibid, p. 84.
[51] Ibid., pp. 126–7.
[52] Ibid., pp. 134–5.
[53] Ibid., p. 162.
[54] Ibid., p. 82.

had enjoyed an almost unparalleled position as a power in the land following the accession of her son. She had been a great heiress in her own right, but the Great Grant of lands to her by the king in 1487 made her one of the richest nobles in England.[55] Lady Margaret was regarded as a trusted confidante of the king,[56] so much so that her household at Collyweston, in Northamptonshire was established as the headquarters of an 'unofficial council of the midlands' between 1499 and 1505.[57] And yet Lady Margaret was apparently afflicted by deep-seated fears about the maintenance of her position and that of the new Tudor dynasty. In his month's mind sermon after her death, Fisher describes Lady Margaret's continual worry that the prosperity of the new dynasty would not last. At times of great rejoicing, she would 'say that some aduersyte wolde folowe – when she was in prosperite she was in drede of the aduerste for to come'.[58] Although the reign of Henry VII has often been characterized as introducing a new stability to English government, particularly by historians of royal finances and household administration, Henry VII's position was by no means secure.[59] Polydore Vergil's account of the reign of Henry VII, the first version of which was written in 1512–13, gives the impression of a reign lurching from one crisis to another, as Henry fends off insurgents and pretenders, political threats from abroad, and from the disorderly Scottish and Welsh borders.[60] The anxious masculinities of *Fulgens and Lucres* might then represent the dynastic anxieties of the Tudors, concerned with justifying their new royal status and maintaining their line.

Lady Margaret also had to negotiate legal and political ideologies in assuming so much political authority for the governance of the Midlands. Henry VII and Lady Margaret used various means to construct an identity for her as a political governor. Margaret was provided with the basis for her political power in the Great Grant,[61] which necessitated political relationships of good lordship and service between Lady Margaret and people in the locality.[62] However, as the wife of Thomas Stanley, earl of Derby, Lady Margaret was in a notably powerless position in terms of legal and political theory. Under common law, for example, married women were regarded as merged with the person of their husband, so that all legal business had to be conducted through him. Noblewomen only came into their own as lords of their lands when they became widows. Lady Margaret and Henry VII took several steps to establish Lady Margaret as a power in her own right. The first parliament of

---

55 Ibid., p. 100.
56 Ibid., pp. 75–6.
57 Ibid., pp. 86–90.
58 J. Fisher, *The English Works of John Fisher, Bishop of Rochester*, EETS ES 27 (1876), pp. 305–30.
59 Watts, 'Introduction', pp. 1–22.
60 P. Vergil, *The Anglica Historia of Polydore Vergil, 1485–1537*, ed. and trans. D. Hay, Camden Society 3rd s. 74 (1950).
61 Jones and Underwood, *King's Mother*, p. 100.
62 Mertes, 'Aristocracy', pp. 49–50.

Henry's reign conferred on her the status of *femme sole*,[63] which had been adopted up until this point only by married women of the middling sort because it allowed them to trade as if they were single women.[64] It gave Margaret the right to sue, to have lawful title and property, to take and receive feoffments, deeds, presentments and sales of property.[65] In other words, it gave Lady Margaret the opportunity to manage her estates as a male noble would. Lady Margaret had no need of the economic benefits of *femme sole* status, as the women of London did. In her case, it had an important symbolic function: by ensuring her unfettered authority over her property, *femme sole* status also signalled her capacity to exercise without reference to a husband's authority the political agency that went with the ownership of great estates.

Margaret Beaufort's independence of her husband was further emphasized through a vow of chastity taken in 1499.[66] Jones and Underwood suggested that her vow was an indication of Henry VII's suspicion of the Stanley family's loyalty, and a symbolic way of distancing her from them.[67] It coincided with Lady Margaret's establishment of a separate household at Collyweston.[68] The rebuilding of the manor house at Collyweston was itself a political act, which emphasized that Lady Margaret's new household was fitted for her role as a political governor of the region, since the new building incorporated a council chamber and a prison, and so was clearly designed in practical terms to facilitate the business of Lady Margaret's council as the 'unofficial council of the midlands'.[69] Lady Margaret's vow and the rebuilding of Collyweston can be seen as a series of strategic moves, designed to create an ideological as well as a physical space in which she could operate as an independent political ruler. The fact that they needed to be undertaken at all reveals a level of anxiety about gender and power. They are the tactics of those who are attempting to forestall any attacks on Lady Margaret's authority on the basis of her gender and married status.

How might Lady Margaret's anxieties about power be related to the negotiations of noble masculinity in *Fulgens and Lucres*? As we have seen, the ability to exercise political authority was thoroughly gendered, since it was related to the development of male bodies. Young men represented political incompetence, because their reason – the intellectual facility which enables men to be wise, prudent and so on – was underdeveloped. They were held to be ruled instead by their passions, incited by the humoral make-up of the young male body, while old male bodies produced the qualities connected with effective rule. In this discourse, women were often equated with the young in terms of

63 Jones and Underwood, *King's Mother*, p. 99.
64 C. M. Barron, 'The "Golden Age" of Women in Medieval London', *Reading Medieval Studies* 15 (1989), 35–58.
65 Jones and Underwoood, *King's Mother*, pp. 98–9.
66 Ibid., pp. 153–4.
67 Ibid., p. 154.
68 Ibid., pp. 154–70.
69 Ibid, pp. 154–70; Jones, 'Collyweston'.

their ability to rule, because of their 'natural' lack of reason. Trevisa's translation of Giles of Rome's *De regimine principum* states that, 'In sum wise femeles ben, oþer semeþ þat þei ben, in comparisoun to maules as children of inparfit age to men of fol age [. . . because] children cunneþ not so moche resoun as men of ful age, for a child is as it were a man not compleet and parfit'.[70] The text continues that 'Wymmen counsaile is feble [. . .] For as a child haþ vnparfitȝ counsaille for he faileth of perfeccioun of man, so a womman haþ feble counsaile for þei ben feble of complexioun and faillen of þe strengþe of man.'[71] Female bodies render women unfit for rule, just as male bodies (eventually) produce political aptitude. The text, however, suggests that women enter old age more quickly than men, in both body and mind, so that they are able to give counsel sooner.[72]

Lady Margaret would have considerable difficulty in calling on the discourses of good government to support her new role as a governor, indeed they would provide scope for calling her governance into question, and this might account for the unusual features of *Fulgens and Lucres* in comparison with the other interludes of youth discussed in this book. The play does not work by presenting the life course of a young man as do *Nature*, *The Worlde and the Chylde*, and *The Interlude of Youth*, all of which closely relate the young man's inability to rule to his physical development. Instead it presents two young male characters who are diametrically opposed: Cornelius, the well-born but vicious nobleman; and Gaius the low-born but virtuous nobleman. It is unusual in presenting us with Gaius, who is a positive role model of how to be a noble man, alongside Cornelius, who conforms in many respects to the models of aberrant young masculinity depicted in other plays. As Horner has noted, aspects of both Cornelius's concept of nobility and that of Gaius's are evident in Lady Margaret's way of living.[73] Like Gaius she devoted herself to 'study', a quality to which Fisher draws attention in his month's mind sermon for Lady Margaret.[74] She was a translator of several devotional books, the owner of others, and was associated with the printing of texts.[75] This was not purely intellectual activity, but also the expression of Lady Margaret's piety. Her religious devotion and charity took many other forms, such as the daily round of observances in her household, her patronage of scholars and colleges, her links with the Carthusian order, and her devotion

---

[70] Aegidius Romanus, *Governance of Kings and Princes*, p. 197 (ll. 18–24).

[71] Ibid., p. 206 (ll. 32–5).

[72] Ibid., p. 207 (ll. 16–20).

[73] Horner, '*Fulgens and Lucres*', pp. 73–4.

[74] Ibid., p. 73; Fisher, *English Works*, pp. 291–2.

[75] Jones and Underwood, *King's Mother*, pp. 180–1; J. Summit, 'William Caxton, Margaret Beaufort and the Romance of Female Patronage', in *Women, the Book and the Worldly: Selected Proceedings of the St Hilda's Conference, 1993*, ed. L. Smith and J. H. M. Taylor (Cambridge, 1995), pp. 151–65; S. Powell, 'Lady Margaret Beaufort and her Books', *The Library* 6th s. 20 (1998), 197–240.

to the name of Jesus.[76] Like Gaius she could say that 'I have borne unto God all my daies / His laude and prayse with my due devocion' and shown 'charitable affeccyon' to her neighbours (II.672–5). If Gaius is able to justify the fact that he 'rulyd the comen wele' (I.97) by appealing to these moral virtues, then so could Lady Margaret.

Nonetheless, Lady Margaret also had a great deal in common with Cornelius.[77] She was able to trace her noble lineage back to John of Gaunt (though this connection was tainted by illegitimacy and adultery), and her pride in her family line is evident from the fact that she commissioned a collection of pedigrees.[78] Like Cornelius, she had inherited substantial estates which made her into one of the great heiresses of England and she understood the importance of house-holding to noble power. She was certainly not afraid to show the magnificence expected of a ruler, as accounts of her hospitality and style of living indicate.[79] Unlike Cornelius, Lady Margaret's consumption was carefully counterbalanced by a rigorous round of religious observance in the household, along with prudent financial control of her income.

The political ideologies implicit in *Fulgens and Lucres* allow a figure like Lady Margaret to disclose her own noble nature, and by extension her capacity to govern, in relation to Cornelius and Gaius. In fact, the play allows her to position herself as superior both to Cornelius and to Gaius. She is able to display the nobility of moral virtue, which is fundamental to political competence in Aristotelian thought, and so she is a better kind of governor than Cornelius, absorbed in his lifestyle of conspicuous consumption. At the same time, she enjoys the nobility of ancestry and inherited wealth which make her superior to Gaius. She is that better kind of noble defined by the interlude as 'worthy more lawde and praysyng / Than many of them that hath their begynnyng / Of low kynred' (II.783–5). Her superior nobility is a justification for her exercise of political authority.

The benefit to Lady Margaret of the negotiation of noble identities played out in *Fulgens and Lucres* is that it avoids the biological essentialism so apparent in the interludes *Nature* or *The Worlde and the Chylde*. These plays relate vice and virtue, and by extension the ability to manage servants and households and kingdoms, to the operations of male bodies. This is not a discourse on which Lady Margaret could easily call. Like Gaius, she had to show that she had transcended a nature inimical to good rule. Where Gaius disciplined his essentially youthful nature and made himself into a mature nobleman, Lady Margaret had to transcend her female nature and make herself into a mature nobleman: that is, one able to exercise political authority

---

[76] Jones and Underwood, *King's Mother*, pp. 171–229; M. G. Underwood, 'Politics and Piety in the Household of Lady Margaret Beaufort', *Journal of Ecclesiastical History* 38 (1987), 39–52.

[77] Horner, '*Fulgens and Lucres*', p. 74.

[78] Jones and Underwood, *King's Mother*, pp. 17–35.

[79] Ibid., pp. 154–9, 166.

in a competent way. Unlike traditional noble masculinity based around the martial prowess, the nobility based on political virtues is one which a woman can appropriate – not easily perhaps, but still it is possible to do so. This may also be the reason that Gaius's ability as a soldier and commander is only alluded to briefly in *Fulgens and Lucres*, and is counterbalanced by the references to piety and study. Like Gaius, Lady Margaret would be able to draw attention to these activities as evidence of the reformed inner nature, and therefore of her ability to wield the political power with which she had been invested.

The politics of age

The fact that political competence is both gendered and age-related means that male life-cycles become invested with political significance, and so male bodies can be appropriated in high political contexts in order to make oblique references to personalities and controversies. This means that a play like *Nature* has the potential to serve as sophisticated politically allusive drama, rather than simple moral didacticism. Its topicality would have been more easily apparent in performance at the political centre, where meanings would be brought to the audience's attention through the disposition of space, the gestures of the actors and the associations which prominent figures in the audience carried with them, as we have seen in the case of Wolsey and John Roo's play discussed in the opening of the chapter. This part of the chapter will explore how the politics of age, evident in *Nature* and in *The Interlude of Youth*, might have operated in performance in the households of Cardinal John Morton, archbishop of Canterbury and Henry Algernon Percy, earl of Northumberland respectively.

In the course of a long and eventful political career, John Morton had often found himself at the centre of political controversy.[80] There is some evidence that Morton was used to being the focus of political drama. A record survives of one quasi-dramatic performance before Morton, long before he was established as Henry VII's counsellor and chancellor, which suggests how the presence of this high-profile politician was used to call forth particular political meanings from an apparently innocuous didactic text. At Morton's installation as bishop of Ely in 1478, during the reign of Edward IV, the banquet held in his honour was accompanied by a subtlety which has come to be known as *Pastor bonus*.[81] The subtlety included a dialogue between two characters: Pastor Bonus (Christ) and a bishop, whom Christ charges to look after his

---

80 A. B. Emden, *Biographical Register of the University of Cambridge to 1500* (Cambridge, 1963), pp. 412–13; C. Harper-Bill, *The Register of John Morton, Archbishop of Canterbury, 1486–1500*, 3 vols., Canterbury and York Society 75, 78 and 89 (1987–2000), I, vii–x.

81 A. Brannen, 'Intricate Subtleties: Entertainment at Bishop Morton's Installation Feast', *Records of Early English Drama Newsletter* 22 (1997), 2–11.

sheep, following Christ's injunctions to Peter in John 21:15–17. The bishop acts as a kind of proxy for Morton, who is not only being enjoined to fulfil his duties well, but is made to utter a promise to do so through this character. As Anne Brannen has suggested, it seems likely that there are political undertones to this proto-drama, given the political context of the installation. Due to his support for the Lancastrian cause Morton had been included in the Bill of Attainder of November 1461, but following the Battle of Tewkesbury received a royal pardon in 1471.[82] After the reversal of his attainder in 1472, Morton became Master of the Rolls, and was a royal councillor by the end of 1473. The subtlety reminds Morton that he owes his appointment to the 'habundant grace / Of king Edward' as much as to Christ.[83] In representing the bishop as making promises of faithful service to Pastor Bonus, the subtlety may also be reminding Morton of his obligation of faithful service to his earthly king. The Bishop's promise to 'expel al rebel' from the Church, for example, looks like a particularly pointed reference to Morton's own past rebelliousness towards Edward.[84] This reading of the simple dialogue is only possible because we know that Morton was a figure charged with political significance from his eventful past. For an audience who understood Morton's personal history and recent political adventures, it might well have been difficult not to read a political interpretation into these lines.

By the end of the fifteenth century, when *Nature* may have been performed before him, Morton was a political 'player' of even greater importance, indeed one of the most influential figures in England. Following the death of Edward IV, Morton had escaped imprisonment at the hands of Richard III, and allied himself with the Lancastrian cause during a period of continental exile.[85] Under Henry VII, Morton became Lord Chancellor and archbishop of Canterbury in 1486, and in 1493 was created cardinal priest of St Anastasia. Contemporary observers viewed him as one of a very few who had any significant influence over the king.[86] During this period of his life, there is some further evidence of Morton's patronage of the arts, for political ends. As archbishop of Canterbury, Morton was the patron of entertainers who were rewarded for their performances by towns in Kent. Musicians under his patronage (described in the records as 'mynstrell' or '*ministrall*') are recorded as having visited Dover in 1489–90, and New Romney in 1498–99, 1499–1500 and 1500–1.[87] This patronage is associated with Morton's lordship of the estates of Canterbury. By the fifteenth century wealthy bishops were managing their estates in ways similar to secular noble households, and using the income

---

82 Harper-Bill, *Register*, I, viii.
83 Brannen, 'Intricate Subtleties', p. 6.
84 Ibid., p. 7.
85 Harper-Bill, *Register*, I, viii–ix.
86 Condon, 'Ruling Elites', pp. 128–9.
87 *Records of Early English Drama: Kent: Diocese of Canterbury*, ed. J. M. Gibson, 3 vols. (London and Toronto, 2002), II, 384, 756–7.

from them to express their status through the household, as secular nobles did.[88] The payment of Morton's entertainers was one way in which the towns of Kent acknowledged his good lordship, and the touring of his entertainers acted as a way of managing his relationships with towns in the locality.

Other evidence of entertainments within Morton's household is anecdotal and creates an image of the household as a centre of intellectual life. In the *Life of More*, Roper illustrates More's precocity as a young man, by describing his acting in entertainments before Morton.[89] Roper reports that Morton commented on the 'wit and towardness' which More demonstrated by ad-libbing his lines. The account suggests that dramatic performance may have been a regular feature of Morton's household life, rather than just a seasonal entertainment. Possibly performances were intended to promote the rhetorical skills of the young men being educated in his household. Later in the sixteenth century, young scholars at schools and universities acted in Terentian plays in order to further their education.[90] The poet Barclay also praises Morton for his patronage of the arts, and presents him as a model 'Maecenas' for later and less generous patrons, though he does not indicate the kinds of artistic endeavour which Morton patronized.[91] *Nature* is a sophisticated play which fits into this sophisticated intellectual milieu.

Nature is also a discussion of different kinds of rule and government, and this preoccupation is evident from the range of references to different forms of authority at the beginning of the play. The character Nature describes herself as god's 'mynyster', a term which denotes a servant or more specifically an official carrying out specific functions on behalf of one of higher authority (I.4).[92] Nature appoints Reason to 'governe' Man (I.159–60). Man is, according to The Worlde, 'ordeyned to regne here in thys emptry' of the natural world (I.422). As discussed in Chapter Three, the young Man's choice of the evil counsellor over the good and his failure to govern his servants effectively are shorthand references to later medieval political discourses, where the evaluation of counsel is a key test for rulers. In this discourse, the rule of the body (in terms of maintaining moral self-discipline) and the rule of the household come to stand for the rule of the kingdom. The discussion of different kinds of rule in the play also implies a discussion of political competence, if we under-

---

88 F. R. H. Du Boulay, *The Lordship of Canterbury: An Essay on Medieval Society* (London, 1966), pp. 251–64; F. Heal, *Of Prelates and Princes: A Study of the Economic and Social Position of the Tudor Episcopate* (Cambridge, 1980), p. 4; F. Heal, 'The Archbishops of Canterbury and the Practice of Hospitality', *Journal of Ecclesiastical History* 33 (1982), 544–63; F. Heal, *Hospitality in Early Modern England* (Oxford, 1990), pp. 246–8; Woolgar, *Great Household*, pp. 1–7.

89 W. Roper, *The Lyfe of Sir Thomas Moore, Knighte*, ed. E. V. Hitchcock, EETS OS 197 (1935), p. 5.

90 Grantley, *Wit's Pilgrimage*, pp. 48–54.

91 A. Barclay, *The Eclogues of Alexander Barclay from the Original Edition by John Cawood*, ed. B. White, EETS OS 175 (1928), I.494–550, IV.498–518. See also Fox, *Politics and Literature*, pp. 47, 52.

92 *MED*, *qv.* 'ministre' (n.).

stand rule of the body and the household to symbolize political governance, as it does in later medieval political discourse.

These discussions were relevant to Morton in a number of ways, and it is possible to interpret some elements of the play as veiled references to potentially sensitive issues in which he was concerned. Morton, like many of the characters in the play, was a governor and a ruler in several senses. He was the head of his own noble household, like Man; but in political terms his functions were more akin to those of other figures in *Nature*. As Lord Chancellor, he was responsible, under the king, for the administration of justice 'in equity'. As Horner has pointed out, the judgement of Lucres in *Fulgens and Lucres* is modelled on legal procedures familiar to Morton in his capacity of a judge in the equity courts of Chancery, Star Chamber and the royal council.[93] Courts of equity were considered to be courts of 'conscience', where it was incumbent on judges to give judgements in accordance with the spirit or 'mind' of the law, with a view to righting manifest wrongs, rather than the letter of the law.[94] That is, they were intended to offer redress on a case-by-case basis to any who had been unable to obtain justice in other courts, or whose complaint lay beyond the scope of the legal codes which operated there. Morton's function as a judge in equity is alluded to in *Nature*, when early in the play Sensualyte petitions The Worlde that Reason should be removed from his position as Man's chief counsellor. Sensualyte's request for redress takes a form strongly reminiscent of the petitions which were customarily addressed to Morton in the court of Chancery. Such petitions alleged a wrong done to the plaintiff by a named individual or individuals, and requested a remedy for that wrong.[95] Sensualyte's petition follows this form in alleging that Reason 'hath done me wrong' and requesting a remedy, that the Worlde should 'adnull the sentence / That Nature gave unto me by Reasons advyse' (I.540–6). Sensualyte even adopts a pose familiar from Chancery petitions of being poor and powerless in the face of a wealthy and powerful oppressor: he complains that Reason 'hath kept great estate / And had of me the over hande and strengar' (I.551–3). The court of Chancery existed to ensure that the advantages of wealth and power enjoyed by one party did not skew justice in his favour.

The depiction of The Worlde is a negative *exemplum* of a judge in equity. He does not seem to be swayed by the dictates of conscience, but by those of his long-standing relationship of good lordship with Sensualyte. Sensualyte appeals to The Worlde because of their relationship of mutual obligation, as a

---

93 Horner, '*Fulgens and Lucres*', pp. 61–4; N. Pronay, 'The Chancellor, The Chancery and the Council at the End of the Fifteenth Century', in *British Government and Administration: Studies Presented to S. B. Chrimes*, ed. H. Hearder and H. R. Loyn (Cardiff, 1974), pp. 87–103.

94 Horner, '*Fulgens and Lucres*', p. 62.

95 W. P. Baildon, *Select Cases in Chancery, AD 1364 to 1471*, Selden Society Publications 10 (1896), pp. xii–xv.

noble and a member of his affinity.[96] As he says, the Worlde 'hath ben my good mayster meny a day' (I.244), and this relationship engenders his confidence in redress. The Worlde's partiality is evident when he grants Sensualyte's petition without inviting Reason to respond to it, whereas it was standard Chancery practice to summon such an individual to respond to the charges before a judgement was given.[97] A performance of *Nature* in the presence of Morton therefore almost inevitably acts on one level as a piece of counsel, exhorting him by means of a negative example to fulfil his judicial duties according to the dictates of conscience, rather than those of personal interests.

This part of the play alludes to principles with which Morton apparently wholeheartedly agreed. He is credited with a number of *dicta* which develop the idea of Chancery as a court of conscience, for example.[98] In his capacity as the president of the court of Star Chamber, Morton was the royal official to whom information on maintenance – the illegal retaining of followers by lords – was to be laid.[99] The Worlde's dealings with Sensualyte illustrate the evils of maintenance, in the form of the perversion of justice. The legislation establishing the court of Star Chamber shows that it was intended to combat offences such as retaining because they worked to nullify the beneficial effects intended in the laws of the land.[100] Retaining was understood to produce instability, because it undermined confidence in the law to protect one's person or one's property. The relationship of mutual obligation between The Worlde and Sensualyte perverts justice because Sensualyte enjoys a greater degree of influence over the quasi-legal procedures of the play than Reason. Maintenance renders Chancery practice inequitable, so that it becomes part of the abuses of the powerful, rather than a place of redress *against* the abuses of the powerful.

The play's depiction of the good and bad counsellors of a lord charged with the rule of an 'empry' takes on a particular resonance in the context of Morton's household. Morton was a member of Henry VII's Privy Council, and reputedly one of his most influential councillors at that.[101] As we have seen in Chapter Two, the choice of counsellors and the evaluation of counsel was one of the defining characteristics of a king in later medieval political discourse. The capacity to deal with counsel, and by extension to rule competently is, furthermore, age-related. In *Nature*, the young Man is a good example of the incompetent governance associated with young men, as he readily accepts all kinds of unsuitable counsellors, and is open to manipulation through their flattery and their appeal to his baser instincts. The natural development of

96   Horrox, 'Service', pp. 65–6; Mertes, 'Aristocracy', pp. 47–9.
97   Baildon, *Select Cases in Chancery*, pp. xiv–xv.
98   Horner, '*Fulgens and Lucres*', p. 62.
99   Pronay, 'The Chancellor', p. 99.
100 Horner, '*Fulgens and Lucres*', p. 52.
101 Condon, 'Ruling Elites', p. 128.

male bodies, however, ensures that Man attains the characteristics of a good governor over time. His sensual desires die away naturally as his body ages, and at last Reason is able to rule him. This conventional attribution of partic- ular qualities – moral, intellectual, and political – to particular ages of man's life sets up an opposition between youth and old age. Old age here stands for moral self-discipline, good household order, and an aptitude for the exercise of political authority.

How might the age-related concepts of counsel and good governance relate to Morton as a political figure? The depiction of the male life-cycle in *Nature* is political in the widest sense that it supports a social system where positions of power are reserved for mature men. Late fifteenth and early sixteenth century society was resolutely gerontocratic, as social institutions (particularly in urban contexts) such as life-cycle service and apprenticeship kept young men and women under the authority of older men and women for an extended period, and delayed key events such as marriage.[102] The age-related political ideology of *Nature* justifies the exclusion of young noblemen from political office by referring to their essential nature: young men are simply incapable of ruling others. However, the play also provides young men with a reason to acquiesce in their own exclusion. According to *Nature*, the natural process which at first debars young men from positions of authority will, in time, guarantee their suitability for these same positions. Probably born *c.* 1420, Morton was in his seventies in the 1490s.[103] In all likelihood he was bearing the physical markers of age, which *Nature* invests with such significance. The play in effect glosses Morton's advancing years as a guarantee of his political aptitude.

There was good reason why Morton might have wanted to assure the wider world of his political trustworthiness during this period, and this is connected to *Nature*'s oblique references to the sin of covetousness. As we saw in Chapter Two, the play alludes briefly to this vice in connection with the ageing Man, as the only one of his sins-cum-servants who attends him into old age. However, *Nature* attempts to minimize the role of this sin, by making only a glancing reference to the vice in the form of the character Covetyse in the

---

102 On the later medieval period, see P. J. P. Goldberg, 'Marriage, Migration and Servanthood: The York Cause Paper Evidence', in *'Woman is a Worthy Wight': Women in English Society, c. 1200–1500* (Stroud, 1992), pp. 1–15; Goldberg, 'Masters and Men'; B. A. Hanawalt, *Growing Up in Medieval London: The Experience of Childhood in History* (Oxford, 1993); B. A. Hanawalt, ' "The Childe of Bristowe" and the Making of Middle-Class Adolescence', in *Bodies and Disciplines: Intersections of Literature and History in Fifteenth-Century England*, ed. B. A. Hanawalt and D. Wallace (Minneapolis, 1996), pp. 155–78. On the early modern period, see K. Thomas, 'Age and Authority in Early Modern England', *Proceedings of the British Academy* 62 (1976), 205–48; S. Brigden, 'Youth and the English Reformation', *Past and Present* 95 (1982), 37–67; I. K. Ben-Amos, *Adoles- cence and Youth in Early Modern England* (London, 1994); P. Griffiths, *Youth and Authority in England, 1560–1640* (Oxford, 1996).

103 Harper-Bill, *Register*, I, vii.

space of a few lines, rather than presenting covetousness as a fully realized stage presence, as is the case with the other deadly sins. The minimal presentation of covetousness in *Nature* is a further way of stressing the superiority of old age, at the expense of the period of youth.

Nonetheless, the sin of covetousness disrupts *Nature*'s depiction of old age as the ideal period of a man's life, particularly the life of a governor. Like the other sins, covetousness in *Nature* has a political significance, in that it is evidence of the inability of the character Man to rule both himself and his household effectively. The fact that Man has to keep Covetyse's continued service in his household a secret from Reason is evidence that Man's body is not completely under the control of his rational powers, and that he is practising a form of self-deception with regard to his own moral character. This lack of self-governance is potentially symbolic of a continued inability to rule others effectively. Covetousness was, however, identified specifically in later medieval political texts as a political vice. It is a characteristic of a bad ruler and is opposed to the kingly virtue of magnificence, a liberal expenditure of money which reflects royal status.[104] In this system of thought, covetousness or avarice is a falling off from the ideal of magnificence, as much as is prodigality with money. Magnificence is the moderate mean between these vices. The English translation of *De regimine principum* claims that if a king cannot be magnificent, it is better that he be a prodigal rather than a miser, in part because it views prodigality and covetousness as age-related conditions: prodigality, characteristic of the young man, will be cured naturally over time as the man's body ages.[105] There is no such remedy for covetousness, which strikes just as the physical development of a man has run its course.

As Bevington has noted, the issue of covetousness had a particular resonance for both Henry VII and Morton.[106] According to chroniclers, Henry VII was accused of avarice by his contemporaries. Polydore Vergil, for example, describes the king's rigorous exploitation of his prerogatives as proceeding '*ex cupiditate principis*'.[107] He also reports that in the last few years of his life Morton and Reginald Bray began to be blamed for encouraging, or at least failing to curb, the king's excesses. Vergil claims that Cornish rebels against the imposition of tax for campaigns against Scotland demanded the execution of Morton and Bray, '*illos malos ... consiliarios*'.[108] These passages are typical of the ways in which criticism of royal policy was couched in terms of the language of political vice and virtue; and how critics habitually turned to the criticism of evil counsellors as a way of avoiding a direct attack on the person

---

104   Horner, '*Fulgens and Lucres*', pp. 55–6; Walker, 'Domestic Drama'; Scattergood, 'Skelton's *Magnyfycence*'; Ferster, *Fictions of Advice*, pp. 139–47.
105   Aegidius Romanus, *Governance of Kings and Princes*, p. 77 (ll. 31–5).
106   Bevington, *Tudor Drama and Politics*, pp. 53–4.
107   Vergil, *Anglica historia*, p. 26 (ll. 22–3, 27).
108   Ibid., p. 92 (ll. 10–13); p. 134 (ll. 1–3). See also C. L. Kingsford, *Chronicles of London* (Oxford, 1905), p. 216.

of the king. Criticism of Henry VII could not be expressed with reference to the political incompetence of young kings, as was the case with four-teenth-century criticism of Richard II.[109] Richard's opponents referred to the traditional inability of young men to evaluate counsel and counsellors in order to construct an image of him as a bad king. This strategy was not avail-able to critics of Henry VII, since Henry was not conspicuously young. Instead they seized on the traditional political failings of old age, and recast accusa-tions against the king's counsellors to suit this situation.

In *Nature*, the deliberate minimizing of the sin of covetousness as a sin of old age works to deflect criticism of royal policy and of Morton's role in its implementation. Covetousness is, in this play, a temporary condition hardly worthy of note. Nonetheless the text is careful to establish that Man keeps his chief counsellor, Reason, ignorant of Covetyse's service. As Sensualyte puts it, 'Reason may not therof know' (II.982). This is a way of absolving Reason of any responsibility for Covetyse. *Nature* may act in one sense as a kind of *apologia* for Morton, a protestation that he, though councillor to the king, is not responsible for the king's political failings. It may, on the other hand, be intended as a more hard-hitting form of political counsel for Morton. *Nature* implies that, had Man's counsellor Reason known about the continuing pres-ence of Covetyse in Man's household, he would have taken forceful action against him. Covetyse is only secure while Reason remains ignorant of his ongoing service. This acts as an oblique reminder to Morton of his own duties to the king. Assumed to be fully cognizant of Henry's avaricious tendencies, he has an overriding obligation as the king's councillor to combat them, no matter how unpleasant or difficult a task this may be.

It is clear that the positive connotations of old age might work to the benefit of any mature nobleman who wished an interlude like *Nature* to affirm his political competence. As we have seen in the discussion above, however, the conventional characteristics of old age might also be exploited to introduce potentially uncomfortable counsel – particularly when, as in the case of Morton, it is apparent that others apart from interlude writers were seizing on motifs from political discourse in order to voice their own criticism. Conversely, it is also clear that the negative connotations of youth offer a powerful vehicle for criticizing young kings and noblemen. As Ian Lancashire has pointed out, despite the fact that the depiction of Youth in *The Interlude of Youth* is in many ways utterly conventional, it nonetheless has the potential to offer a powerful critique of young rulers. Lancashire located the performance of the interlude in the household of Henry Algernon Percy, fifth earl of Northumberland, and in this context the negative depiction of Youth can be understood as a critique of the young Henry VIII and his policies in the north, or as a critique of the young Lord Henry Percy and his youthful excesses.[110]

---

[109] Ferster, *Fictions of Advice*, pp. 108–26.
[110] *Two Tudor Interludes*, ed. Lancashire, pp. 28–9, 53–7.

The Interlude of Youth can also be understood as exploiting the political rhetoric of youth for positive ends: that is, in order to construct an image of both the fifth earl of Northumberland and his son as competent rulers. Northumberland, it has been argued, was engaged in a process of bidding for political office in the early part of the sixteenth century.[111] He evidently felt that he possessed a strong claim to offices such as the lieutenancy of the north, which had been held by his father, the fourth earl. The fifth earl's lifestyle of conspicuous consumption centred in his residences at Leconfield and Wressle and his investment in the household can be understood as ways of advertising his ability to undertake such offices.[112] Through it, Northumberland displayed the resources in terms of wealth and manpower which would enable him to take up these roles; and he displayed his political competence through the orderly conduct of household life.

How might *The Interlude of Youth* contribute to this kind of political image-making in the Northumberland context? Lancashire has pointed out that the inclusion of the character Riot in the play may well function as an oblique reference to the earl's grievances. As Youth's companion and one who incites him to violence and disorder, Riot stands not only for the instability conventionally associated with the young, but for political instability in the north.[113] The play hints that such unrest may only be assuaged by the strong hand of someone like the earl of Northumberland, rather than the licence permitted by the young king.

As we saw in Chapter Three, *The Interlude of Youth* is also a text attuned to the political discourse of the princely mirror. The character Youth is a type of the bad governor, as well as the type of the sinful man. The text alerts us to the political significance of the figure Youth by presenting him as one who chooses evil counsel over good; and as one who submits to the manipulation of his own servant, rather than ruling his servant effectively. Youth's failures bespeak a political incompetence which ought to debar him from the political offices to which Northumberland aspired. However, as we saw in Chapter Two, the narrative of Youth's progress differs significantly from those depicted in *Nature, The Worlde and the Chylde* and the earlier *Castle of Perseverance*. *The Interlude of Youth* focuses on only one stage of life. This Age – youth – becomes the key Age in the life-cycle, where man faces the defining crisis of his life, as Youth repents and makes a decisive break with his previous way of life. In *Nature, The Worlde and the Chylde* and *The Castle of Perseverance*, the repentances of the young are unsatisfactory and short lived, as the central characters soon lapse. In these plays, only the repentance of old age is true and lasting. By locating a true and lasting repentance in the period of youth, *The Interlude of Youth* therefore rebuts the age-related norms which associate male

111 M. E. James, *A Tudor Magnate and the Tudor State: Henry Fifth Earl of Northumberland* (York, 1966).

112 Larsen, 'Expressions of Nobility'.

113 *Two Tudor Interludes*, ed. Lancashire, pp. 56–7.

youth with sinfulness. Young men may be naturally prone to sin, but that does not mean that young men must remain sinful and that old age is the only period appropriate to holy living, as Riot and Pride contend. The figure of Youth is therefore not a wholly negative one. Rather Youth manages to transcend his natural sinful nature, in an unusual and admirable way. Youth's capacity to reform himself is figured in his dismissal of Pride and Riot (ll. 742–61). Youth shows the ability to discipline his own moral nature, putting from him his sinful inclinations. But since the sinful aspects of his nature are represented as Youth's servant and companion, Youth's moral reformation is also a household reformation. These actions, by extension, demonstrate a capacity for effective governance.

This clearly has implications for the kinds of political messages *The Interlude of Youth* might be sending. If we read the presentation of Youth in the early part of the play as satire of Henry VIII, then its conclusion acts as a form of counsel for the king. It proposes a course of action to remedy personal, household and public disorder, which begins with the king's personal reform. Once the king has set the realm of his body in good order by disciplining his unruly youthful nature, a household reform will follow, as he repudiates evil influences, whether evil servants or intimate friends. These reforms imply that, by extension, good order may then be established at the level of the kingdom.

In fact, Henry VIII was receiving advice couched in similar terms at around the time of the first performance of the interlude, in an English translation written in 1513–14 of Frulovisi's *Gesta Henrici Quinti*.[114] The prohem of the translation rather self-consciously denies that the text is intended for 'reproof of vice nor defaulte of vertue' in Henry, but nonetheless presents the life of Henry V as a positive *exemplum* for Henry VIII to follow.[115] The translation's primary aim is that Henry VIII 'maie in all thinges concerninge his person and the reigement of his people, conforme himselfe to his [i.e. Henry V's] life and manners, wch he vsed after his coronacion, and be councelled by the example of his greate wisdome and discretion in all his common and perticular Acts'.[116] This text implicitly links self-rule with the rule of nations, and implies that moral reform of the kind evinced in the story of Henry V's reformation at his coronation makes a better ruler. Moreover, the translator urges Henry VIII to emulate specific kingly virtues demonstrated by Henry V: the virtues of justice, sexual continence, and humility.[117] As in princely mirrors, these virtues are not just those associated with good men, but they are political virtues 'most necessarie to euerie prince to insue'.[118] Henry V becomes an ideal king, in part by undergoing a spiritual process of repentance, after

---

114 G. Walker, *Persuasive Fictions: Faction, Faith and Political Culture in the Reign of Henry VIII* (Aldershot, 1996), pp. 14–26.
115 *The First English Life of King Henry the Fifth*, ed. C. L. Kingsford (Oxford, 1911), p. 3.
116 Ibid., p. 4 (ll. 10–14).
117 Ibid., pp. 4–5.
118 Ibid., p. 5 (l. 2).

following the promptings of his youthful nature. On changing his life, he confesses his past excesses to a 'vertuous Monke' and 'in all things [. . .] reformed and amended his life and his manners'.[119] His acts no longer show 'youth nor wildnes' but the 'grauitie and discretion' of a mature man.[120] He summons his former friends, and though he rewards them, urges them to repent if they wish to remain in the court. He forbids his presence to any who refuse to forsake their old ways.

This piece of political advice literature indicates how easily a moral discourse elides with a political one in the sixteenth century, and shows how readily *The Interlude of Youth* might be read as a kind of princely mirror. Like the English life of Henry V, *The Interlude of Youth* promotes sexual continence and humility, which can be understood as political virtues. It depicts a young nobleman undergoing a process of repentance, and commitment to a life of prayer and the instruction of others, which may have a political significance as much as a moral one. The depiction of moral reform in *The Interlude of Youth* could well act as a piece of political counsel for the young Henry VIII, as much as that in the *Life* of Henry V. The play teaches him how to make himself into a better ruler; and, perhaps more importantly, how to signal his political competence to a watching world, in a language which the political establishment would understand. Walker has argued that Skelton's *Magnyfycence*, which also depicts a process of moral and political reform by a prince, is a way of advertising Henry VIII's political competence, by drawing attention to Henry's household reform in the Expulsion of the Minions of 1519.[121]

The ideology of youth apparent in *The Interlude of Youth* might equally have a more immediate application to the Northumberland household. The earl was adept at appropriating the literature of youth and noble education to transmit messages about the political competence of himself and his heir. Several verse texts apparently directed at the young with didactic purpose were added in the early sixteenth century to the Percy manuscript (London, British Library, Royal MS 18.D.II) while it was in the possession of the earl.[122] Like the earl's household books, this text was intended for display as much as instruction of the young: he was responsible for the addition to the manuscript of elaborate miniatures in Flemish style, and the new texts were written in display scripts.[123] The rubrics to the educational texts in the manuscript indicate that they were also displayed as inscriptional verse on the walls of Northumberland's manors at Leconfield and Wressle. Clearly the earl was interested in advertising his investment in this style of literature.

---

[119] Ibid., p. 17 (ll. 29–31).

[120] Ibid.

[121] Walker, 'Domestic Drama'.

[122] G. F. Warner and J. P. Gilson, *Catalogue of the Western Manuscripts in the Old Royal and King's Collections*, 4 vols. (London, 1921), II, 308–10. The verses are printed in E. Flügel, 'Kleinere Mitteilungen aus Handschriften, 3: Die Proverbs von Lekenfield und Wresil (Yorks.)', *Anglia* 14 (1892), 471–97.

[123] Warner and Gilson, *Catalogue of the Western Manuscripts*, II, 310.

In part, the texts in the manuscript help to convey an impression of the earl's household as a well-ordered and efficiently governed institution. For example, the lyric 'Drede god and fle from syn' advises the reader carefully to regulate his behaviour within the household.[124] Though these injunctions are framed in moral terms – in terms of the pursuit of vice and the suppression of virtue – they promote behaviours familiar from fifteenth-century courtesy texts discussed in Chapter Two. For instance, the text instructs the reader to be restrained in speech: to 'Speke thy wordis discretely'; to 'Speke littill and trewly'; to 'Talke at thy dyner honestly', and to 'Discretly kepe thy tunge still'.[125] It encourages people to 'After thy degree pretend', a command which advises the young man to know his place.[126] The text also expresses a disapproval of boastfulness, advising 'Avaunt neuyr of thy degree / If thoue haue a goode properte / Let other men comend & prayse the'.[127] The text demonstrates that Northumberland subscribes to the values of self-control and observance of rank. This is turn reflects on the earl's ability to regulate the behaviour of his household, and promotes an image of him as an able governor. A performance of *The Interlude of Youth* in the Northumberland household offers further opportunities to draw attention to the good manners exhibited by the earl's household, since the behaviour exhibited by Youth in the play stands in such stark contrast to them. Youth's boastfulness and vaunting of his own current status, his ambition for a higher status to which he has no real claim, and his violence towards Charity draw attention to the social conventions of great-hall space by breaching them in a spectacular fashion.[128] The figure of Youth throws the good order of the earl's household into sharp relief.

The reforming narrative of *The Interlude of Youth*, as a kind of princely mirror, may well have been addressed to Northumberland's heir, Lord Henry Percy. At least one of the verse-texts from the Percy Manuscript is specifically associated with him. The rubric at the beginning of this text – 'He that made this hous for contemplacion' – tells us that the original was inscribed on 'the rouf of my lorde percy closet' at Leconfield Manor.[129] The text is presented as educational one, intended to encourage the young nobleman in the 'exercyse of lernynge and vertuus occupation', the activities for which the closet has been explicitly designed, according to the opening lines of the text.[130] The manuscript text goes out of its way to create an image of the young Percy poring over his books in the private space of the closet. In other words, it makes visible activities which by their very nature would remain invisible to

---

124 Flügel, 'Kleinere Mitteilungen', pp. 485–7.
125 Ibid., pp. 485, 487.
126 Ibid., p. 486.
127 Ibid., p. 487.
128 *Interlude of Youth*, ll. 57–9, 308–10, 591–6.
129 Flügel, 'Kleinere Mitteilungen', pp. 482–5.
130 Ibid., p. 482. On closets as private rooms for study and devotion, see Girouard, *Life in the English Country House*, p. 56.

others. As the text itself makes clear, these activities are connected with the obtaining of political offices, of the kind to which the earl aspired for himself and his son.

Moreover, 'He that made this hous' relates learning and the obtaining of offices to a narrative of repentance. Like *The Interlude of Youth*, the verse-text is a debate that centres on the issue of whether repentance and the pursuit of learning and virtue are necessary and possible for the young nobleman. It takes the form of a dialogue between two voices. The first voice advocates learning. The second acts as a devil's advocate, arguing that learning is unnecessary, particularly for a young nobleman, and that it can be postponed to a later period of life. This debate mirrors the concluding scenes of *The Interlude of Youth*, where Charity and Humility urge repentance upon Youth, while Riot and Pride insist that repentance is unnatural to the young man, and in any case may be put off to a more convenient season (ll. 589–795).

In the verse-text, both voices assume that powerful age-related norms apply to the young. The second voice in this poem refers to the same body of knowledge about the moral nature of young men as Riot and Pride do in *The Interlude of Youth*, in order to argue that young nobles need not pursue, or can afford to postpone, their application to learning and virtue. He contends that 'youthe of nature is inclynede to play' and that the young 'by supposycion to sport will applye'.[131] Instead he presents old age as the age appropriate to study and virtue, since 'Youthe in his flowres may lyue at liberte / In age it is conuenient to grow to grauite'.[132] The first voice of the Percy poem certainly regards the young man as naturally inclined to sin, since he says that 'It is supposede by olde practyse that youthe will folow sensualite'.[133] However, this voice also asserts that the young man is still educable, in both the intellectual and the moral sense. In advocating study and self-discipline in youth, he is concerned with the future of the young man. He bases his concern for the young on the assumption that what one is in youth determines what one is in age: 'As youthe is ordorid and accustomede in his yeris grene / So after warde in his olde age it shall be seane'.[134] This is an attitude familiar from other moral texts, particularly those urging parents to take the moral education of their children seriously. Study is in this sense a disciplining activity which combats idleness, the 'moder of all vice'.[135] Indeed, this phrase is a close echo of *Fulgens and Lucres*, where Gaius presents study in similar terms (II.679–80). Through it one may construct oneself into 'youthe of condiciones aunciente': that is, one who in imitating the manners and adopting the values of the mature has made himself into an old man. Such a one stands in opposition to 'them which in age be yonge and negligent': those individuals who, even late

---

[131] Flügel, 'Kleinere Mitteilungen', p. 482.

[132] Ibid., p. 483.

[133] Ibid., p. 482.

[134] Ibid.

[135] Ibid.

in life, are trapped in the behaviours associated with the young. It is possible, in other words, to transcend the natural inclinations of young bodies, as a young man. This is exactly what Youth achieves in *The Interlude of Youth*, becoming at the end of the play a soberly dressed man, committed to a life of prayer and the instruction of other sinful men (ll. 762–80).

Further comparison of the poem with *The Interlude of Youth* shows that the interlude puts forward a similar message, and uses a similar means to do so. Instead of an exchange between two characters, the interlude presents a conflict between two groups of characters: the representatives of good (Charity and Humility) and the representatives of evil (Riot and Pride). While these groups are at loggerheads throughout the play – indeed Pride and Riot lay violent hands on Charity and stock him – the climactic scene of the play features all four characters seeking to sway Youth through argument and counter-argument. Charity and Humility appeal to Youth to repent. Riot and Pride attempt to refute their arguments by calling on ideas of what is natural to young and old men. Riot appeals to the 'young saint old devil' proverb, to emphasize that sin is natural to young men, and that it would be unnatural to repent at this age (ll. 612–15). Both the play and the poem seek to discredit these assumptions by putting them in the mouths of the agents of evil and by demonstrating that it is quite possible for the young man to take on the qualities associated with the old man. They assert that holiness in the young is not some monstrous aberration but something which each young nobleman ought to set his mind to attaining.

However, unlike the interlude, the poem goes on to make the pursuit of learning and virtue into an issue of status and power. The second voice (the opponent of virtuous occupation) proposes that the pursuit of 'cunnynge and lernynge' may be good in themselves, but 'Yet nobillnes nedithe not so mych as pore degre'.[136] This voice presents learning as a pragmatic accomplishment – a professional qualification, only required by those who need to earn a living through it. He stigmatizes learning by associating it with labour, asking 'Where plente is what nedith travayle / For hym thatt hathe littil lernynge dothe well'. The young nobleman, it is implied, should be characterized by his leisured lifestyle. This argument reminds us of Cornelius in *Fulgens and Lucres*, who draws disparaging comparisons between his own life of leisure and the need of his rival Gaius to work for a living (II.543–70). Youth of *The Interlude of Youth* also has negative associations with learning. These negative associations do not arise out of a link between learning and labour as much as a link between learning and a clerical identity. Youth associates Charity's Latin 'gibb'rish' with being 'clerkish' (ll. 113–14). Youth's hostility to Charity appears to arise because he suspects Charity of attempting to make him 'clerkish' too (ll. 115–22).[137] This kind of learning finds no place in Youth's conception of his noble identity.

---

[136] Ibid., p. 483.
[137] Grantley, *Wit's Pilgrimage*, p. 141.

These views stand in opposition to the attitude to learning and noble status articulated by the first voice in 'He that made this hous'. This speaker counters the arguments of his opponent by pointing to the fact that the nobility have an equally pragmatic use for learning and for the pursuit of virtue. He maintains that 'cunnynge withe vertu makithe nobilnes more excellent', just as gold sets off a precious stone.[138] Virtue and learning are excellencies which are not just fitting to noble birth, but somehow intensify it, so that the virtuous and learned noblemen is a better kind of nobleman. The first voice also maintains that it is 'a great lac' if a nobleman does not have an accomplishment that a 'poore man' has.[139] Learning and virtue are necessary for the nobleman to maintain his claim to his innate superiority to those of low status. However, in addition, they offer him an opportunity to demonstrate through visible gestures superiority to other men of noble status who are vicious and igno-rant. The first voice goes on to spell out the concrete benefits of cultivating learning and virtue in terms of the competition for advancement. He points out that 'He that hathe litill yet by lernynge may / Cum to greate honoures we se euery day'.[140] The attainment of learning enables the low-born or poor man to encroach upon the kinds of offices which noblemen also desire. Such 'honoures' – positions of authority and influence which confer honour on their holder – would be the privilege of the nobleman automatically, if only he possessed the necessary intellectual qualities. As the first voice puts it, 'As noblenes withoute cunnynge is dyssolate / So cunnynge withoute maners is reprobate'.[141] In this passage, 'maners' stands as a kind of synonym for 'noblenes'. 'Maners', the modes of courtly behaviour, are presented as the rightful preserve of the nobleman, presumably because it is assumed that innate noble nature expresses itself naturally through a particular set of gestures. The nobleman will always enjoy an advantage over the low-born man, but only provided that he also cultivates his intellectual abilities. The nobleman's social accomplishments are on their own insufficient to win him the honours which otherwise he might be entitled to claim as his due. Only learning will guarantee him an absolute advantage over the 'pore man', and indeed over other noblemen who have not had the good sense to acquire it.

Both the verse-text and *The Interlude of Youth* open an opportunity for Northumberland to make a powerful statement about his own and his son's capacity for 'honoures', those offices which are the due of learned noblemen capable of moral and intellectual self-discipline. The texts establish the earl's commitment to the pursuit of learning and moral virtue through the very fact of his investment in them. As we have seen, the earl advertised his ownership of educational verse-texts by putting them on show in a display manuscript and on the walls of his residences. A performance in the Northumberland

---

138 Flügel, 'Kleinere Mitteilungen', p. 483.
139 Ibid.
140 Ibid.
141 Ibid.

household of *The Interlude of Youth*, which also asserts the importance of the self-disciplining man, would of course also represent a very public statement of the earl's identification with these principles.

Youth's progress can also be interpreted as a piece of counsel or a kind of princely mirror offered to Lord Henry Percy, Northumberland's heir. As Northumberland's Orders for Twelfth Night show, the earl's procession into the hall on this festive occasion served to draw attention to the young Henry Percy, through his proximity to his father. Once he had come of age, Henry Percy would have followed immediately after his father.[142] This arrangement emphasizes the importance of the male line for the continuance of the dynasty and the preservation of Percy power in the North; but it also stresses the importance of the legal age of majority for status and authority. The text of *The Interlude of Youth* offers Henry Percy advice on how to comport himself once he has inherited his lands from his father. The play works to emphasize the importance of the self-disciplining model of noble masculinity for Percy's benefit. However, the verse-text 'He that made this house' implies that Henry Percy was already this kind of self-disciplining young nobleman, by inviting us to imagine the young Lord Henry secluded in this private space, devoting himself to the study of this or other similar texts. In this context, *The Interlude of Youth* may act less as a piece of advice literature, intended in all earnest to reform an aberrant young man, than as a way for Northumberland to draw his audience's attention to the fact that Percy has already overcome his youthful nature – at least, so a text like 'He who made this house' would have us believe. Percy is already demonstrating a fitness for government and political office. In this sense the text may as part of Northumberland's programme to obtain important political offices in the North for his son, as much as for himself, and reflects the earl's attempts to appropriate the political 'court idiom' to press his claims to these honours, as James has suggested he did in other ways.[143]

The discourses of youth are useful to interlude writers because they allow them to discuss sensitive political issues in symbolic terms. As in much later medieval political literature, the symbolic values of youth are developed in the context of works which are ostensibly pragmatic, educational texts directed at the young. The problematic transitions to noble adulthood and the anxious masculinities the interludes depict can be read as expressions of noble anxieties about the preservation of aristocratic status, power and privilege in the face of social change. The representations of young nobles can also be understood as part of a system of political shorthand which enables writers to make comments on politics and personalities in an allusive, oblique and often highly ambiguous way. These works employ familiar features of political rhetoric – references to the concepts of rule and governance, good and evil

[142] Lancashire, 'Orders for Twelfth Day and Night', pp. 32–3.
[143] James, *Tudor Magnate*, p. 26.

counsel, the old and the young – in a way which treads a fine line between criticism and flattery. It is possible to view depictions of the young rulers of the plays both as offering truth-telling criticism with urgent exhortations for reform, and as insinuating favourable images of noble patrons. In other words they exhibit exactly the same 'combination of deference and challenge' which Ferster sees as characteristic of much later medieval literature of advice to princes.[144]

144 Ferster, *Fictions of Advice*, p. 3.

CONCLUSION

The interludes *Nature, Fulgens and Lucres, The Worlde and the Chylde, The Interlude of Youth* and *Calisto and Melebea* contain finely nuanced discussions of what it means to be a noble and a man at the turn of the fifteenth century. The plays are highly conscious of different kinds of identity generated by the varying intersections of age, gender and status at this time. This book has considered only one of the identity categories represented in these texts in any detail, yet even this limited examination suggests important conclusions.

First, the interludes are intensely aware of the performative nature of the identities they present. Noble masculine nature is only apparent through external signs. It has to be disclosed in appropriate gestures – literally to be acted out. This self-conscious theatricality is not a new idea in the sixteenth century: it is inherited from late medieval traditions of thought about the self, and about how an individual can act out identity in public arenas like the great hall of a household, and the ways in which audiences are fundamental to its construction, as one adapts one's performance, for instance to avoid censure. The plays were performed in the very public spaces where, according to fifteenth-century courtesy texts, individuals were already attuned to observing and evaluating behaviour (both their own and that of others), so they contribute to and comment on the process of constructing a socialized self.

The artificial nature of this type of identity is also apparent in the journeys which the young noblemen of the plays make. They have to undergo a process of 'self-fashioning', to borrow Greenblatt's phrase, to tame their natural selves and to make themselves appropriate adult masculinities. Noble masculinity is something which has to be learned. In common with much late medieval moral and didactic writing, these interludes show an ambiguous attitude to male bodies: young male bodies produce instability and sin, violence and disorder; adult male bodies may be the capable of producing reason, self-control and good order; but a lack of self-discipline in youth will mean, at the very least, that their capacity for doing so is postponed into old age. Even those young characters who achieve a reformation of themselves, like Youth in *The Interlude of Youth*, have to undergo a painful process full of conflict, within and without. The disciplines of repentance, religious devotion and study are advanced in the interludes as practical methods of reforming 'natural' youthful masculinity into a more acceptable form. Above all, these texts make the *processes* of self-disciplining central to adult and noble masculinity, since they are presented as equivalent to political competence. It does not matter so much which regime the aristocrat uses to govern his unruly body – it is more that he needs to show the ability for self-rule at all.

Interludes furthermore stress that households and house-holding are crucial to the performance of noble identities. The texts discussed in this book are aware of the problematic nature of some signs of aristocratic status like dress, conspicuous consumption and perhaps even manners for the purpose of transmitting messages about a nobleman's essential nature and point him towards a more reliable, more exclusive system of signs available in the noble household. Noble masculinity is predicated on the idea of rule – the ability to govern both oneself and others – and that ability (or its lack) is demonstrated in the plays through the interaction of young noble masters with household servants. Successful adult aristocrats, the plays imply, are those who produce order in the potentially unruly social groups for which they are responsible, in the same way as they produce order in their own unstable bodies. The plays exploit the negative examples of young men who readily accept the counsel of unworthy servants, and are susceptible to flattery and artful manipulation of subordinates. Gaius in *Fulgens and Lucres* is an unusual example of a self-disciplining young noble who demonstrates an astute ability to deploy an alternative set of gestures and so establish himself as a superior brand of aristocrat.

In *Nature*, *The Interlude of Youth* and *The Worlde and the Chylde* the link between the rule of noble households and the rule of noble bodies is figured in the fact that the servants who gradually control the young nobleman are also the sins which gradually degrade man's soul. This emphasizes the close link between moral self-discipline and the ability to exercise authority, and highlights the symbolic power of servants and household life, which act as gestures transmitting messages about an aristocrat's noble nature.

The plays deliberately provoke anxiety about young noblemen, and through them the future of noble masculinity, in order to stimulate nobles to preserve their privileges by constantly performing their noble masculinity. It seems likely that this kind of anxiety should be located in the established nobility: those, in other words, with the most to lose from the erosion of noble privilege. Seen from this point of view, the interludes represent an attempt to redefine and reinforce noble identities in the face of social change at the end of the fifteenth century and beginning of the sixteenth century. Noble lifestyles were being appropriated by an increasingly wealthy population, and this represented a substantive threat to nobles and nobility, precisely because historically the question of who was noble had depended so much on being able to live like a noble.[1] The efforts of these plays to reorientate noble masculinity away from display and conspicuous consumption and towards the rule and government of a noble household show a recourse to an alternative set of signs for an innate noble nature which is born to rule others. In this system, the noble household is important not so much as a place of extravagant expenditure, but as a place where the nobleman can disclose his noble nature through

---

[1] H. Kaminsky, 'Estate, Nobility, and the Exhibition of Estate in the Later Middle Ages', *Speculum*, 68 (1993), 684–709.

the maintenance of order and harmony in household space, and through the quality of the service rendered to him. The *familia* and the decorous, ceremonious style of living practised by it comes to represent the noble at its head. It is a valuable sign of nobleness, precisely because it is difficult for those of lower status to appropriate it, in the way in which they could appropriate noble dress, noble manners or even noble offices.

The plays stress the importance of the household as a site of noble signification to the exclusion of other elements of traditional noble masculinity. There is not much room in these interludes for – for example – martial prowess and military exploit. While the exemplary Gaius in *Fulgens and Lucres* has been responsible for several military successes, these are alluded to only briefly. Elsewhere violence is shown only in the form of the dangerous and disruptive violence of unruly young men, or inappropriate and even ridiculous masculine competition.

Since anxiety about noble masculinity is an anxiety about noble power, it is possible to read the renegotiations of noble masculinity in the plays as a means for addressing obliquely the problems of exercising power. These were particularly acute for nobles at the beginning of the sixteenth century, following the disastrous upheavals of the Wars of the Roses and while a new royal dynasty was being established. In this context, it is perhaps understandable that a text such as *Fulgens and Lucres* represents the key to noble masculinity and noble power as being the disciplining activities of religious devotion and study (while minimizing references to military prowess and unstable young male biology), when advocating aggressive forms of masculinity might make a noble patron perceived as a threat to the stability of the realm.

Precisely because the direct discussion of power and governance might be perceived as contentious and dangerous, it becomes necessary to mask the plays' contemporary relevance by referring back to long-standing, widely accepted concepts. The interludes can be seen in the context of what David Lawton has called the 'dull' literature of the fifteenth century, works which on the surface appear concerned with rehearsing sententious commonplaces, but which actually represent a lively communal intellectual culture, based on discussion and debate.[2] In the later Middle Ages, noble households are often represented as places where the reading aloud and discussion of chronicles, romances, morally improving works, and other worthy texts takes place.[3] The young noblemen of the plays are a discursive site where ideologies of conduct, moral virtue, status and politics meet, and which seem designed to provoke comment and to offer audiences the opportunities of reading their own sub-texts into them, rather than closing down meanings. The performance of household interludes is a natural complement to other kinds of literate prac-

---

[2] D. Lawton, 'Dullness and the Fifteenth Century', *Speculum* 54 (1987), 761–99.

[3] J. Coleman, *Public Reading and the Reading Public in Late Medieval England and France* (Cambridge, 1996), pp. 128–40; Jones and Underwood, *King's Mother*, p. 176.

tices in the household – a rehearsal of apparently conventional but potentially subversive ideas, in a convivial setting amongst a household community. Perhaps the printing of these early interlude texts even reflects their usefulness as reading material in this kind of communal context, outside the festive seasons when interludes were most frequently performed.

The association of the period of youth with political incompetence, and of the period of old age with political competence, allows interludes to engage with current political debates. This is possible given the fact that the literature of political advice current in the period offers political commentary couched in similar terms. So criticism of Henry VII's taxation policies is expressed in moral terms, as criticism of the age-related sin of avarice; and in the form of attacks on evil counsellors, in the person of individuals like John Morton. A performance of the interlude *Nature* in the presence of Morton then can be seen as politically charged. The play may be read as a defence of Morton, an assertion of his political competence, guaranteed, as it is for Man in the text, by advancing years. It might also represent an attempt to minimize the significance of the avarice of the old as a potential political failing of Henry VII's regime, and to assert that the positive connotations of age override this flaw. The use of the rhetoric of counsel in the play, and in particular the association of the good counsellor Reason with Man's old age appears as a defence of Morton's role as a loyal and trustworthy counsellor. But the play may also represent coded warnings or hard-hitting counsel for Morton, reminding him of the standards by which his performance as judge and counsellor is being evaluated by the elites who used this idiom.

In *The Interlude of Youth*, on the other hand, the capacity of the young nobleman to reform himself is also invested with powerful political meanings. In the context of the Northumberland household, the progress of Youth in the play may well represent political counsel for the young Henry VIII, on how to govern himself, his household and, by extension, his kingdom. Alternatively, the play can be seen in terms of the attempts of the earl of Northumberland to attain important political offices under the crown for himself and his son. In this context, Youth's reformation in the play draws attention to the capacity of the earl and his heir for the government of themselves and others, in line with the image the earl of Northumberland constructed of himself and his son through his investment in other educational literature and his commitment to the ideology of the household.

The plays imply that, far from being secure monolithic concepts, concepts of nobility were always unstable and precarious. Aristocratic masculinity had constantly to be renegotiated in the face of threats, real or imagined; and it always had to be remade in the lives of individuals, as much as through the medium of abstract theorizing. The form of noble masculinity advanced in the interludes of youth is innovative in some senses. They attempt to reinterpret some traditional aspects of medieval nobility, such as conspicuous consumption, as essentially ignoble, though it is worth noting that the texts are rather vague on what should be considered excessive consumption for nobles, and what is appropriate consumption to display the aristocratic virtue of liberality. The strong emphasis on governance as the defining activity of the nobleman, where increasingly the discipline of one's own body and inner nature is related to wider spheres of rule, and the lack of reference to traditional aspects of aristocratic masculinity such as military prowess, probably reflect a broader change in English society, as the political turmoils of the fifteenth century died away. Just as noble houses increasingly deployed architectural features like crenellations for symbolic reasons, rather than practical, military ones, so military prowess, though still prized as a marker of nobility, becomes less and less important to the actual day-to-day business of being noble. Nonetheless, the idea that governance of oneself and others is central to nobility is not itself new, but recurs in political and educational literature throughout the late medieval period. This harking back to long-standing concepts is of course a vital strategy to make noble identities *appear* to be ahistorical and immutable, even while they are in the process of change.

The figure of the young nobleman in the early interludes is particularly useful as a site for the renegotiation of noble masculinity in the late fifteenth and early sixteenth centuries, because it is capable of embodying competing and even contradictory ideas. The young nobleman is naturally fitted to rule as a man and a nobleman, yet naturally comes to represent disorder and an inability to rule; he represents the future for noble families and their dynastic strategies, yet he himself is the strongest threat to the continuity of the noble line and the preservation of noble power and wealth. The young man is the natural site for disclosing anxieties about social and political change and influence because he is conventionally the symbol of instability and transience. He is, paradoxically, a safe place to put the formless fears of those mature noblemen who had to work so hard to maintain the fiction of the solidity and unchanging nature of noble power.

BIBLIOGRAPHY

Primary Sources

Aegidius Romanus (Giles of Rome). *The Governance of Kings and Princes: John Trevisa's Middle English Translation of the* De regimine principum *of Aegidius Romanus*. Ed. D. C. Fowler, C. F. Briggs and P. G. Remley. Trans. J. Trevisa. New York and London, 1997.

Axton, R., ed. *Three Rastell Plays: Four Elements, Calisto and Melebea, Gentleness and Nobility*. Cambridge and Totowa, 1979.

Baildon, W. P., ed. *Select Cases in Chancery, AD 1364 to 1471*. Selden Society Publications 10. 1896.

Banks, M. M., ed. *An Alphabet of Tales*. 2 vols. EETS OS 126, 127. 1904, 1905.

Barclay, A. *The Eclogues of Alexander Barclay from the Original Edition by John Cawood*. Ed. B. White. EETS OS 175. 1928.

Bartholomaeus Anglicus. *On the Properties of Things, A Critical Text: John Trevisa's Translation of Batholomaeus Anglicus'* De proprietatibus rerum. Ed. M. C. Seymour. Trans. J. Trevisa. 2 vols. Oxford, 1975.

Boas, F. S., ed. *Five Pre-Shakespearean Comedies*. London, 1934.

Brown, C., ed. *Religious Lyrics of the Fifteenth Century*. Oxford, 1939.

Cawley, A. C., ed. *Everyman*. Manchester, 1961.

Caxton, W. *Caxton's Book of Curtesye*. Ed. F. J. Furnivall. EETS ES 3. 1868.

Davidson, C., and Happé, P., eds. *The Worlde and the Chylde*. Kalamazoo, 1999.

Davis, N., ed. *Non-Cycle Plays and Fragments*. EETS SS 1. 1970.

Dean, J. M., ed. *Richard the Redeless and Mum and the Sothsegger*. Kalamazoo, 2000.

Dudley, E. *The Tree of Commonwealth*. Ed. D. M. Brodie. Cambridge, 1948.

Eccles, M., ed. *The Macro Plays*. EETS OS 262. 1969.

Edgeworth, R. *Sermons Very Fruitfull Godly and Learned by Roger Edgeworth: Preaching in the Reformation*. Ed. J. Wilson. Cambridge, 1993.

Elyot, T. *Dictionary*. Menston, 1970.

Fisher, J. *The English Works of John Fisher, Bishop of Rochester, Part One*. Ed. J. E. B. Mayor. EETS ES 27. 1876.

Flügel, E., ed. 'Kleinere Mitteilungen aus Handschriften, 3: Die Proverbs van Lekenfield und Wresil (Yorks.)'. *Anglia* 14 (1892), 471–97.

Furnivall, F. J., ed. *The Babees Book*. EETS OS 32. 1868.

———, ed. *Hymns to the Virgin and Christ; The Parliament of Devils; and Other Religious Pieces*. EETS OS 24. 1868.

———, ed. *Quene Elizabeths Achademy*. EETS ES 8. 1869.

Gibson, J. M., ed. *Records of Early English Drama: Kent: Diocese of Canterbury*. 3 vols. London and Toronto, 2002.

Giles of Rome (Aegidius Romanus). *The Governance of Kings and Princes: John Trevisa's Middle English Translation of the De regimine principum of Aegidius Romanus*. Ed. D. C. Fowler, C. F. Briggs and P. G. Remley. Trans. J. Trevisa. New York and London, 1997.

Ginsberg, W., ed. *Wynnere and Wastoure and The Parlement of the Thre Ages.* Kalamazoo, 1992.

Greville, F. *Fulke Greville: The Remains.* Ed. G. A. Wilkes. Oxford, 1965.

Hall, E. *The Union of the Two Noble and Illustre Families of Lancaster and Yorke.* Ed. H. Ellis. London, 1809.

Harper-Bill, C., ed. *The Register of John Morton, Archbishop of Canterbury, 1486–1500.* 3 vols. Canterbury and York Society 75, 78, 89. 1987, 1991, 2000.

Hearne, T., ed. *Liber Niger.* London, 1774.

Herrtage, S. J. H., ed. *Catholicon Anglicum: An English-Latin Wordbook.* EETS OS 75. 1881.

Hoccleve, T. *Hoccleve's Works: The Minor Poems.* Ed. F. J. Furnivall and I. Gollanz. Rev. J. Mitchell and A. I. Doyle. 2 vols. EETS ES 61, 73. 1970.

—— *Hoccleve's Works: The Regement of Princes and Fourteen Minor Poems.* Ed. F. J. Furnivall. EETS ES 72. 1897.

Kingsford, C. L., ed. *Chronicles of London.* Oxford, 1905.

——, ed. *The First English Life of King Henry the Fifth.* Oxford, 1911.

Kurath, H., and Lewis, R. E., eds. *Middle English Dictionary.* 118 fascicles. Ann Arbor, 1953–2001.

Kymer, G. *Dietarium. Liber Niger.* Ed. T. Hearne. London, 1774.

Lancashire, I., ed. *Two Tudor Interludes: Youth and Hick Scorner.* Manchester, 1980.

Lydgate, J. *The Minor Poems of John Lydgate.* Ed. H. N. MacCracken. EETS ES 107, OS 192. 1911, 1934.

Mannyng, R. *Handlyng Synne.* Ed. I. Sullens. Binghampton, 1983.

Manzalaoui, M. A., ed. *Secretum secretorum: Nine English Versions.* EETS OS 76. 1977.

Mayhew, A. L., ed. *Promptorium parvulorum.* EETS ES 102. 1908.

Medwall, H. *Fulgens & Lucres: A Fifteenth-Century Secular Play by Henry Medwall.* Ed. F. S. Boas and A. W. Reed. Oxford, 1926.

—— *The Plays of Henry Medwall: A Critical Edition.* Ed. M. E. Moeslein. New York and London, 1981.

Medwall, H. *The Plays of Henry Medwall.* Ed. A. H. Nelson. Cambridge and Totowa, 1980.

More, T. *The Complete Works of St Thomas More.* Ed. A. S. G. Edwards. 15 vols. New Haven, 1963–1997.

Morris, R., ed. *The Pricke of Conscience: A Northumbrian Poem by Richard Rolle de Hampole.* Berlin, 1863.

——, and Gradon, P., eds. *Dan Michel's Ayenbite of Inwyt, or Remorse of Conscience.* 2 vols. EETS OS 23, 278. 1965, 1979.

Myers, A. R., ed. *The Household of Edward IV: The Black Book and the Ordinance of 1478.* Manchester, 1959.

Nelson, A. H., ed. *Records of Early English Drama: Cambridge.* 2 vols. Toronto, 1989.

Record Commission. *Statutes of the Realm.* 11 vols. London, 1963.

Roper, W. *The Lyfe of Sir Thomas Moore, Knighte.* Ed. E. V. Hitchcock. EETS OS 197. 1935.

Ross, W. O., ed. *Middle English Sermons.* EETS OS 209. 1940.

Simpson, J. A., and Weiner, E. S. C., eds. *The Oxford English Dictionary.* 2nd edn. 20 vols. Oxford, 1989.

Society of Antiquaries of London. *A Collection of Ordinances and Regulations for the Government of the Royal Household.* London, 1790.

Steele, R. R., ed. *Three Prose Versions of the Secreta secretorum*. EETS ES 74. 1898.
Vergil, P. *The Anglica Historia of Polydore Vergil, 1485–1537*. Ed. and trans. D. Hay. Camden Society, 3rd Series 74. 1950.
Ward, J., ed. and trans. *Women of the English Nobility and Gentry, 1066–1500*. Manchester, 1995.
Wenzel, S., ed. and trans. *Fasciculus morum: A Fourteenth-Century Preacher's Handbook*. University Park PA, 1989.
Woodbine, G. E., and Thorne, S. E., eds. *Bracton on the Laws and Customs of England*. 4 vols. Cambridge MA, 1968.

Secondary sources

Aers, D., ed. *Culture and History, 1350–1600*. Detroit, 1992.
——— 'A Whisper in the Ear of Early Modernists'. *Culture and History, 1350–1600*. Ed. D. Aers. Detroit, 1992. Pp. 177–202.
Alford, J. A., ed. *From Page to Performance: Essays in Early English Drama*. East Lansing, 1995.
——— ' "My Name is Worship": Masquerading Vice in Medwall's *Nature*'. *From Page to Performance: Essays in Early English Drama*. Ed. J. A. Alford. East Lansing, 1995. Pp. 151–77.
Altman, J. B. *The Tudor Play of Mind: Rhetorical Inquiry and the Development of Elizabethan Drama*. Berkeley, 1978.
Amos, M. A. ' "For Manners Make Man": Bourdieu, De Certeau, and the Common Appropriation of Noble Manners in the *Book of Courtesy*'. *Medieval Conduct*. Ed. K. Ashley and R. L. A. Clark. Minneapolis and London, 2001. Pp. 23–48.
Ashley, K., and Clark, R. L. A., eds. *Medieval Conduct*. Minneapolis and London, 2001.
Barr, H., and Ward-Perkins, K. ' "Spekyng for one's sustenance": The Rhetoric of Counsel in *Mum and the Sothsegger*, Skelton's *Bowge of Court*, and Elyot's *Pasquil and Playne*'. *The Long Fifteenth Century: Essays for Douglas Gray*. Ed. H. Cooper and S. Mapstone. Oxford, 1997. Pp. 249–72.
Barratt, D. M. 'A Second Northumberland Household Book'. *Bodleian Library Record* 8 (1967–72), 93–98.
Barron, C. M. 'Centres of Conspicuous Consumption: The Aristocratic Town House in London, 1200–1550'. *London Journal* 20 (1995), 1–16.
——— 'The "Golden Age" of Women in Medieval London'. *Reading Medieval Studies* 15 (1989), 35–58.
Baskervill, C. R. 'Conventional Features of Medwall's *Fulgens and Lucres*'. *Modern Philology* 24 (1905), 419–42.
Beadle, R., ed. *The Cambridge Companion to Medieval English Theatre*. Cambridge, 1994.
Beattie, C., Maslakovic, A., and Rees Jones, S., eds. *The Medieval Household in Christian Europe, c. 850–1550: Managing Power, Wealth and the Body*. Turnhout, 2003.
Ben-Amos, I. K. *Adolescence and Youth in Early Modern England*. London, 1994.
Bernard, G. W. *The Power of the Early Tudor Nobility: A Study of the Fourth and Fifth Earls of Shrewsbury*. Brighton, 1985.
———, ed. *The Tudor Nobility*. Manchester, 1992.

Bevington, D. *From Mankind to Marlowe: Growth of Structure in the Popular Drama of Tudor England*. Cambridge MA, 1962.

—— *Tudor Drama and Politics: A Critical Approach to Topical Meaning*. Cambridge MA, 1968.

Binsky, P. *Medieval Death*. London, 1996.

Boas, F. S. *Introduction to Tudor Drama*. London, 1933.

Böll, F. 'Die Lebensalter'. *Neue Jahrbücher für das klassische Altertum* 31 (1913), 89–145.

Brackman, A., ed. *Papstum und Kaisertum*. Munich, 1926.

Brannen, A. 'Intricate Subtleties: Entertainment at Bishop Morton's Installation Feast'. *Records of Early English Drama Newsletter* 22 (1997), 2–11.

Breitenberg, M. *Anxious Masculinity in Early Modern England*. Cambridge, 1996.

Bremmer, J., and Roodenburg, H., eds. *A Cultural History of Gesture*. Oxford, 1991.

Brigden, S. 'Youth and the English Reformation'. *Past and Present* 95 (1982), 37–67.

Briggs, C. F. *Giles of Rome's* De regimine principum: *Reading and Writing Politics at Court and University, c. 1275–c. 1525*. Cambridge, 1999.

Burrow, J. A. *The Ages of Man: A Study in Medieval Writing and Thought*. Oxford, 1986.

—— ' "Young Saint, Old Devil": Reflections on a Medieval Proverb'. *Review of English Studies* 30 (1979), 385–96.

Butler, J. *Gender Trouble: Feminism and the Subversion of Identity*. New York, 1990.

—— 'Imitation and Gender Insubordination'. *Inside/Out: Lesbian Theories, Gay Theories*. Ed. D. Fuss. New York, 1992. Pp. 13–31.

Cadden, J. *The Meanings of Sex Difference in the Middle Ages: Medicine, Science and Culture*. Cambridge, 1993.

Camille, M. *Mirror in Parchment: The Luttrell Psalter and the Making of Medieval England*. Chicago, 1998.

Chambers, E. K. *The Mediaeval Stage*. 2 vols. London, 1903.

Chew, S. C. *The Pilgrimage of Life*. Port Washington, 1962.

Chrimes, S. B. *Henry VII*. London, 1972.

Coleman, J. *Public Reading and the Reading Public in Late Medieval England and France*. Cambridge, 1996.

Colley, J. S. '*Fulgens and Lucres*: Politics and Aesthetics'. *Zeitschrift für Anglistik und Amerikanistik* 23 (1975), 322–30.

Condon, M. M. 'Ruling Elites in the Reign of Henry VII'. *Patronage, Pedigree and Power in Later Medieval England*. Ed. C. Ross. Gloucester, 1979. Pp. 109–42.

Cooper, H., and Mapstone, S., eds. *The Long Fifteenth Century: Essays for Douglas Gray*. Oxford, 1997.

Cox, J. D., and Kastan, D. S., eds. *A New History of Early English Drama*. New York, 1997.

Craik, T. W. *The Tudor Interlude: Stage, Costume, and Acting*. Leicester, 1958.

Crupi, C. W. 'Christian Doctrine in Henry Medwall's *Nature*'. *Renascence* 34 (1982), 100–12.

Cullum, P. H., and Lewis, K. J., eds. *Holiness and Masculinity in the Middle Ages*. Cardiff, 2004.

Curry, A., and Matthew, E., eds. *Concepts and Patterns of Service in the Later Middle Ages*. Woodbridge, 2000.

Davenport, T. ' "Lusty Fresch Galaunts" '. *Aspects of Early English Drama*. Ed. P. Neuss. Cambridge and Totowa, 1983. Pp. 111–28.

Davis, N. 'The Meaning of the Word "Interlude": A Discussion'. *METh* 6 (1984), 5–15.

Debax, J. ' "God Gyve You Tyme and Space" ': Toward a Definition of Theatrical Space in the Tudor Interludes'. *French Essays on Shakespeare and His Contemporaries: 'What Would France With Us?'*. Ed. J. Maguin and M. Willems. Newark and London, 1995. Pp. 50–65.

Dillon, J. *Language and Stage in Medieval and Renaissance England*. Cambridge, 1998.

Douglas, M. *Purity and Danger: An Analysis of concept of Pollution and Taboo*. 2nd edn. London and New York, 2002.

Dove, M. *The Perfect Age of Man's Life*. Cambridge, 1986.

Dronzek, A. 'Gendered Theories of Education'. *Medieval Conduct*. Ed. K. Ashley and R. L. A. Clark. Minneapolis and London, 2001. Pp. 135–59.

Du Boulay, F. R. H. *The Lordship of Canterbury: An Essay on Medieval Society*. London, 1966.

Dyer, C. *Making a Living in the Middle Ages: The People of Britain, 850–1520*. New Haven and London, 2002.

Emden, A. B. *Biographical Register of the University of Cambridge to 1500*. Cambridge, 1963.

Ferster, J. *Fictions of Advice: The Literature and Politics of Counsel in Late Medieval England*. Philadelphia, 1996.

Fichte, J. O. 'The Presentation of Sin as Verbal Action in the Moral Interludes'. *Anglia* 103 (1985), 26–47.

Forstater, A., and Baird, J. L. ' "Walking and Wending": Mankind's Opening Speech'. *Theatre Notebook* 26 (1971–72), 60–4.

Foucault, M. *The Archaeology of Knowledge*. Trans. A. M. S. Smith. London, 1972.

—— *Discipline and Punish: The Birth of the Prison*. Trans. A. Sheridan. Harmondsworth, 1979.

Fox, A. *Politics and Literature in the Reigns of Henry VII and Henry VIII*. Oxford, 1989.

Fuss, D., ed. *Inside/Out: Lesbian Theories, Gay Theories*. New York, 1992.

Girouard, M. *Life in the English Country House*. New Haven and London, 1978.

Godfrey, R. A. 'Nervous Laughter in Henry Medwall's *Fulgens and Lucres*'. *Tudor Theatre* 3 (1996), 81–96.

Goldberg, P. J. P. 'Marriage, Migration and Servanthood: The York Cause Paper Evidence'. *'Woman is a Worthy Wight': Women in English Society, c. 1200–1500*. Ed. P. J. P. Goldberg. Stroud, 1992. Pp. 1–15.

—— 'Masters and Men in Medieval England'. *Masculinity in Medieval Europe*. Ed. D. M. Hadley. London and New York, 1999. Pp. 56–70.

—— 'What Was A Servant?'. *Concepts and Patterns of Service in the Later Middle Ages*. Ed. A. Curry and E. Matthew. Woodbridge, 2000. Pp. 1–20.

——, ed. *'Woman is a Worthy Wight': Women in English Society, c. 1200–1500*. Stroud, 1992.

Grantley, D. *Wit's Pilgrimage: Drama and the Social Impact of Education in Early Modern England*. Aldershot, 2000.

Green, R. F. *Poets and Princepleasers: Literature and the English Court in the Late Middle Ages*. Toronto, 1980.

Greenblatt, S. J. *Renaissance Self-Fashioning: From More to Shakespeare*. Chicago, 1980.

Greenfield, P. H. 'Festive Drama at Christmas in Aristocratic Households'. *Festive Drama*. Ed. M. Twycross. Cambridge, 1996. Pp. 34–40.

Grenville, J. *Medieval Housing*. Leicester, 1997.

Griffiths, P. *Youth and Authority in England, 1560–1640*. Oxford, 1996.

Gunn, S. J., and Lindley, P. G. 'Charles Brandon's Westhorpe: An Early Tudor Courtyard House in Suffolk'. *Archaeological Journal* 145 (1988), 272–89.

Guy, J. A. 'The Rhetoric of Counsel in Early Modern England'. *Tudor Political Culture*. Ed. D. Hoak. Cambridge, 1995. Pp. 292–310.

Hadley, D. M., ed. *Masculinity in Medieval Europe*. London and New York, 1999.

Hanawalt, B. A. 'The Childe of Bristowe and the Making of Middle-Class Adolescence'. *Bodies and Disciplines: Intersections of Literature and History in Fifteenth-Century England*. Ed. B. A. Hanawalt and D. Wallace. Minneapolis, 1996. Pp. 155–78.

—— *Growing Up in Medieval London: The Experience of Childhood in History*. Oxford, 1993.

——, and Wallace, D., eds. *Bodies and Disciplines: Intersections of Literature and History in Fifteenth-Century England*. Minneapolis, 1996.

Happé, P. *English Drama Before Shakespeare*. London, 1999.

Harris, B. J. *Edward Stafford, Third Duke of Buckingham, 1478–1521*. Stanford, 1986.

Hasler, A. J. 'Hoccleve's Unregimented Body'. *Paragraph* 13 (1990), 164–83.

Heal, F. 'The Archbishops of Canterbury and the Practice of Hospitality'. *Journal of Ecclesiastical History* 33 (1982), 544–63.

—— *Hospitality in Early Modern England*. Oxford, 1990.

—— *Of Prelates and Princes: A Study of the Economic and Social Position of the Tudor Episcopate*. Cambridge, 1980.

Hearder, H., and Loyn, H. R., eds. *British Government and Administration: Studies Presented to S. B. Chrimes*. Cardiff, 1974.

Hepburn, F. 'Arthur, Prince of Wales and his Training for Kingship'. *The Historian* 55 (1997), 4–9.

Hicks, M. A. *Bastard Feudalism*. London, 1995.

Hoak, D., ed. *Tudor Political Culture*. Cambridge, 1995.

Hofmeister, A. '*Puer, Iuvenis, Senex*: Zum Verständnis der mittelalterlichen Altersbezeichnungen'. *Papstum und Kaisertum*. Ed. A. Brackman. Munich, 1926. Pp. 288–316.

Horner, O. '*Fulgens and Lucres*: An Historical Perspective'. *METh* 15 (1993), 49–86.

Horrox, R., ed. *Fifteenth-Century Attitudes: Perceptions of Society in Late Medieval England*. Cambridge, 1994.

—— 'Service'. *Fifteenth-Century Attitudes: Perceptions of Society in Late Medieval England*. Ed. R. Horrox. Cambridge, 1994. Pp. 61–78.

James, A., Jenks, C., and Prout, A. *Theorizing Childhood*. Cambridge, 1997.

James, M. E. *A Tudor Magnate and the Tudor State: Henry Fifth Earl of Northumberland*. York, 1966.

Jenks, C. *Childhood*. London, 1996.

Johnson, R. C. 'Audience Involvement in the Early Tudor Interlude'. *Theatre Notebook* 24 (1970), 101–11.

Jones, M. 'Early Moral Plays and the Earliest Secular Drama'. *The Revels History of Drama in English, Vol. 1: Medieval Drama*. Ed. L. Potter. London and New York, 1983. Pp. 213–91.

Jones, M. K. 'Collyweston: An Early Tudor Palace'. *England in the Fifteenth Century*. Ed. D. Williams. Woodbridge, 1987. Pp. 129–41.

——, and Underwood, M. G. *The King's Mother: Lady Margaret Beaufort, Countess of Richmond and Derby*. Cambridge, 1992.

Jones, R. C. 'The Stage World and the "Real" World in Medwall's *Fulgens and Lucres*'. *MLQ* 32 (1971), 131–42.

Kaminsky, H. 'Estate, Nobility, and the Exhibition of Estate in the Later Middle Ages'. *Speculum*, 68 (1993), 684–709.

Kay, S. and Rubin, M., eds. *Framing Medieval Bodies*. Manchester, 1994.

Keen, M. *Chivalry*. New Haven and London, 1984.

Kenny, A. *Aquinas on Mind*. London and New York, 1993.

Kipling, G. *The Triumph of Honour: Burgundian Origins of the Elizabethan Renaissance*. Leiden, 1977.

Kretzmann, N. 'Philosophy of Mind'. *The Cambridge Companion to Aquinas*. Ed. N. Kretzmann and E. Stump. Cambridge, 1993. Pp. 128–52.

——— and Stump, E., eds. *The Cambridge Companion to Aquinas*. Cambridge, 1993.

Lancashire, I. 'The Auspices of *The World and the Child*'. *Renaissance and Reformation* 12 (1976), 96–105.

Lancashire, I. 'Orders for Twelfth Day and Night *circa* 1515 in the Second Northumberland Household Book'. *ELR* 10 (1980), 7–45.

Larsen, R. 'Expressions of Nobility: Conspicuous Consumption and Segregation in the Household of the Fifth Earl of Northumberland'. Unpublished M.A. dissertation, University of York, 1998.

Lascombes, A. 'Time and Place in Tudor Theatre: Two Remarkable Achievements – *Fulgens and Lucres* and *Gorboduc*'. *French Essays on Shakespeare and His Contemporaries: 'What Would France With Us?'*. Ed. J. Maguin and M. Willems. Newark and London, 1995. Pp. 66–80.

Lawton, D. 'Dullness and the Fifteenth Century'. *Speculum* 54 (1987), 761–99.

Leech, C, and Craik, T. W., eds. *The Revels History of Drama in English, Vol. 2: 1500–1576*. London and New York, 1980.

Lewis, I. M., ed. *Symbols and Sentiments*. London, 1977.

Lewry, P. O. 'Study of Ageing in the Arts Faculty of the Universities of Paris and Oxford'. *Ageing and the Aged in Medieval Europe*. Ed. M. M. Sheehan. Toronto, 1990. Pp. 23–38.

Loades, D. *Tudor Government: Structures of Authority in the Sixteenth Century*. Oxford, 1997.

McDonald, N. F., and Ormrod, W. M., eds. *Rites of Passage: Cultures of Transition in the Fourteenth Century*. York, 2004.

McFarlane, K. B. *The Nobility of Later Medieval England*. Oxford, 1973.

MacKenzie, W. R. 'A Source for Medwall's *Nature*'. *PMLA* 29 (1914), 189–99.

McSheffrey, S. 'Men and Masculinity in Late Medieval London Civic Culture: Governance, Patriarchy and Reputation'. *Conflicted Identities and Multiple Masculinities: Men in the Medieval West*. Ed. J. Murray. London and New York, 1999. Pp. 243–78.

Maguin, J., and Willems, M., eds. *French Essays on Shakespeare and His Contemporaries: 'What Would France With Us?'*. Newark and London, 1995.

Marks, R., and Williamson, P., eds. *Gothic: Art for England, 1400–1547*. London, 2003.

Mauss, M. 'Body Techniques'. *Sociology and Psychology*. Trans. B. Brewster. London, Boston and Henley, 1979. Pp. 95–123.

Medcalf, S., ed. *The Later Middle Ages*. London, 1981.

Mertes, K. 'Aristocracy'. *Fifteenth-Century Attitudes: Perceptions of Society in Late Medieval England*. Ed. R Horrox. Cambridge, 1994. Pp. 42–60.

——— *The English Noble Household, 1250–1600: Good Governance and Politic Rule*. Oxford, 1988.

Miller, H. *Henry VIII and the English Nobility*. Oxford, 1986.

Mullally, E., and Thompson, J., eds. *The Court and Cultural Diversity*. Cambridge, 1997.

Murray, J., ed. *Conflicted Identities and Multiple Masculinities: Men in the Medieval West*. New York and London, 1999.

Neal, D. 'Masculine Identity in Late Medieval English Society and Culture'. *Writing Medieval History*. Ed. N. Partner (London, 2005). Pp.171–88.

Nelson, Alan H. ' "Of the seuen ages": An Unknown Analogue of *The Castle of Perseverance*'. *Comparative Drama* 8 (1974), 125–38.

Neuss, P., ed. *Aspects of Early English Drama*. Cambridge and Totowa, 1983.

Nicholls, J. *The Matter of Courtesy: Medieval Courtesy Books and the Gawain-Poet*. Cambridge, 1985.

Norland, H. B. *Drama in Early Tudor Britain, 1485–1558*. Lincoln NB, 1995.

Nuttal, J. 'Household Narratives and Lancastrian Poetics'. *The Medieval Household in Christian Europe, c. 850–1550: Managing Power, Wealth and the Body*. Ed. C. Beattie, A. Maslakovic and S. Rees Jones. Turnhout, 2003. Pp. 91–106.

Orgel, S. *The Illusion of Power: Political Theater in the English Renaissance*. Berkeley and London, 1975.

Orme, N. 'Children and the Church in Medieval England'. *Journal of Ecclesiastical History* 45 (1994), 563–87.

——— 'The Education of Edward V'. *BIHR* 57 (1984), 119–30.

——— *From Childhood to Chivalry: The Education of the English Kings and Arsitocracy, 1066–1530*. London and New York, 1984.

——— *Medieval Children*. New Haven and London, 2001.

Ormrod, W. M. 'Coming to Kingship: Boy Kings and the Passage to Power in Fourteenth-Century England'. *Rites of Passage: Cultures of Transition in the Fourteenth Century*. Ed. N. F. McDonald and W. M. Ormrod. York, 2004.

Owst, G. R. *Literature and Pulpit in Medieval England*. Cambridge, 1933.

Partner, N., ed. *Writing Medieval History*. London, 2005.

Paster, G. K. *The Body Embarrassed: Drama and the Disciplines of Shame in Early Modern England*. Ithaca NY, 1993.

Patterson, L. 'On the Margin: Postmodernism, Ironic History, and Medieval Studies'. *Speculum* 65 (1990), 87–108.

Petersen, J. E. 'The Paradox of Disintegrating Form in *Mundus et Infans*'. *ELR* 7 (1977), 3–16.

Phillips, K. M. *Medieval Maidens: Young Women and Gender in England, 1270–1540*. Manchester, 2003.

Pollock, F., and Maitland, F. W. *The History of English Law Before the Time of Edward I*. 2 vols. 2nd edn. Cambridge, 1898.

Posner, D. M. *The Performance of Nobility in Early Modern European Literature*. Cambridge, 1999.

Potter, L., ed. *The Revels History of Drama in English, Vol. 1: Medieval Drama*. London and New York, 1983.

Potter, R. *The English Morality Play: Origins, History and Influence of a Dramatic Tradition*. London and Boston, 1975.

Powell, S. 'Lady Margaret Beaufort and her Books'. *The Library* 6th s. 20 (1998), 197–240.

Pronay, N. 'The Chancellor, the Chancery and the Council at the End of the Fifteenth Century'. *British Government and Administration: Studies Presented to S. B. Chrimes*. Ed. H. Hearder and H. R. Loyn. Cardiff, 1974. Pp. 87–103.

Pugh, T. B. 'Henry VII and the English Nobility'. *The Tudor Nobility*. Ed. G. W. Bernard. Manchester, 1992. Pp. 49–110.

Rawcliffe, C. 'Baronial Councils in the Later Middle Ages'. *Patronage, Pedigree and Power in Later Medieval England*. Ed. C. Ross. Gloucester, 1979.

———, and Flower, S. 'English Noblemen and their Advisers: Consultation and Collaboration in the Later Middle Ages'. *Journal of British Studies* 25 (1986), 157–77.

Reed, A. W. *Early Tudor Drama: Medwall, The Rastells, Heywood, and the More Circle*. London, 1926.

Riddy, F. 'Mother Knows Best: Reading Social Change in a Courtesy Text'. *Speculum* 71 (1996), 66–86.

Righter, A. B. *Shakespeare and the Idea of the Play*. London, 1964.

Ross, C., ed. *Patronage, Pedigree and Power in Later Medieval England*. Gloucester, 1979.

Rossiter, A. P. *English Drama From Early Times to the Elizabethans*. London, 1950.

Sanders, N. 'The Social and Historical Context'. *The Revels History of Drama in English, Vol. 2: 1500–1576*. Ed. C. Leech and T. W. Craik. London and New York, 1980. Pp. 3–67.

Scattergood, J. 'Fashion and Morality in the Late Middle Ages'. *England in the Fifteenth Century*. Ed. D. Williams. Woodbridge, 1997. Pp. 255–72.

——— 'Skelton's *Magnyfycence* and the Tudor Royal Household'. *METh* 15 (1993), 21–48.

Schell, E. T. 'On the Imitation of Life's Pilgimage in *The Castle of Perseverance*'. *JEGP* 87 (1968), 235–48.

Schmitt, J.-C. 'Introduction'. *Gestures, History and Anthropology* 1 (1984), 1–23.

——— 'The Rationale of Gestures in the West: Third to Thirteenth Centuries'. *A Cultural History of Gesture*. Ed. J. Bremmer and H. Roodenburg. Oxford, 1991. Pp. 59–70.

Schultz, J. A. 'Medieval Adolescence: The Claims of History and the Silence of German Narrative'. *Speculum* 66 (1991), 519–39.

Sears, E. *The Ages of Man: Medieval Interpretations of the Life Cycle*. Princeton, 1986.

Shahar, S. 'The Old Body in Medieval Culture'. *Framing Medieval Bodies*. Ed. S. Kay and M. Rubin. Manchester and New York, 1994. Pp. 160–86.

Sheehan, M. M., ed. *Ageing and the Aged in Medieval Europe*. Toronto, 1990.

Siemens, R. G. ' "As Strayght as Ony Pole": Publius Cornelius, Edmund de la Pole and Contemporary Court Satire in Henry Medwall's *Fulgens and Lucres*'. *Renaissance Forum* 1.2 (1996). URL: http://www.hull.ac.uk/renforum/v1no2/siemens.htm.

Siraisi, N. G. *Medieval and Early Renaissance Medicine: An Introduction to Knowledge and Practice*. Chicago, 1990.

Smith, L., and Taylor, J. H. M., eds. *Women, the Book and the Worldly: Selected Proceedings of the St Hilda's Conference, 1993*. Cambridge, 1995.

Southern, R. 'The Technique of Play Presentation'. *The Revels History of Drama in English, Vol. 2: 1500–1576*. Ed. C. Leech and T. W. Craik. London and New York, 1980. Pp. 72–89.

Spivack, B. *Shakespeare and the Allegory of Evil: The History of a Metaphor in Relation to his Major Villains*. New York, 1958.

Sponsler, C. 'Conduct Books and Good Governance', in *Drama and Resistance: Bodies, Goods and Theatricality in Late Medieval England*. Minneapolis and London, 1997. Pp. 50–74.

—— *Drama and Resistance: Bodies, Goods and Theatricality in Late Medieval England*. Minneapolis and London, 1997.

Starkey, D. 'The Age of the Household'. *The Later Middle Ages*. Ed. S. Medcalf. London, 1981. Pp. 225–90.

——, ed. *The English Court From the Wars of the Roses to the Civil War*. London, 1987.

—— 'Intimacy and Innovation: The Rise of the Privy Chamber, 1485–1547'. *The English Court From the Wars of the Roses to the Civil War*. Ed. D. Starkey. London, 1987. Pp. 71–118.

—— 'Representation Through Intimacy: A Study of the Symbolism of Monarchy and Court Office in Early Modern England'. *Symbols and Sentiments*. Ed. I. M. Lewis. London, 1977. Pp. 187–224.

Strohm, P. 'Hoccleve, Lydgate and the Lancastrian Court'. *The Cambridge History of Medieval English Literature*. Ed. D. Wallace. Cambridge, 1999. Pp. 640–61.

Summit, J. 'William Caxton, Margaret Beaufort and the Romance of Female Patronage'. *Women, the Book and the Worldly: Selected Proceedings of the St Hilda's Conference, 1993*. Ed. L. Smith and J. H. M. Taylor. Cambridge, 1995. Pp. 151–65.

Symonds, J. A. *Shakspere's Predecessors in the English Drama*. London, 1900.

Thomas, K. 'Introduction'. *A Cultural History of Gesture: From Antiquity to the Present Day*. Ed. J. Bremmer and H. Roodenburg. Oxford, 1991. Pp. 1–20.

—— 'Age and Authority in Early Modern England'. *Proceedings of the British Academy* 62 (1976), 205–48.

Tristram, P. *Figures of Life and Death in Medieval English Literature*. London, 1976.

Twycross, M., ed. *Festive Drama*. Cambridge, 1996.

—— 'The Theatricality of Medieval English Plays'. *The Cambridge Companion to Medieval English Theatre*. Ed. R. Beadle. Cambridge, 1994. Pp. 37–84.

Tydeman, W. *English Medieval Theatre, 1400–1500*. London, 1986.

Underwood, M. G. 'Politics and Piety in the Household of Lady Margaret Beaufort'. *Journal of Ecclesiastical History* 38 (1987), 39–52.

Ungerer, G. *Anglo-Spanish Relations in Tudor Literature*. Madrid, 1956.

Walker, G. 'A Domestic Drama: John Skelton's *Magnyfycence* and the Royal Household', in *Plays of Persuasion: Drama and Politics at the Court of Henry VIII*. Cambridge, 1991. Pp. 60–101.

Walker, G. 'Household drama and the art of good counsel', in *The Politics of Performance in Early Renaissance Drama*. Cambridge, 1993. Pp. 51–75.

—— *Persuasive Fictions: Faction, Faith and Political Culture in the Reign of Henry VIII*. Aldershot, 1996.

—— 'Playing by the Book: Early Tudor Drama and the Printed Text', in *The Politics of Performance in Early Renaissance Drama*. Cambridge, 1998. Pp. 6–50.

—— *Plays of Persuasion: Drama and Politics at the Court of Henry VIII*. Cambridge, 1991.

—— *The Politics of Performance in Early Renaissance Drama*. Cambridge, 1998.

Wallace, D., ed. *The Cambridge History of Medieval English Literature*. Cambridge, 1999.

Warner, G. F., and Gilson, J. P. *Catalogue of the Western Manuscripts in the Old Royal and King's Collections.* 4 vols. London, 1921.

Wasson, J. 'Professional Actors in the Middle Ages and Early Renaissance'. *Medieval and Renaissance Drama* 1 (1984), 1–11.

Watkins, J. 'The Allegorical Theatre: Moralities, Interludes, and Protestant Drama'. *The Cambridge History of Medieval English Literature.* Ed. D. Wallace. Cambridge, 1999. Pp. 767–92.

Watts, J. L., ed. *The End of the Middle Ages? England in the Fifteenth and Sixteenth Centuries.* Thrupp, 1998.

—— 'Introduction: History, The Fifteenth Century and the Renaissance'. *The End of the Middle Ages? England in the Fifteenth and Sixteenth Centuries.* Ed. J. L. Watts. Thrupp, 1998. Pp. 1–22.

—— 'Politics, War and Public Life'. *Gothic: Art for England, 1400–1547.* Ed. R. Marks and P. Williamson. London, 2003. Pp. 26–36.

Wells, S. 'Food in the City: An Interdisciplinary Study of the Ideological and Symbolic Uses of Food in the Urban Environment in Later Medieval England'. Unpublished Ph.D. thesis, University of York, 2002.

Westfall, S. R. ' "A Commonty a Christmas gambold or a tumbling trick": Household Theater'. *A New History of Early English Drama.* Ed. J. D. Cox and D. S. Kastan. New York, 1997. Pp. 39–58.

—— *Patrons and Performance: Early Tudor Household Revels.* Oxford, 1990.

Whigham, F. *Ambition and Privilege: The Social Tropes of Elizabethan Courtesy Theory.* Berkeley, 1984.

Williams, D., ed. *England in the Fifteenth Century.* Woodbridge, 1987.

Wilson, F. P. *The English Drama, 1485–1585.* Oxford, 1969.

Womack, P. 'Imagining Communities: Theatres and the English Nation in the Sixteenth Century'. *Culture and History, 1350–1600.* Ed. D. Aers. Detroit, 1992. Pp. 91–145.

Wood, M. *The English Mediaeval House.* London, 1965.

Woolf, R. *English Religious Lyrics in the Middle Ages.* Oxford, 1968.

Woolgar, C. M. *The Great Household in Late Medieval England.* New Haven and London, 1999.

INDEX

III *Religion and Medicine in the Middle Ages*, ed. Peter Biller and Joseph Ziegler (2001)

IV *Texts and the Repression of Medieval Heresy*, ed. Caterina Bruschi and Peter Biller (2002)

York Manuscripts Conference

Manuscripts and Readers in Fifteenth-Century England: The Literary Implications of Manuscript Study, ed. Derek Pearsall (1983) [Proceedings of the 1981 York Manuscripts Conference]

Manuscripts and Texts: Editorial Problems in Later Middle English Literature, ed. Derek Pearsall (1987) [Proceedings of the 1985 York Manuscripts Conference]

Latin and Vernacular: Studies in Late-Medieval Texts and Manuscripts, ed. A. J. Minnis (1989) [Proceedings of the 1987 York Manuscripts Conference]

Regionalism in Late-Medieval Manuscripts and Texts: Essays celebrating the publication of 'A Linguistic Atlas of Late Mediaeval English', ed. Felicity Riddy (1991) [Proceedings of the 1989 York Manuscripts Conference]

Late-Medieval Religious Texts and their Transmission: Essays in Honour of A. I. Doyle, ed. A. J. Minnis (1994) [Proceedings of the 1991 York Manuscripts Conference]

Prestige, Authority and Power in Late Medieval Manuscripts and Texts, ed. Felicity Riddy (2000) [Proceedings of the 1994 York Manuscripts Conference]

Middle English Poetry: Texts and Traditions. Essays in Honour of Derek Pearsall, ed. A. J. Minnis (2001) [Proceedings of the 1996 York Manuscripts Conference]